SOURCES OF SECESSION

by

Gerrit J. tenZythoff

The Historical Series of the Reformed Church
in America

No. 17

SOURCES OF SECESSION

The Netherlands Hervormde Kerk on the Eve
of the Dutch Immigration to the Midwest

by
Gerrit J. tenZythoff

Wm. B. Eerdmans Publishing Co.
Grand Rapids, Michigan

Copyright © 1987 Wm. B. Eerdmans Publishing Co.
255 Jefferson S.E., Grand Rapids, Michigan 49503

Library of Congress Cataloging in Publication Data

Gerrit J. tenZythoff
Sources of Secession, the Netherlands Hervormde Kerk on the
Eve of the Dutch Immigration to the Midwest

(The Historical Series of the Reformed Church in America,
No. 17, Donald J. Bruggink, Editor)
Introduction, Martin E. Marty
Endnotes: p. 139-181.
Includes index.
1. The Reformed Church in America; 2. The Netherlands
Reformed Church; 3. The Secession of 1834
ISBN 0-8028-0328-8

[author's birthday: February 17, 1922]

[editor's birthday: June 30, 1929]

To
The Reformed Church in America

The Historical Series of the Reformed Church in America

This series has been inaugurated by the General Synod of the Reformed Church in America, acting through its Commission on History, for the purpose of encouraging historical research and providing a medium wherein this knowledge may be shared with the academic community and with the members of the denomination in order that a knowledge of the past may contribute to right action in the present.

General Editor

The Rev. Donald J. Bruggink, Ph.D., Western Theological Seminary

The Author

Gerrit J. tenZythoff was born and raised in The Netherlands. His schooling was interrupted during World War II when in 1943 he was arrested by the Nazis. Having made good his escape from Berlin and Nazi Germany, he graduated from the University of Utrecht after the war. Mr. tenZythoff married Elizabeth C. Bok in 1951. This was also the year they came to Canada to serve as home missionaries for the Reformed Church in America among the immigrants then arriving from The Netherlands. While in Vancouver, British Columbia, he earned the S.T.M. degree at the Union College of British Columbia. He joined the teaching staff at Western Theological Seminary in 1960 and earned both the M.A. (1961) and Ph.D. (1967) degrees at the University of Chicago.

In 1966, tenZythoff accepted a teaching position in the history department on the Mansfield campus of Ohio State University. In 1969, he became the first head of the newly-opened Department of Religious Studies at Southwest Missouri State University, serving in that position until 1982, when physical disability forced him to retire from administration. Under tenZythoff's leadership, the department grew to ten full-time faculty, annually attracting over a thousand students. Dr. tenZythoff continues as Professor of Religious Studies at Southwest Missouri State University.

Contents

Foreword

Some day the dictionaries may have to do with the Reformed part of Christendom what they have done with the Byzantine sector: coin a new use for the adjective. Thus *A Supplement to the Oxford English Dictionary* adds this definition to "Byzantine: reminiscent of the manner, style, or spirit of Byzantine politics. Hence, intricate, complicated, inflexible, rigid, unyielding." The non-Reformed historian who appraises the Calvinist traditions of Scotland, the Netherlands, and the United States, finds good reason to apply some of those adjectives—particularly "intricate" and "complicated" to the Reformed tradition.

How does one keep track? The very names of denominations and parties suggests something of the complexity. On the pages that follow the reader will learn the names of groups in the Netherlands. In the United States there is not only the Reformed Church in America, which figures centrally in the plot of this book's hero, Albertus Christiaan Van Raalte. There is a split off called the True Dutch Reformed Church. In the 1920s one must learn of the Antithetials and people best described as AntiAntitheticals, Confessionalists and, one presumes, Anti-Confessionalists. (I should talk: we Lutherans once generated a Norwegian-American church body in opposition to the Missouri Synod. It was called, sweetly, the Anti-Missourian Brotherhood!)

We can deride these intricacies and complexities if we will, and we will. But derision is not the only proper attitude, and certainly not the best. In the spirit of Spinoza, if one wishes to do justice, there is a need to come to such phenomena not to laugh, not to cry, but to understand. For it happens that, shrouded behind and coded in such party names were (and sometimes are) real flesh and blood people of great spirit and dedication. Some of their battles are no longer relevant, but others are. In any case, the intense disputes that led to schisms or involved, as in Van Raalte's case, secession, were marks not only of human stubbornness but of desires to display Christian faithfulness. Yet having said those moderating words, it still remains to be noted that both those who are direct heirs of the strugglers and those who look on need much help in sorting them out.

Gerrit tenZythoff's book, *Sources of Secession,* is a very valuable con-

tribution to our understanding of one set of people who witnessed in
Europe and then came to America and played their part in church life
here. He captures well both the spirit of old controversy and the pas-
sions that survive. I remember my astonishment when I first read in
his introduction that he experienced some frustration over the sources.
The reason was not linguistic: he has mastery of the languages in question. Nor historical: Professor tenZythoff knew where to go for sources,
and how to handle them. His problem was that he could not gain access
to them all. No secretive Vatican stood in the way. Instead, "some
institutions and certain persons are averse and even unwilling to make
their extant holdings available for historical research. Persons thus reluctant to divulge historical information are still embarrassed by the
actions of their forefathers in the ecclesiastical controversies and quarrels
of the time."

Fortunately for us, there were plenty of unembarrassed divulgers
who, after a century or a century and a half, found no reason to protect
old reputations or cover up old controversies. One finds here no "smok-
ing gun" of the sort Americans are trained to pounce upon as evidence.
One does find here a story of doctrinal, polity, and personal dispute
that came to have great consequence. It is Professor tenZythoff's special
gift to be able to sort out the doctrinal fighters, the polity debaters, the
tacticians and diplomats of the various bodies and to treat them properly.

Ideas have consequences. So do doctrines and polity positions. Some
of these take the form of commitments so profound, so unyielding, that
those who hold them have to inconvenience themselves. It is always
wrenching to participate in the disruption of a church body, to secede,
to go into exile. Today we are coming to understand more and more,
through the pursuit of social history, what was the daily life of the
American immigrant who came for reasons of both churchly conviction
and practical necessity in hard times in the Netherlands.

Once upon a time not only heirs of contenders but heirs in general
were easily embarrassed by stories of their immigrant ancestors. Today
many if not most citizens figuratively wear the recall of their trials as
badges of honor. Blacks proudly reflect on the nameless slave ancestors
who were, against their will, uprooted from African homes and sold into
American slavery. Jews do not mind hearing of their ragpicker great
grandparents on New York's Lower East Side. They know that behind
them stood the Hebrew prophets, generations ago, and they take pride.
Once there was assimilation, the cherishing of the melting pot, the
covering up of peculiarities among grandparents. Today people try both
to escape the blandness of mass produced culture and to get a sense of

identity and guidance from the humble migrants of the 19th century and even later.

In that context the Dutch-background Reformed are these days retracing their ancestors' steps. But this story is not only for the Van Raalteites, very few of whom would know that that is what they are. It is for all the Reformed, many other Michiganders, students of history, participants in church life, who need case studies beyond their own. Case study: the word sounds cold. We remind ourselves again of real people acting out their human dramas on the Reformed ecclesiastical stage.

This is the time also to pay tribute to the author. Professor tenZythoff explains why others have avoided this important story. He knows that time may be running out for American citizens to bring their curiosities to bear on the sources: they are quite distanced from the nuances of the old languages of the sources. He is an intellectual and spiritual citizen of both Netherlandish and American worlds, and has moved with ease between them. He has had a distinguished career as an historical scholar, a teacher at a state university, a friend to fellow (post World War II) immigrants, an exemplar to and stimulator of students who learned from him what conscientiousness, fairness, and scrupulousness in historical work look like. Now readers can join this company of beneficiaries. They will walk away from this reading informed about church life in two countries by learning more about what it was like among the people who left the Netherlands to come to America. They may learn more about how to think about others who made such pilgrimages—or how to think about themselves, their past, and what they might hope for in the continuing drama of our "intricate, complicated" national life.

Martin E. Marty

Editor's Preface

Sources of Secession began its life at the University of Chicago as a doctoral thesis titled *The Netherlands Reformed Church: Stepmother of Michigan Pioneer Albertus Christiaan Van Raalte*. The Historical Commission of the Reformed Church in America soon became aware of its excellence and voted to publish it, after some stylistic alterations. Dr. tenZythoff had taken all of his studies through college and seminary with Dutch as his primary language, and had now written an exceedingly complex doctoral thesis in one of his other languages, in this case, English.

The lucid flow of the present text is the work of the Rev. Dr. Milo Dean Van Veldhuizen, Campus Minister for Portage Lake United Ministries in Higher Education at Michigan Technological University, Houghton, Michigan. Only a person who has dealt with a text, grammatically correct, yet not written in the idiom peculiar to one's native tongue, can understand the difficulty in transforming that which is already "right" into something that consistently reads more naturally to an American audience. For the finesse with which that difficult task has been accomplished, we owe a tremendous debt (which as in most scholarly tasks, is repaid only in the knowledge of a job well done) to Dr. Van Veldhuizen.

To Harriet Bobeldyk, who retyped the manuscript, keeping an already busy faculty secretary even more busy, a debt of thanks is owed (this debt being met only by the friendship of author and editor). Dr. tenZythoff has persevered in this publication while creating, de novo, a religion department larger than many seminaries, and one which religiously informs and challenges over a thousand students each year, while at the same time struggling with physical infirmities which would have forced most of us into retirement. For both his scholarship and perseverance, we give thanks to God.

Donald J. Bruggink
Editor

Author's Preface

Since having completed my doctoral thesis for the University of Chicago, interest in the materials I covered has markedly increased. In The Netherlands the *Documentatieblad voor de Nederlandse Kerkgeschiedenis van de Negentiende Eeuw* was created, joining and expanding the goals of the *Stichting Het Réveil*. Excellent studies have been produced touching upon many aspects of my earlier work. The centennial of Abraham Kuyper's *Doleantie* (1886-1986) has raised further interest in the nineteenth century as evidenced by many publications that document and probe the relation of the *Doleantie* and the earlier Secession of 1834.

In addition, easier contacts between The Netherlands and North America have enabled such denominations as the Reformed Church in America and the Christian Reformed Church to be much more active in studying roots and sources. The thousands of post World War II immigrants from The Netherlands and their offspring in North America have added to the need for understanding ecclesiastical roots on both sides of the Atlantic. Learned societies for the advancement of Netherlandic studies have been created in Canada and the USA. Their scholarly pursuits are making an impact.

My profound gratitude and enthusiasm for these and other significant developments are tempered by regret over my inability to participate more fully in these historic changes. Physical disabilities because of severe illnesses combined with remoteness from sources make it impossible for me to keep up with the wealth of materials and publications now available. My study does not reflect this later scholarship. But it is my profound hope that my work will facilitate access to the vigorous dialogues of earlier scholars about the sources of secession and their meaning.

It is a joy to acknowledge the help of many without whom I would have been unable to complete my study. My parents and grandparents of blessed memory kindled in me an early interest in the church and its history. That interest was later ably stimulated, broadened, and guided by an outstanding faculty: Dr. H. Bouwmeester at the Doetinchems Gymnasium; professors M. van Rhijn, A. A. van Ruler, and

S. F. H. J. Berkelbach van den Sprenkel at the University of Utrecht; professor John Webster Grant at the Union Theological Seminary in Vancouver, British Columbia; professors Martin E. Marty, Jerald C. Brauer, Sidney E. Mead, James Hastings Nichols, and Karl Weintraub at the University of Chicago. In addition, I was influenced and helped by the doctors M. Elisabeth Kluit, H. Berkhof, J. M. de Jong, O. J. de Jong, Donald J. Bruggink, Eugene Osterhaven, Elton Bruins, Karel Hanhart, and H. J. Ponstein.

It would not have been possible to do my work in three different countries without the significant help of Dr. P. J. Schram; N. J. Prinsen; The Prins Bernhard Fonds; the Gereformeerde Kerk te Ommen; Mr. Klaas Schaap and the Gemeentelijk Museum at Arnhem; the Netherlands Museum at Holland, Michigan; Willard C. Wichers; George Cook; Mildred Schuppert; Jantina Holleman; Barbara Lampen; Third Reformed Church at Holland, Michigan; T. J. Koldewijn; Hope Reformed Church at Vancouver, British Columbia; Dr. Harold Englund; Robert deBruyn and Dr. Robert Bruce Flanders.

A most unique influence was exerted by the Derk Jan Wilpshaar family and Mans Grendelman without whose bravery I could not have survived in World War II. More importantly, their exemplary devotion to the Lord of the Church added a dimension of the eternal to my appreciation of the history of the Church that was never matched or duplicated elsewhere.

What I owe to the unswerving love of my wife, Elisabeth, daughter, Cora-Joan, and my brothers and sisters can be expressed best in the words of Old Hundredth: "Praise God from Whom all blessings flow . . . ."

Gerrit J. tenZythoff

Introduction

Several studies have been written on the Dutch settlers who arrived in the American Midwest after 1846. None of these describe in depth the ecclesiastical background in The Netherlands, in particular that of the Netherlands Reformed Church. It is not surprising that this should be the case. Many of the Dutch immigrants, and especially the eminent clergymen among them, were in the old country members of the Christian Seceded Church, not of the Netherlands Reformed Church. Most of the members belonging to the Christian Seceded denomination arrived in America with vivid memories of having broken away from the Netherlands Reformed Church to establish a purer church. As a result, even recent studies of the Dutch emigration tell far more about the secession and the Seceded Church than about the Netherlands Reformed Church. Understandable as this preoccupation may be, the Netherlands Reformed Church should not be ignored. The history of the emigrants, not only in The Netherlands but especially in Michigan, cannot be fully understood unless one comprehends the relationship between the seceders and the Netherlands Reformed Church.

The congregation of Pastor Albertus Christiaan Van Raalte is a case in point. Upon settling in Michigan he encouraged his followers to join the Reformed Church in America, members of which had befriended the immigrants upon their arrival in the United States. In 1857 the *Ware Hollandsche Gereformeerde Kerk* in Michigan, now known as the Christian Reformed Church, broke away from Van Raalte and the Reformed Church in America. The attempts to explain this secession within the American frame of reference have not been successful. For example, the claim has been made that Freemasonry was the real issue over which Van Raalte's church divided. However, there is no evidence to support such a contention. More to the point is the fact that Van Raalte was always a reluctant seceder. His love for the Netherlands Reformed Church in which his father had been a pastor manifested itself in strong emotional ties with that church. Although Van Raalte never denied that the Secession of 1834 had been necessary, some of his followers in Michigan, reviving old charges originating in The Netherlands, accused Van Raalte of having been a half-hearted seceder. Those who left Van

Raalte's Reformed Church in the Secession of 1857 stated as their principal reason that, unlike Van Raalte, one should have no question at all about the secession from the Netherlands Reformed Church. Of the five additional reasons advanced by the seceders of 1857, two refer directly to issues only relevant to the Secession of 1834, namely, the singing of hymns and participation in the Lord's Supper on the part of Christians not affiliated with the Reformed Church.

There are additional reasons for providing this history of the Netherlands Reformed Church. One of them became manifest when in 1963 the municipal Netherlands Museum at Holland, Michigan, formed the Dutch-American Historical Commission. Calvin College and Seminary of the Christian Reformed Church, together with Hope College and Western Theological Seminary of the Reformed Church in America, joined the Netherlands Museum in creating this research and archival organization. Naturally the group tends to stress the American experience of their forebears more than the history of the mother church in The Netherlands. In spite of a genuine interest in their own history, few people of Dutch descent continue to speak or read the Dutch language, and English translations of source material in The Netherlands are seldom available. Moreover, the American descendants of Van Raalte's followers have not authored works on the ecclesiastical history of The Netherlands and as a consequence a mythology exists about the ancestral church in The Netherlands which is hard to reconcile with historical facts.

Dutch historians, moreover, have in general paid little attention to the nineteenth-century emigration to the United States. The emigrants represented such a small percentage of the population in The Netherlands that they could be ignored with impunity. Even historians concentrating on the Secession of 1834 have slighted the emigrants. They write almost exclusively about the conflicts and developments within the Christian Seceded Church in The Netherlands. As a result, the Netherlands Reformed Church has not been studied as the historical precursor of the Protestant Dutch settlers in the American Midwest.

The question of how Van Raalte was related to both the Netherlands Reformed Church and the Christian Seceded Church after 1835, however, involves problems which cannot be solved at this time. What is left of the records is scattered far and wide, making it difficult to determine whether sufficient material is available. In addition, some institutions and certain persons are unwilling to make their holdings available for historical research.

The following study concentrates therefore on the Netherlands Reformed Church in the period of the last decade of the eighteenth century to the fourth decade of the nineteenth century.

I

The French Revolution Changes
The Netherlands

On October 17, 1811, Albertus Christiaan Van Raalte[1] was born at Wanneperveen, a small village in what was then known as the *departement des bouches de l'Issel*. France had imposed that name upon the province of Overijssel after annexing The Netherlands in 1810.[2] Had Napoleon succeeded in his desire to reduce the former Republic of the United Netherlands to a permanent and integral part of his French empire, Albertus Christiaan would have grown up a Frenchman.

THE STATE PRIOR TO THE NAPOLEONIC CONQUEST

The Dutch nation had responded to the emperor's grand designs without enthusiasm. Powerful segments within the republic had, indeed, lent eager support to revolutionary ideas, but that was prior to 1795 and the overthrow of the House of Orange. Idealists, merchants, adventurers, and others had found themselves together in the *Patriotten* movement that opposed the Orange party.[3]

Orange

The stadholder, William V of Orange, resisted the advance of French influence and ideas and in this action was encouraged by Great Britain and Prussia. He was even urged to assume monarchical powers, but the last of the hereditary princes of Orange lacked the character to inspire his followers to take so bold a step. Nor was the stadholder willing to accept a constitutional monarchy. He felt that this would be no more than "a king under a guillotine."[4] Thus William V failed to place himself in either of the two positions which would attract large numbers of supporting Dutch.

The seven provinces had been federated only loosely through the Union of Utrecht (1579). Her larger neighbors, England and France, had become strong centralized states and threatened the survival of the Dutch republic. But a constitution that would transfer the governing

1

power from the rather independent provinces to a central government was unthinkable to the Dutch because they had fought their Eighty Years War against Spain (1568-1648) to resist the centralizing policies of the Hapsburg Monarchy. A new constitution that was to unify the provinces would be acceptable only if the rights of all the citizens were safeguarded and strengthened.

William V lacked both the will and the wisdom to champion the democratic rights of the ordinary citizens and to be the force behind national unification. He preferred to rely on the oligarchy of regents who through the years had gradually limited the citizens' privileges and rights, in the very defense of which the war of independence against Spain had been fought. Since traditionally the House of Orange had championed these privileges and rights, it was popular with those classes who frequently found themselves disenfranchised. By refusing for himself a constitutional monarchy in favor of allying himself with the ruling oligarchy, however, Stadholder William V strained the popularity of the Oranges and forced the democratic supporters of his house into the waiting arms of those who were inspired by the ideals of the American and French revolutions. The *Patriotten* included, therefore, not only republican elements who were traditionally opposed to any constitutional role for the House of Orange but also those who had originally supported Orange. Many Orange-Democrats were still willing to maintain the Oranges, but William V was unable and unwilling to use what support he had remaining to bring these factions together into a unified, democratic state. The words of Johan Huizinga are appropriate:

> The national consciousness of our old United Provinces was dualistic like the state itself: half monarchical, half republican, half Prince [of Orange], half States [General]. . . .[5]

The stadholder's wife, Frederika Sophia Wilhelmina, a niece of Prussia's Frederick the Great, had much greater ability than her husband; but under the constitution she lacked the opportunity to substitute for him.[6] When she finally did intervene in the deteriorating situation, the *Patriotten* had gained enough military strength to prevent her from reaching the country's capital where she might have seized power. Her brother, King William Frederick II of Prussia, interpreted this incident as an "insult" grave enough to demand satisfaction. He seized the opportunity to solve the Dutch constitutional crisis in a manner favorable to both Prussia and England. In September 1787 he invaded The Netherlands and restored the House of Orange and its party to power.

The Orange party, and especially the House of Orange itself, was still very popular with the lower classes,[7] but it failed to grant the liberties which had stirred the *Patriotten* to rebellion. Backed by both Prussia and England,[8] the party pushed through a policy of revenge that forced the exodus of more than five thousand *Patriotten* who found refuge in Brussels, Antwerp, and Paris.[9] The Orangists also translated the external support of England and Prussia into effective internal control. This could be accomplished only by manipulating a precarious power-balance among the several provinces.[10]

Gijsbert Karel van Hogendorp, one of the ablest Orangists, urged moderation, but the restorationists had not the slightest interest in reestablishing democracy.[11] With Van Hogendorp the party's more enlightened supporters continued to insist upon expansion and modernization of ancient democratic rights, but they were a minority and lacked the strength to bring about reforms. That left them nowhere to turn but to the *Patriotten*.[12] Thus, popular support of the House of Orange failed to gain constitutional expression. On the other hand, the autocratic portion of the Orange party felt so threatened that it sought to entrench itself more firmly. As a ruling clique, it staved off the democratic element and in the name of loyalty to Orange it began to usurp power formerly belonging to the people. Against these intruding regents the lower classes no longer had a defense.[13]

Patriotten

Like the Orange-Democrats, the *Patriotten* desired to maintain and expand the rights and privileges of the Dutch burghers. They, too, interpreted the War of Independence against Spain as justifiable and necessary opposition against Hapsburg absolutism. But they differed in their attitude toward the House of Orange. The Orange-Democrats tended to be lenient toward a ruling Orange which assumed too much power. The *Patriotten* would not hesitate to dispense with the House of Orange altogether, should it encroach on citizens' rights and privileges. Both parties found ample justification for their views in Dutch history. Orange-Democrats would stress the important roles individual princes of Orange had played in the life of the Dutch nation, and *Patriotten* reminded the burghers that the Dutch on several occasions had removed the Oranges from any and all offices in the republic for the sake of civil liberty.

Religiously, most Orange-Democrats were not adverse to interpret the House of Orange as a visible sign of God's grace, even special grace, toward The Netherlands. Most *Patriotten* were more apt to believe that the benevolent Supreme Being had provided wise, rational systems for men, and especially Dutchmen, to govern themselves.

4 *Sources of Secession**Sources of Secession*

The differences between these parties could erupt into fierce battles, but their common interest in the people's good could quickly unite them. The Dutch in the last quarter of the eighteenth century witnessed both.

Foreign ambassadors, very much aware of the conflicting factions, seized the opportunity to advance their countries' cause at the expense of the Dutch republic.[14] England and Prussia worked through the House of Orange and its ruling oligarchy, France and the United States of America through the *Patriotten*. Interference on the part of these foreign powers increased hostility between the Dutch parties.[15] The cleavage could not be repaired, and in the absence of national unity the country's independence could not be defended.

The destruction of the Dutch republic did not bring to an end the dispute as to which party had been truly indigenous. The debate continued through the nineteenth century and into the twentieth. Some historians have argued that the democratic movement exemplified by the *Patriotten* was foreign to The Netherlands and had been imported from France.[16] Other writers have argued the very opposite.[17] The quarrels of the historians are reflections of the deep divisions which the French Revolution have added to the strife of The Netherlands. Few areas of Dutch life were left untouched, and this divisive spirit certainly was a factor in the Secession from the Reformed Church of 1834 into which was drawn Albertus Christiaan Van Raalte.

THE STATE AFTER THE NAPOLEONIC CONQUEST

The actual end of the Dutch republic came with the French armies invading across the solidly frozen Rhine and Meuse rivers in December 1794 and January 1795. But even the *Patriotten* did not unreservedly welcome the democracy of the French. Reports of the regime of horrors at Paris and of cruelties committed in Belgium by French liberators had dampened earlier enthusiasm.[18] However, even at this late hour the Orange party failed to display enough political acumen and military power to capitalize on its opponent's momentary weakness.[19] In addition, neither England nor Prussia showed any readiness to stand up to France,[20] and defense forces under English control behaved so abominably that many Netherlanders preferred the presence of French troops.[21] French armies easily overcame the republic's inadequate defenses. On January 18, 1795, Prince William V fled from The Hague. Ice in the rivers and canals had blocked all escape routes save the one to England. He joined his family there, never to return to The Netherlands.[22]

Moderation

On January 19, 1795, French delegates issued their refusal of the
Dutch capitulation in the following proclamation:

> We do not come to you in order to place a yoke upon you: the French
> nation shall respect your independence. Exercising their sovereignty,
> the Batavian people shall have sole authority to change or improve the
> mode of their government. . . .[23]

French generosity later proved to have been far less altruistic than
it appeared to be at the time. The Treaty of The Hague recognized the
"liberated" Republic of The Netherlands as a sovereign state, but it was
only temporarily honored by the French, and involved very heavy financial burdens and considerable territorial loss.[24] In response to Dutch
wishes, France consented to guarantee the colonies, but that became
an empty gesture when in England Prince William V ordered Dutch
colonial authorities to welcome the British navy.[25] When England's men
of war imposed a crippling blockade on Holland's harbors, The Netherlands was further compelled to share the burdens of France's conflict
with Great Britain.

Nonetheless, the new regime in The Hague did gain for The Netherlands the advantage of a considerable degree of independence. In
spite of frequent humiliation, Dutch authorities were in charge of the
"velvet revolution"[26] that was to "improve the mode of their government."[27] For example, the new rulers were not so dependent upon
French precedent that they had the members of the *ancien régime*
guillotined. On the contrary, no executions occurred. The former magistrates were spared, along with a considerable portion of their rights
and privileges. Their arrogance came to an end, but for two reasons
these so-called perpetrators succeeded in aligning themselves with the
new authorities.

The first reason was that a true democracy was not established at this
time. The Federalists, who were in the majority among the *Patriotten,*
had wanted to continue as much autonomy for the seven provinces as
possible, but the *Unitarissen,* who were in the minority, wanted a centralized regime and managed to eliminate their opponents by a series
of political coups in which the French ambassador, De la Croix, and his
military attaché, General Joubert, were deeply involved.[28] However,
radicalization of the revolution did not take place. The Dutch general,
Daendels, one of the most ardent among the *Patriotten,* carried out a
counter-coup, bringing a moderate regime to power in The Hague.[29]
That this coup won quick recognition in Paris was not the result of

France's whim. France adhered to the enduring grand design of its foreign policy earlier stated by the radical Danton: "Let us take Holland, and Carthage [i.e., England] is ours."[30] To obtain that objective the *Directoire* at Paris had secretly, though without definite commitment, encouraged General Daendels. France, where Napoleon had become first consul in 1799, needed a quiet and docile Holland. For that reason Daendels's moderate rulers were able to go so far in 1801 as to offer the Orangists a general pardon and subsequently honor it.[31]

The second reason was that the exiled House of Orange was forced to clarify its relation to The Netherlands. A restoration seemed very unlikely. Prussia, which supported the House of Orange in 1789, had made an agreement with the French to remain neutral. Thus a Dutch invasion force, under the able Prince Frederik of Orange, could not be maintained on the eastern border of The Netherlands.[32] In addition, when a combined English-Prussian force invaded North Holland in 1799, a general uprising in favor of the House of Orange did not occur.[33] Napoleon's star was beginning its phenomenal rise and neither Great Britain nor Prussia was willing to put up a strong defense on behalf of the House of Orange. Prince William VI, the heir apparent, then deserted his father's rigid position and made his way to Paris. In a settlement of Orange's claims, he accepted from Napoleon certain properties in Germany.[34] William V thereupon had no choice but to discharge his faithful followers in The Netherlands from exclusive allegiance to his house.[35] In doing so, the desperate William V unknowingly expanded the Orange influence in The Netherlands as his followers made their presence felt in various other areas of Dutch politics.

For the time being, however, Orange's direct role in active politics had come to an end. It was not even a participant when England and France permitted the Batavian Republic to join the peace treaty of Amiens.[36] But Orange had been so intertwined with Dutch life and history that many Netherlanders continued their loyalty, although not in pre-revolutionary forms. And, strangely enough, the French themselves provided the incentive for continued Orange loyalty.

As Napoleon's power increased, The Netherlands was more and more treated as a French colony. That policy alienated even France's most ardent supporters among the Dutch. Support was further eroded by the refusal of the radical revolutionaries to adopt Napoleon's conservatism.[37] Although the majority of moderates welcomed such a farewell to extremism, they also resented France's colonizing schemes. In defense of their country, moderate *Patriotten* were willing to join Orangists in the formation of a national front.[38] Its combined power was insufficient to obviate French encroachments upon Dutch sovereignty, but it did provide the will to survive that enabled the Dutch to resume national independence in 1813.

Louis Napoleon Bonaparte

To fight England in a renewed war, Napoleon needed all the support he could wrest from his Dutch ally.[39] Outright annexation would have given him quick access to Dutch resources, but he was held back by his fear of Prussia, now awakening to the dangers of its neutral position.[40] He found a subterfuge by elevating his brother, Louis Napoleon Bonaparte, to the sovereignty of a newly constituted Kingdom of Holland.[41] To make this move appear legal, he forced the Dutch government to go through the farce of begging him for this favor.[42] On June 22, 1806, the new "King of Holland" made his official entry into The Hague.

Once on the throne, however, Louis identified himself with his new people to an unexpected degree.[43] Not only did he try to learn their language,[44] but he also shielded them as best he could against his extortionist brother in France. Although the emperor had warned him that his true friends would be ". . . les catholiques; apres eux les hommes qu'on appelle les jacobines . . . ,"[45] King Louis made deliberate efforts to establish good relationships with other churches as well. Besides, he was eager to include in his circle of friends the nobility and the former regents. When he did not exclude the Orangists, and even permitted them to display their ancient coats of arms, he drew stern warnings from his brother. Napoleon feared that King Louis might be so blind as to select for his government pro-Orange ministers who in turn might adopt a pro-British policy.

The emperor was determined to enforce his continental blockade, although by 1809 the economic situation in The Netherlands had deteriorated to such a degree that in Amsterdam no less than 100,000 persons, almost half of the population, were on relief of some sort. Napoleon continued to demand that his royal brother yield more and more of Holland's national production in behalf of France's defense. But Louis was not without pity for "his" people. In addition to resisting these demands, he had the audacity to think of making a bargain with England. The emperor prevented such a move by calling him to Paris, where he was placed under virtual arrest. Napoleon's attitude toward all his relatives had changed by this time; their egotism and shortcomings had embarrassed the emperor and had harmed his political designs. To destroy England his continental system would have to be carried out in minute detail. Thus Napoleon ordered "his custom officers into

Holland" and legalized that action by annexing Louis's Kingdom of Holland to France.[46]

Annexation

The imperial government began operations in Holland with care and restraint.[47] Relatively few Frenchmen were installed in key positions. *Patriotten* and Orangists alike were utilized as administrators. Only a handful of men such as G. K. van Hogendorp and A. R. Falck were principled enough to refuse cooperation. The collaborators defended their involvement by pointing to the advantages of unification, for uniform structures of law and taxation were being imposed upon all the provinces. Indeed, the population appeared to be far from hostile when Napoleon and the Empress visited The Netherlands in 1811. He was welcomed as "le héros de l'universe" who would restore "the golden age of Saturn."[48]

Even Bilderdijk, a self-appointed spokesman of the Orangists, did not hesitate to praise Napoleon for taming the monstrous revolution. If only the Prince of Orange could have been a monarch like that![49] Absolute monarchy, thought Bilderdijk, best expressed God's authority over mankind. Consequently, Bilderdijk gave his support to Napoleon. He described him in messianic terms as "the hero who struck the death-blow at the monster of terror."[50]

Soon, however, The Netherlands was forced to meet military requirements that made the return of any golden age impossible. The country was flooded with administrative personnel from France who highhandedly enforced the newly-imposed taxation, customs regulations, censorship, and conscription. Thus the dream of French-administered messianic times came to an end. But revolution did not burst forth, even though Napoleon was defeated in Russia and high French officials began to flee The Netherlands after the "Moniteur" carried the news, on October 30, 1813, that the Allies had defeated Napoleon at Leipzig.

Gijsbert Karel van Hogendorp, strictly loyal to the House of Orange during all these years, foresaw the danger of such passivity.[51] Freedom and independence would have to be won by affirmative action. Already in 1812 he had composed his famous *Schets* for a constitution that was later to become the political backbone of the restored Netherlands. When Napoleon released the 29th Army Bulletin, Van Hogendorp judged the time was ripe to form a committee that would act as an interim government in an emergency.[52] While a lack of communication made a general uprising impossible, nevertheless, on October 17, 1813, the committee formed a temporary government that filled the power vacuum and recalled the House of Orange from exile.[53]

William I, Sovereign Ruler

Prince William, the son of William V, returned to Scheveningen-The Hague on November 30, but he did not bring back the old times prophesied by Van Hogendorp and his committee. The prince adopted the title Sovereign Ruler of The Netherlands, thus laying the foundation for an authority greater than the former United Republic had granted the House of Orange.[54] But William was at the same time wise enough to continue the constitutional tradition of the republic, namely that sovereignty rested in both the House of Orange and the States General. This constitutional approach proved to be capable of uniting in a common cause the former archenemies: Orangists and *Patriotten*. What had taken place under French domination had prepared each party to accept the other as a partner.[55] The Orangists were satisfied because an Orange would hold executive power; the *Patriotten* were satisfied because a parliament would share sovereign power. Nonetheless, there was little cause for rejoicing. Van Hogendorp complained that the nation "was so tired of resolutions and disagreements that it left everything to the Prince."[56] Officially, the prince accepted "what The Netherlands offered him . . . only under guarantee of a wise constitution that guarantees your freedom against possible abuses in the future. . . ."[57] Unofficially, however, the prince commented that "the constitution needs only to be seen as a toy in the hands of the people in order to give them the illusion of freedom, while in reality one moulds it [i.e., the constitution] according to the circumstances."[58]

The strong support from England for a sentinel on France's northern boundaries made it possible for the Congress of Vienna to add Belgium to the territory of the former republic.[59] To formally unite Belgium and The Netherlands into one political body, a new constitution was required. Napoleon's escape from Elba precipitated the final action: the Congress of Vienna recognized William I as "King of The Netherlands" on March 22, 1815.[60] It was under this king and a subsequent organic law that in 1816 the Reformed Church was completely reorganized.

THE CHURCH PRIOR TO THE NAPOLEONIC CONQUEST: UNITY AND DIVISION

Van Hogendorp's slogan "old times are returned" did not fit the churches either. Although the uncertainties which had plagued The Netherlands since 1795 came to an end, the relationship between church and state which had prevailed under the United Republic was not restored.

Dordrecht, 1618-19

The Netherlands Reformed Church had gained definite form and status even before The Netherlands acquired its internationally recognized independence at the Peace of Westphalia in 1648. During a lull in the Eighty Years War against Spain the government of the United Provinces, in collaboration with the Reformed Church, called a National Synod at Dordrecht: 1618-19. There the orthodox scholastic party led by Gomarus was victorious over the biblical-humanistic wing of Arminius's followers. Ministers and officers in the Reformed Church were compelled to accept and sign the anti-Arminian Canons of Dordt.[61]

The synod was far less successful in expressing its victory in the national constitution. Dissenters were formally excluded from public office, but exceptions were made. The republic's central government lacked the constitutional strength to enforce a test act, nor could the provincial authorities prevail at will in local situations.[62] Erasmian humanism had deeply penetrated Dutch civilization, and the long-established concepts of freedom were not to be exterminated.[63] Unlimited freedom of religion did not formally exist, although in practice one could usually worship as one saw fit.

The United Republic underwent no fundamental changes with respect to this religious situation when the Peace of Westphalia was concluded in 1648. Compromises that had been instituted during the struggle with Spain were respected. Already during that war, the republic had become a haven for refugees: English Quakers and Puritans (including America's Pilgrim fathers), Salzburger Lutherans, Hernhutters of the *Unitas Fratrorum*, Ashkenazim or German-Polish Jews, and French Huguenots—the latter being served at one time by more than forty ministers in Amsterdam alone.[64] The presence of so many divergent groups made futile repeated attempts to retreat from established tolerance and freedom.

Division Within Dordt: Coccejus and Voetius

The Dordtian party presented no unbroken phalanx in opposition to the sundry theologies and modes of worship practiced in the land. Already at the synodical session of 1618-19, divergent views had come to light, and one of the major rifts occurred over the understanding of man's fall as related to predestination. Gomarus, Voetius, Trigland, and others were supralapsarians, believing that God had rejected the unsaved prior to the Fall. Most of the foreign delegates joined the infralapsarian position, defended by Walaeus, Kerckhoven, and others, that such an eternal rejection by God had come after the Fall.[65] The orthodox further lost ground when Coccejus in his covenant theology made use of Rene Descartes's philosophy.[66] Professor Gisbertus Voetius, at the University of Utrecht, put up a strong counterattack using the forms of scholastic orthodoxy. He found a helpmate in the piety imported from English Puritanism, but that alliance proved to be self-defeating.

Coccejus and Voetius differed with respect to their emphasis on biblical exegesis. Voetius was certainly not unbiblical, but his exegetical method was drawn from scholasticism. Coccejus refused to adhere to an exegetical method that could ignore biblical context if that were necessary to support a dogmatic decision. Yet both Coccejus and Voetius aimed at the *praxis pietatis,* the practice of piety. Thus it was possible that both sides established natural links with the practical mysticism ingrained in Dutch religion since the days of the Brethren of the Common Life. For that reason the dispute failed to generate consistent heat among church people. Fierce flare-ups did occur, but the fire smoldered mainly in academic circles which comprehended the theological issues involved.

The academic dispute broke out in the church at large in the form of the question of Sabbath observance. The Coccejans adopted the more liberal attitude because they interpreted the covenant of works as having been abrogated in the successive stages of the history of salvation. Voetians, however, equated the New Testament Sunday with the Old Testament Sabbath and observed it accordingly. During the many years that the church was engaged in this inner battle, both parties began to develop certain characteristics. In public prayers, Voetians would ask God's blessing upon the Oranges, but not upon the States General; Coccejans would transpose these entreaties for blessing. The two were separated even outwardly. Voetians had their hair clipped short, and, if bald, they wore a simple black cap. Coccejans, on the other hand, let their hair grow to their shoulders and did not hesitate to wear wigs. Thus contending for the truth, both parties refused to leave the church. Because of equal strength a stalemate developed that compelled them to live with each other. The civil authorities hastened this process by occasionally issuing court injunctions forbidding eristical publications on either side. But however welcome, peace of this sort exacted its price. Within the one church two distinct modes of theological thinking coexisted, now without real communication. Dordtian orthodoxy lost its uniformity in the bifurcation of a right and left wing.

Dordt's Left: Balthasar Bekker

Representative of the left was Balthasar Bekker (1634-98), who served
as a minister of the Reformed Church in the provinces and, after 1680,
in Amsterdam. In his view revealed religion and human reason could
ultimately not disagree because God, who was the Revealer as well as
the Creator with respect to man's reason, could not possibly contradict
himself. In the search for truth, however, Bekker would not permit the
biblical revelation, literally understood, to prevail over human reason
in such a way as to obliterate it. He accepted the Cartesian method of
doubt and the radical separation of spirit and matter. An educator and
catechist of rare ability, Bekker attacked the superstitions of his age by
explaining natural phenomena in rational terms. His explanation of comets was a case in point. Many orthodox ministers, Voetius among them,[67]
interpreted the appearance of comets as God's revelatory action. They
were taken as warnings of impending doom. Bekker readily admitted
that the Bible portrays comets as being God's messengers, but he insisted upon the importance of understanding them in natural and rational terms.[68]

Bekker's earlier defense of Cartesian philosophy as harmless for theology and good for learning had already evoked strong protests.[69] When
he published his *De Betooverde Wereld*,[70] the opposition became fu-
rious and, accusing him of atheism, the church began disciplinary proceedings against him. What Bekker had done was to apply the Cartesian
method of seeking rational explanations for natural occurrences. The
principal purpose of *De Betooverde Wereld* was to expose the widespread belief in spirits, witches, and devils as irrational and therefore
unbiblical. Bekker granted that sorcery and other satanic works occur
in the Bible but he explained them away as God's accommodation to
the level of civilization at that time. His opponents, Voetians and anti-
Cartesians, attacked this view of Scripture, ignoring Bekker's valiant
struggle against the superstitious belief in witches among their contemporaries. Bekker steadfastly refused to accept the literal interpretations
of his opponents, and they succeeded in having him deposed from the
ministry in 1692. Unlike the condemnation of the Arminians at the
Synod of Dordrecht which resulted for the condemned in loss of liberty
and citizenship, the disciplinary action against Bekker had no such civil
consequences. He was no longer permitted to partake of the Lord's
Supper, but his salary continued till his death in 1698. The whole episode did very little to stop Descartes's influence. As time went on,
fewer Christians were willing to uphold the condemnation of Bekker
and his ideas. Judicial processes against witches were discontinued and

other superstitions diminished as a result of Bekker's work. The Dordtian party was capable of developing "liberalism" within its own ranks.

Dordt's Right: De Labadie and Koelman

Aberrations from true doctrine occurred no less on the right. The orthodox desire to reform the church to perfection revealed its unbiblical aspects clearly in Jean de Labadie (1610-74).[71] This Frenchman was a Roman Catholic priest who had been trained by the Jesuits, although he never joined their order. After his conversion to the Reformed Church in 1650, he became famous for his fiery sermons and strict pastoral methods. In 1666 he came to Utrecht where Voetius and his friends welcomed him as an ally. That same year De Labadie accepted a call to the French Huguenot church at Middelburg, but he found himself ill at ease because of the many unconverted among the church's membership. In his strenuous efforts to have none but the saved in the church De Labadie did not hesitate to bar even his colleague Du Moullin from the Lord's Supper. But it was De Labadie whom the Reformed Church deposed in 1669 because of his refusal to sign the *Confession* and *Discipline*. Undisturbed, De Labadie quickly established his own church in which each member claimed individual conversion and sanctification. His group attracted considerable attention but actual membership never grew very large.[72] Following De Labadie's death in 1674, a small but dedicated group continued meeting until the dwindling membership disbanded in 1732.[73] Ironically, De Labadie established a larger and more permanent following within the Reformed Church. They shared his concern for a church more truly reformed according to the Scriptures. They saw their contemporary world as evil and to be avoided.

Although many within the Reformed Church equaled De Labadie's concern for a continuing reformation of Christ's body, the orthodox brethren were divided in their own ranks with respect to what constituted the true church. This was made especially clear by Voetius's favorite student, Jacobus Koelman (1632-95).[74] A minister since 1657, Koelman attacked the claim of De Labadie's group that they were the true church consisting of the elect and the saved. He agreed with their emphasis on piety, but he insisted that the church of Jesus Christ was a *corpus christianum* in which, as in Noah's ark, clean and unclean would dwell together.

And yet, in 1675, the church deposed Koelman, too. He had continually refused to use the prescribed liturgical forms and prayers on the ground that those forms were at best examples for the inexperienced.

No minister, argued Koelman, should be forced to cloak his faith in the words and forms of other Christians. When Koelman also refused to honor any day as holy except the Lord's Day, the civil authorities insisted that he be deposed, and the church readily complied. Like De Labadie, Koelman was convinced of being absolutely right; but, unlike De Labadie, he did not secede. In spite of being deposed, he continued to consider himself and his audience members of the Reformed Church. Abstaining from separately organizing his followers, he interpreted his deposition as abundant proof that the Reformed Church needed further, more thorough reform. Thus, instead of creating a church of his own, Koelman preached and taught in the many conventicles, or house congregations. It was unthinkable for him to resign from the church *semper reformanda*. That had been De Labadie's sin, of which Koelman wanted no part.

Conventicles

Over the years, the conventicles had become the haven of many believers who sought the church's continuing reformation. Reasons for the existence of these conventicles varied, but concern for the Reformed Church was always one of them. The origin of the conventicles is noted because they played a part in the Secession of 1834. Although conventicles could and did become seceded churches, they primarily provided a spiritual home of hope and prayer for the concerned. The necessity of secession was always discussed in the midst of this ambivalence.[75]

A. C. Duker blamed the Voetians for starting the conventicles as a practice of partisan religious fellowship; indeed fellowship within the church, but without active participation in worship services conducted by the rival Coccejans.[76] K. Groot explained the origin of conventicles not in terms of ecclesiastical quarrels but as an attitude intrinsically present in Voetian and similar piety. The feeling of contrition leads naturally to the conviction that one is as nothing before God. It is typical for the pietists to transcend this feeling in and through the spiritual delight resulting from the withdrawal from this world and "participation in brief devotions and prayer services for those who share the same spirit; in short: withdrawal into the conventicles."[77]

However, J. C. Kromsigt demonstrates that conventicles had an even more natural birth in the Reformed Church.[78] He calls attention to the early gatherings for prophesying which long before the Synod of Dordrecht were often the means by which local churches reformed themselves from Roman error. These gatherings served a double purpose: they enabled church members and ministers to discuss the content and applications of the sermon. On the other hand, the meetings could also involve the study and discussion of a portion of Scripture unrelated to the Sunday worship service.

When the Synod of Dordrecht, in its seventeenth session, carefully regulated how children and converts were to be catechized, it included a provision encouraging pastors to conduct adult instruction classes for those who were concerned about the status of their soul. Voetius and his friends seized this new possibility which while in some ways similar to the earlier prophesyings, was now domesticated, for in accordance with synodical ordinance the gatherings had closed membership and were placed under theologically trained leadership. The number of these meetings began to multiply rapidly because of De Labadie and Koelman and received an added impetus in 1672 when King Louis XIV almost crushed The Netherlands, causing many Dutchmen to meet in conventicles to inquire into the will of the Lord for their country.

By this time, however, a bifurcation had taken place between the *gezelschap*, or company, and the *oefening*, or exercise. The *gezelschap* resembled the prophesyings only insofar as the members were able to freely exchange their views. The sermon and its application, the "cases of conscience," were no longer the subjects of exchange. In their place came the private religious experience of each member. Attention turned from the Word of God to the word of the converted sinner. On the other hand, the *oefening*, or exercise, more closely resembled the church service, because it was opened and closed with prayer, and Scripture was read and explained. As both forms of worship attracted the mystically inclined, the quietists would frequent the *gezelschap* while others found in the *oefening* their spiritual home. Both had in common that they could equally well serve the needs of either satisfied or dissatisfied church members. Thus conventicles could be separatistic or they could serve to curb secession. The dissatisfied found in them an opportunity to be in contact with God outside the regular channels of the church without having to secede. As Koelman demonstrates, the unity of the church could thus be believed as well as practiced. For the Labadists, the purity of the church took precedence over its unity. Because of their ambiguous status, the conventicles could develop in either direction.[79] Were the Reformation and its aftermath considered a failure, one would sooner or later start the church *de novo* by transforming the conventicle into a seceded church. But if the members understood the Reformation as a process to be continued in their time too, conventicles would prevent a secession by becoming a temporary home.[80]

Civil Authority

The conventicles were not the only adhesive force which prevented the Reformed Church from splintering into many factions. The Synod

of Dordrecht had granted civil authorities considerable weight in ecclesiastical matters, and thus in 1619, the orthodox party could gain state
sanction in its condemnation of the Arminians. But it was a Pyrrhic
victory, for the magistrates took advantage of their influential position.
A case in point was the action of Prince William III of Orange, also King
of England, who personally favored the Voetians but in 1694 collaborated with the States General in bringing about a state-imposed ecclesiastical agreement which called for the "conservation of rest and peace
in the churches."[81] A national synod was not called. The republic's
political situation was considered to be so perilous that bitter synodical
controversies over religious issues could not be tolerated.

Toleration

When the times improved and the Dutch republic was in less danger,
a repetition of the contentious spirit of 1618-19 became highly unlikely.
Strong advocates of tolerance like John Locke, Pierre Bayle, and Baruch
de Spinoza provided theories of tolerance to augment existing practice.
Thus the peaceful coexistence of divergent convictions within as well as
without the church could be reinforced and further rationalized. It is
true that these theories were taught primarily at the universities, but
the membership of the church as a whole responded well to these ideas
because the church's piety had been Erasmian to begin with.[82] Because
of its concern for practical piety the church had formed its own indigenous
contribution toward tolerance.[83] Such thoughts were not simply foreign
imports, nor did tolerance sprout and blossom among the liberals alone.
   In defense of the cause of tolerance, the Reverend Johannes M.
Mommers, a Voetian of strong persuasion, published in 1738 his *Eubulus of Goede Raad* in which he pled with Coccejans, Voetians, and
other orthodox to cease quarreling with one another.[84] He did not min-
imize differences, but clearly presented his objections to the views of
those with whom he disagreed while not distorting their opinions. His
counsel of moderation attracted a wide audience.
   Nevertheless the old party spirit refused to die. It was kept alive
because the attitudes of local and provincial authorities often determined
whether or not action would be taken on issues which arose within the
church.[85] So long as these authorities did not act in a unified way strong
church-wide policies could not be developed. The result was that numerous ecclesiastical protests were made and heard at every level in
every province.[86]

In Protest of Toleration

From 1751 until 1760, Alexander Comrie and Nikolaas Holtius wrote vigorously in joint protest against *tolerantie*.[87] Almost two centuries later, in 1934, Professor A. C. Honig characterized these two ministers as the models of the Reverend Hendrik de Cock[88] who started the Secession of 1834. Honig presented this thesis in his farewell address to the Theological School of the Seceded Church located at Kampen, entitling his speech: *Van Comrie tot De Cock of: Het Credo des Afscheiding*.[89] As his main thesis he argued that De Cock, the true servant of the Word, had accepted "the legacy of Comrie and Holtius," which meant that De Cock held to the "obligatory and binding character of the three forms of unity."[90] He offered this value judgment:

> I see the benevolent hand of God over his church, first of all in The Netherlands, but then also in other lands of this world, in the fact that the rather young minister of Ulrum [i.e., De Cock] dared to accept Comrie's and Holtius' legacy and dared to acquaint the membership again with the Five Articles of Dordrecht.[91]

According to Honig, *Tolerantie*[92] was "the blurring of Reformation doctrine, and in our country the effort to put the Canons of Dordrecht aside and to have reason take the place of revelation."[93]

Honig made true nationalists of Comrie and Holtius. He observed that "the idea of *Tolerantie* had ripened abroad" and had therefore been "imported from foreign countries."[94] For Honig it was very clear who favored what: "in general the Orangists were in favor, but the *Patriotten* were against maintaining the Reformed Confession." He continued: "The triumph of *Tolerantie* in the ecclesiastical and confessional domain followed on the heels of the revolutionaries' political victory."[95]

Comrie and Holtius had objected to the articles of reconciliation which had been drawn up by the theological faculty of the University of Leiden at the request of Stadholder Prince William IV of Orange and the provincial authorities of Overijssel in response to a problem in the church at Zwolle.[96] One of Zwolle's four ministers, Anthonie van der Os, had publicly stated that he did not accept Micah 5:1, Psalm 2:7, and John 5:26 as proofs of Christ's eternal Sonship.[97] Not a strict Dordtian, he placed man's justification not prior to but after the act of faith: a subtle modification of the orthodox *ordo salutis*. Leiden judged that this was not unorthodox, but this failed to save Van der Os. In 1755 he was deposed.

Comrie and Holtius had been very suspicious of Leiden, charging that the faculty had been inspired by the desire to introduce a tolerance "by which Remonstrants and Contra-Remonstrants might be united in the friendliest way."[98] They set out to scrutinize this evil design in an anonymous series of pamphlets entitled *Examen van het ontwerp van Tolerantie*.[99] In 1759 the tenth volume carried a scathing attack on the late Professor Johannes van der Honert and his alleged Pelagianism. Upon the faculty's protest to the States General, Holtius was called in by the General Secretary and reminded in no uncertain terms of the agreement to abstain from party politics within the church.

Although the *Examen* ceased immediately, party spirit was not overcome.[100] Several classes had already gone on record in defense of Dordrecht, and one of the seven provincial synods held that "a synod derives the infallibility of its decisions from agreement with God's Word; that was the case with the Dordtian; hence its doctrine is infallible."[101] Other judicatories of the Reformed Church disagreed.

Since neither party was able to drive the other out of the church, a stalemate was reached that lasted until the privileged position of the Reformed Church was lost when the Dutch United Republic fell in 1795. As sparring continued in this twilight period, indifference developed among the membership of the church toward the fine points in doctrine. How they felt was aptly expressed by the last stadholder, Prince William V: "Doctrines need to be taught, but most of them must be considered mysteries of which we, human beings, can form no idea."[102]

Toleration and Reason

As the eighteenth century drew to a close, the intellectual climate was changing. *Tolerantie* resulted not so much from evil plots, but developed as a religious interest which shifted from the *fides quae creditur* to the *fides qua creditur*: from objectivity to subjectivity.[103] Religious and scientific convictions were no longer one unified and eternally valid system. Personal religious convictions became more inviolable while state and church began to lose the right to define and impose a body of truth.[104] Protestant dogma itself was critically evaluated.[105] Comrie and Holtius advocated a return to the Synod of Dordrecht, but many scholars began to employ reason as the most reliable tool with which to appropriate the Father's revelation. People were growing confident that, under God, education could perfect man.[106] That conviction was bolstered by the scholarly and exegetical sermons preached by a generation of ministers trained both to note and avoid the weaknesses of Dordrecht.

The church's membership divorced itself from the past at a slower rate than did the ministerial leadership. Sermons from the pulpit tended to be directed so exclusively to man's reason that the needs of the heart were often neglected. Where the pulpit provided insufficient food for the soul, conventicles would provide what was lacking. Both pulpit and lectern claimed to be reliable ways to understand the Bible. Reason and heart thus came to stand over against each other. In the family of faith it became possible for brothers to know each other as second cousins or as even more distant relatives.[107]

THE CHURCH AFTER THE NAPOLEONIC CONQUEST

Such was the church which the *Patriotten* desired to separate from the state in 1795.[108] The Orangists hardly opposed this move, and the actual change was affected almost without violence, though a few towns went so far as to demolish church pews reserved for use by officials of the *ancien régime*, or to remove them at the owner's expense.[109] Anti-religious sentiment was hardly involved. At the very first meeting of the new National Assembly president Pieter Paulus closed his opening speech with a solemn prayer.[110] But the National Assembly did take action against the privileged position of the Reformed Church. On August 5, 1796, the citizen-representatives at The Hague divorced the Reformed Church from the Dutch state. Representative Guljé, a Roman Catholic, called it a Mohammedan marriage because the husband-state espoused one denomination as sultana and kept others as concubines. The definite terms of the divorce had to be provided by a new constitution, and May 30, 1797, was set as the deadline for submission of constitutional amendments. The Reformed Church's polity was still geared to a system of separate, loosely-federated provinces in which each province had its "own" Reformed Church. They could not react fast enough. An arbitrary gathering of ministers at Utrecht composed a memorandum addressed to the National Assembly, but even that arrived too late. It requested no more than provisions for places of worship, enforcement of Sunday observance, and state-paid salaries and pensions for ministers. The separation of church and state was not protested. When eighteen ministers at Haarlem and Amsterdam refused to swear the required oath of allegiance to the new republic, the new government showed its determination by deposing all eighteen.[111]

What the Reformed Church could not do on the national level, however, was done by the now free and sovereign Batavian people. On August 8, 1797, they rejected the proposed constitution by an overwhelming vote: 108,761 to 27,955.[112] Ecclesiastical opposition showed its strength at the polls, the Reformed Church in defense of its former position and the Roman Catholics in disappointment that the present equality still favored the Protestants.

Radicalization

The second National Assembly convened on September 1, 1797, and adopted policies more radical than those of its predecessor. The 215,000 signatures on a petition requesting continuation of and subsidies for the Reformed Church were completely ignored. The *Unitarissen* had engineered a coup that ousted the Federalists.[113] Intensifying the revolution, they quickly imposed a new constitution that lacked a chapter dealing with religion. An organic law soon followed, requiring every denomination to provide for itself. The Reformed Church was the least prepared to meet this situation. The blow was somewhat softened by the proposed interim: during the first three years the state was prepared to pay ministerial salaries. Meanwhile, municipal governments were given possession of the steeples and church bells within their territory. Congregations were permitted to keep their buildings only if they had been the original builders. This provision affected all former Roman Catholic churches now in Reformed or other hands. Very democratically, the parish with the highest membership could claim title; thus, especially in the southern part of The Netherlands, many churches changed hands.[114] Ecclesiastical possessions other than sanctuaries were to be nationalized in order to pay for national education and the care of the poor. The theological faculties no longer continued as separate departments of the universities to train ministers for the Reformed Church but were relegated to the faculties of philosophy.

Daendels's coup of January 22, 1798, brought no changes for the church. The new constitution was quickly pushed through. It separated church and state and firmly established religious and political freedom. The Reformed Church was forced to meet the new situation.

Committees were soon established in every classis and provincial synod, mainly for the purpose of collecting the money that would be required to support the church after the three-year interim. There was little success. Sacrificial giving had been superfluous for so long that the lethargy was extremely hard to overcome. Although the church's internal strife had more or less come to a standstill, lack of unity and vision greatly hampered unified action. Furthermore, the last nationwide synod had been held in 1618-19. Nor should it be overlooked that the nation's economic situation was steadily worsening. Amsterdam alone had to feed more than 80,000 indigents in the year 1800. Many members who were perhaps willing to pay for their church lacked the means.

Restoration

Oddly enough, it was the state that saved the Reformed Church from disaster. A reaction had begun in France that also affected The Netherlands. On February 5, 1801, the National Assembly extended the interim state support of the church by a year. It was during this year that The Netherlands yielded to Napoleon's strong pressure for a modification of the revolutionary constitution. As the country regressed into oligarchic rule, the modified constitution again provided for the separation of church and state, but the two were considered as allies in the provision that "all denominations which honor and glorify a Supreme Being with the purpose to foster virtue and good morals, enjoy equal protection of the laws."[115] The law required that each person fourteen years and older had to register with the denomination of his choice, thus enabling the government to support the churches from the headmoney collected. No civil privileges could be claimed on the basis of church membership. The Reformed Church did profit, however, by the provision that each denomination was guaranteed title to properties held at the turn of the century, since transfers had not been made at a rapid pace.

Restoration went even further. On August 11, 1803, the Executive Authority declared religion to be of great importance to the commonwealth and made worship of the Supreme Being a concern of the state. Sundays were to be observed; the calling of a minister required again the magistrate's approval; in several congregations the right of approving the call of a minister was returned to the family so privileged under the *ancien régime*; deputies of the body politic returned to ecclesiastical meetings; theological faculties reopened in the service of the Reformed Church. Not only were the eighteen deposed ministers reinstated, but the special pews for civil authorities were returned to the churches. This was far more than the belated memorandum from Utrecht had requested.[116]

The churches were not adversely affected when Napoleon managed to establish a unified government in 1805. However, the Reformed Church did not regain the privileged position lost in 1795.

When King Louis Napoleon ascended the throne of Holland in 1806,[117] the rewritten constitution provided that "the king and the law equally protect all religions practiced in the country."[118] Though a Roman Catholic, the new monarch interpreted this provision literally and attended to the confused financial matters of the Reformed Church. Thus, he ordered all provincially administered funds of the church placed in an account of the central government. Ministerial salaries were to be paid from this account.

The plan did not succeed, however, because of the increasing debts contracted by the state. In 1807 expenditures were twice as high as income. King Louis avoided bankruptcy, but at the price of suspending all ministerial salaries. Nevertheless, some improvements were made as small congregations, unable to support their own ministers, were combined with others.

The king also permitted his minister of public worship, J. H. Mollerus, and his assistant, J. D. Janssen, to start work on a new polity for the Reformed Church that would be adequate for the contemporary situation. Mollerus and a committee completed plans in 1809. Implementation never took place, however, because the emperor recalled his brother and annexed The Netherlands to France.

Unification

Napoleon intended to govern his new addition to *l'Empire* by French law.[119] On January 24, 1812, he ordered a representative committee from the churches to reduce the number of denominations by combining the Remonstrants with the Reformed Church, the Old Catholics[120] with the Roman Catholic Church, and the Restored Evangelical Lutherans with the Evangelical Lutheran Church. The committee completed its preliminary report by August 1812, but Napoleon's reign did not last long enough to actualize this type of ecumenicity.

Napoleon's plan was not entirely without relation to ideas present in the churches. As early as 1796 the *Remonstrantse Broederschap* had invited all Protestants to consider a union "through the bond of love with all men who willingly confess the name of Jesus Christ, so that differences in understanding of the abstract would be henceforth excluded."[121] The union did not take place. Churches considered it with sympathy, but agreement on certain doctrines was held as an absolute requirement for union. For example, the Reformed Church's Synod of North Holland demanded, as a minimum, agreement on these three doctrines: (1) that the human race is born in sin and therefore doomed; (2) that substitutionary atonement is the only way to salvation; (3) that the internal recreative operation of the Holy Spirit is necessary.

The Remonstrants tried again in 1797, but the results were virtually the same. Only at Dokkum did a Remonstrant congregation effect a union, but with the Mennonites and not with the Reformed Church. The new body called itself the United Christian Congregation and set as its goal "the exhortation to and aid in the exercise of virtue based on rational conviction."[122]

A similar but unrelated effort was made through the *Christo Sacrum* Society at Delft,[123] which consisted of a small body of young people from different church backgrounds who at first retained membership in their respective denominations.[124] They refused to oppose any dogma and concentrated on the improvement of worship and liturgy. Although their weekly services were not held on Sundays, the denominations at Delft nonetheless felt threatened and condemned this intraconfessional body. When it was learned that *Christo Sacrum* had gone so far as to celebrate the Lord's Supper, the churches excommunicated known participants and thus forced the society, against its intention, to become a separate denomination. Although its example was followed in three or four other places, the new denomination failed to arouse popular support. At Delft it existed from 1797 to 1836 and attracted no more than 117 members.

Even as these voluntary attempts at unity were thwarted, so the churches resisted Napoleon's pressure for unity. However, their victory did not stem primarily from spiritual strength. That was evident even prior to Napoleon's annexation.

Thus, the institutional churches were bypassed when the Netherlands Missionary's Association came into existence.[125] J. Th. van der Kemp, the founder of the association, did not deem it necessary to communicate with denominational officials. When he translated the "Appeal to the religious inhabitants of The Netherlands" that had been issued by the London Missionary Society he addressed it to the population in general.[126]

Similarly, when the Netherlands Missionary's Association was established on December 19, 1797, it addressed itself not to individual denominations, but to "all genuine worshippers of our Lord . . . in The Netherlands."[127] The association admitted that the majority of the ministers on its board served the Reformed Church, but it insisted that this should not be a hindrance to the members of other "Christian denominations."[128] The address pointed to the urgency caused by "increasing unbelief and irreligion"; it therefore called for prayer "on the first Monday of each month at approximately seven o'clock in the evening"; it solicited financial support "without taking away from other pious expenditure"; and it expressed the hope that "different dogmas not pertaining to the essence of the Christian religion . . . would not prevent support . . . because what matters is the general cause of the Christian religion and the salvation of immortal souls."[129]

In reaction to this appeal the faithful in the denominations began to fear that "persuasions would be mixed," and the initial denominational support declined considerably. Nevertheless, the association weathered the storm, stating on May 21, 1799, that it "adhered to the Old and New Testaments as the foundation from which alone truth must be derived and as the sole rule of faith and action, as well as to the Twelve Articles of faith."[130] The association always remained suspect in the eyes of some, but it was able to perform its task without support from institutional churches. Missions could be done without the church, and that was indicative of the church's disunity.

Moderation

Following the moderate temper of the times, the churches refused to be greatly moved or to be deeply involved.[131] Allard Pierson, a most astute observer, described this moderate temper:

> One was so happily together, each in his high political or religious feather. Why should some eccentric make a spectacle of himself and climb over the wall? By nature and by tradition oligarchic, the civilized portion of the Dutch population, the thinking part of the nation, formed readily a clique that lacked nothing, spiritually distinguishing itself by the calmness typical of people who have partaken of an abundant meal. The restlessness of the hungry after better and higher, in any case after something else, was obviously exaggeration, going too far.[132]

J. H. van der Palm, who served on Leiden's theological faculty both in the French period and after the restoration of 1813, exemplified this attitude.[133] One of Van Raalte's teachers, he was considered "the most eloquent speaker in the possession of whom the fatherland may pride itself."[134] His colleague, A. des Amorie van der Hoeven, rightly characterized him as "the man of the true middle road."[135]

In this spirit of moderation King William I restored the Reformed Church. Albertus Christiaan Van Raalte was to take an active part in the protest against this spirit of moderation.

II

The Church Order of 1816

Albertus Christiaan Van Raalte grew up in a parsonage, and was taught strict obedience to the authorities ordained by God. He affirmed this in a letter written from the United States in April 1862:[1]

> From the cradle my father inculcated in me obedience to the powers ordained over me; all my soul breathed therefore nothing but to obey the ecclesiastical authorities too, for in my parental home I had grown up with the hymns, many of which had become precious to me, although I did desire congregational freedom for others; but this much did my Father teach me indeed that obedience, if it did not debase me, must be rendered for God's sake, and that it therefore had its limits where it would run contrary to his command.[2]

The minutes of the Reformed Church at Wanneperveen confirm that strict Christian discipline was exercised in Van Raalte's upbringing.[3] Albertus Christiaan's father had served there from 1811 to 1820 and acted as both chairman and secretary of the consistory.[4] Thus, the minutes were signed by him and always appear in the same handwriting. They testify to a careful pastorate. House visitation always preceded the quarterly celebration of the Lord's Supper. The poor were provided for. Few references to the ecclesiastical and political upheavals were made, except for those which recorded the consequent required changes or modifications. Only once was the consistory involved in a controversy. It concerned the elementary schools owned and operated by the Reformed Church.[5] In order to understand why the father of Albertus Christiaan dared to deviate from his strict obedience to the powers ordained by God, it will be necessary to briefly review the issue concerning the schools. This issue later became a factor in the seceders' decision to emigrate to the United States.

STATE, CHURCH, AND EDUCATION

Napoleon had ordered radical changes in secondary and higher education when he made the Dutch nation a part of his empire.[6] He excused the elementary school system because of the excellent revisions implemented within it by the Education Law of 1806.[7] Even King William I adopted the law of 1806 when he established his restored kingdom of The Netherlands.[8]

The Education Law of 1806

The Education Law of 1806 provided that elementary schools could be either public or private. Municipal governments were responsible for the former, although the federal government exercised comprehensive control over the quality of education by setting standards for the curriculum as well as teachers.[9] Private schools could be financed by tuition charges, a foundation, or a society established for the express purpose of running such a school.[10] Private schools could also be operated and, if necessary, subsidized by the deacons of a congregation. Such schools were invariably for the poor.[11]

The teaching of so-called dogmatic Christianity was outlawed in the public schools, while private schools were under no such restrictions. However, the new law did not totally ban religion from the public schools. It required that pupils were to be taught "all civil and Christian virtues."[12] Under this provision the public school opened and closed its day with prayer, a hymn, and the reading of a portion of the Bible.[13] Further, the church was urged to provide catechetical instruction for those pupils who wished to receive it on a voluntary released-time basis.[14] The "velvet revolution" stipulated the separation of church and state in a surprisingly moderate manner.

Prior to 1795 the public schools were permeated with Reformed theology. The United Republic had from its inception been concerned "that for the building up of a good republic and for the well-being of the country it matters not a little that young people from the cradle be educated in the fear and the right knowledge of God and be trained in every good art and virtue of youth."[15] The Synod of Dordrecht defined what constituted "the right knowledge of God" and the United Provinces purged that which did not conform to Dordrecht's definition from public education.[16] Children in the public schools were required to learn the questions and answers of the Heidelberg Catechism. Roman Catholics were sometimes excused,[17] but when not, were taught the difference between the Lord's Supper and the "Popish Mass" in the words of Answer 80 of the Catechism: "and thus at bottom the Mass is nothing else than a denial of the one sacrifice and passion of Jesus Christ, and an accursed idolatry."[18]

The civil authorities, together with those of the Reformed Church, worked out a separate school system in each of the seven provinces.

Thus each province placed its own particular character on its public education. But it is equally true that this character was comprehensively and deeply influenced by the Reformed Church. The States General was representative of this influence when it assigned the respective provinces the task:

> to educate and bring up the children (being the seed from which every advantage in Church and Republic is to be expected) in the Christian, Reformed Church, in the fear of God, all morality, and obedience, and also in learning and crafts, each one according to his opportunity and potential for the sake of God's glory, the well-being of the Churches, the commonwealth, and to the comfort and pleasure of everyone, both communally and individually, who may expect and enjoy the fruits thereof unto posterity.[19]

Religious Equality and Natural Religion

The public school discontinued teaching Calvinistic doctrines when the Reformed Church lost its privileged position in 1795. But the Reformed Church lost another means of influence. For almost three centuries the civil authorities had exercised control over the admission of teachers to private as well as public schools.[20] Such supervision had prevented militant indoctrination of the students in private institutions of denominations other than the Reformed Church. The tradition of such government control took deep roots and it was natural that the Velvet Revolution did not question putting private schools teaching Reformed doctrine under similar supervision. Control by the state had in former days been beneficial insofar as it produced some degree of religious toleration. To achieve the fullest measure of liberty, equality, and brotherhood, the state needed to reduce the Reformed Church to a status similar to that of other religious bodies. The new rulers were inspired by a natural religion which primarily served as "a source of virtue and a pillar of happiness and prosperity."[21] They believed that without this type of religion the nation would perish. This new principle replaced the old and it was enforced in the manner which had worked so well in the old republic—government control over the appointment of teachers. The new rulers could thus ensure that religious instruction in the public schools would be deistic and non-sectarian. It considered natural religion of vital importance in an education that

> through development of the children's rational faculties should be suitable to form them into reasonable beings and in addition to impress upon their hearts the knowledge and understanding of all that they owe to the Supreme Being, society, their parents, themselves, and their fellow men.[22]

The decision concerning the extent of government control that should be exercised over private schools was complicated by the possibility that such schools might become an avenue of escape from instruction in the state-supported non-sectarian religion. That possibility was reduced, however, by the clause in the Education Law of 1806 which stipulated that "admission of teachers in private schools can be made dependent upon no other conditions than those connected with their own behavior and ability."[23] Under this provision, municipal authorities could refuse to admit a teacher to a private school if such an admission "through partisanship and self-interest would abrogate the established rights of others."[24] Furthermore, the law required that municipalities both operate public schools and pass judgment on a teacher's request for admission to a private school within their boundaries. The local government could therefore act as both judge and jury. Great difficulties arose later, however, since the manner of appeal to be utilized by a teacher refused admission had not been clearly spelled out.

Like Napoleon, King William I adopted the law of 1806 for his Dutch realm, and also applied it to Belgium when it was added to the kingdom.[25] The Roman Catholics in that newly added territory were apprehensive about the Protestant North and did not welcome the new school system with its deistic religion. Jesuits and *Frères ignorants,* often imported from France, were hired in private schools to counteract the state-imposed religious emphasis. But the law's sections governing the admission of private school teachers served as a deterrent to the wholesale transfer of pupils to the private schools.[26]

Similarly, Protestants could be hampered in their desire to continue in private schools the kind of religious instruction outlawed in the official sessions of the public schools. The seceders of 1834, among them Albertus Christiaan Van Raalte, found that the municipal authorities often adjudicated requests for private schools with the same bias that opposed Roman Catholic aspirations in Belgium.[27] The two groups were too far separated in geography and in principle to be able to unite forces against their common enemy. The Roman Catholics in the North, unlike those in Belgium, were not in the majority. Thus, they favored the law of 1806. It had delivered them from the kind of public school which had taught Reformed doctrine, and they supported the ruling liberal party in order to prevent a return to that situation.[28] Protestant objections, on the other hand, were inspired by the desire to combat the spirit of the age and to return to the republic which had allied itself firmly with the confessions of the Reformed Church.[29]

It is thus clear why the Reverend Albertus Van Raalte and his consistory at Wanneperveen wanted to continue complete control of their private school. If it became a public school, as Mayor Acker wanted, religious instruction would have to comply with the law of 1806. At this point the elder Van Raalte examined his principle of obedience, for God's sake, and began to make inquiries whether or not the proposal could be resisted. The church's minutes state no more than that pastor and mayor were ordered to work out a reasonable arrangement. The available evidence indicates that the private school continued to be controlled solely by the church during Van Raalte's pastorate. The civil authorities avoided a showdown.

Little documentation is available on the other pastorates held by Albertus Van Raalte. Thus there is no need to doubt his son's statements about the spirit of obedience pervading the parsonage. More than twenty-seven years after his secession, and more than sixteen years after his emigration to the United States, the son was still so deeply impressed by his father's loyalty to the Reformed Church that he stated in his letter of April 1862:

> As for me, I hated it to be able no longer to occupy the pulpits of my father, to become a shame unto my relatives and to my mother during her lifetime; for me it was the most painful sacrifice to give up the so fervently desired preaching from the country's pulpits.[30]

That loyalty also explains why the minutes of Wanneperveen's Reformed congregation contain no negative comments concerning changes brought about in the Reformed Church. Only when he was directly hampered in his service to God did the elder Van Raalte dare to resist the divinely ordained powers of church and state. Because he could freely preach and teach in the Reformed Church, he considered it his Christian duty not to protest but to serve diligently.

This attitude of unquestioning obedience to government and church leaders may partly explain what Jan Romein has called one of the most difficult problems in Dutch history—the lethargy on the part of the Dutch population after its restoration to independence.[31] That this attitude prevailed is acknowledged by every observer, but explanations for it differ widely.[32] Romein feels that the nation's two most important groups, the paupers and those who lived from private investments, had a common lack of interest in politics and therefore welcomed King William's leadership. The Reformed Church shared in this lethargy, and the Reverend Hendrik de Cock, who in 1834 was the first minister to secede, considered it to be an evil consequence of the departure from the Dordtian establishment.

STATE CHURCH RELATIONS

Political compromises made by the Reformed Church during the time of the republic had made it quite docile, and the Velvet Revolution of 1795 became a conservative movement so rapidly that the church escaped the necessity of a radical self-examination as to how it was to function properly in the new situation. Even if the clergy *had* wanted to protest Napoleon's settlement, their financial status made it virtually impossible. The emperor's war machine had required so much money that even ministerial salaries were paid irregularly and many pastors found themselves compelled to sell their libraries. Often they had to beg for a living,[33] and one is said to have starved to death.[34] When King William by his decree of January 19, 1814, made certain that salaries were regularly paid, the clergy became less than willing to protest against further royal guardianship over their church.[35]

Great was the enchantment with the monarch who had triumphantly returned after the French upheavals. He enjoyed such confidence that, in the words of Huizinga: "after cheering a bit, the tired nation quietly laid itself to sleep under the shadow of the Orange tree."[36] But more than exhaustion was involved, for the nation wanted to enjoy the dream:

> that the best had now been reached. Thankful for peace, for the reopened sea, for the partly restored colonies; thankful for the tempered application of liberal ideas to church and state, the fathers were satisfied to live in the now best of all worlds, infused as in the days of old by that national self-satisfaction that had indeed received quite a blow and therefore perhaps discontinued to boast of their own country as "the delight of the Supreme Majesty" but a self-satisfaction that still liked to speak of [that country] as the throne of religion and civil virtue, of freedom, and people's happiness.[37]

The same spirit prevailed at the universities. It is perhaps best exemplified in the life of Professor J. H. van der Palm, one of Van Raalte's teachers at Leiden. A former *Patriot* and revolutionary, Van der Palm had been a very active participant in the government of the Batavian Republic and was one of the principal architects of the Education Law of 1806. He returned to Leiden's theological faculty in 1806 as professor *poesos et oratoriae sacrae*.[38] Van der Palm became a very popular lecturer and enjoyed even more popularity as university preacher.[39] His enthusiasm for the revolution ebbed away as French domination increased, and in 1813 his collaboration with the enemy was overshadowed by the benefits he was able to obtain for the country. So great was his fame that on December 6, 1813, King William appointed him

as secretary of the fully restored university. When Leiden's alumni of
the class of 1790 needed a speaker at their reunion in July 1828, no
more logical choice could have been made than Van der Palm. King
William requested that the meeting be held at The Hague so that he
could attend,[40] and Van der Palm assured the monarch:

> The Netherlands is everywhere called and praised as the happiest coun-
> try on earth. . . . You respect everybody's rights and guard the interest
> of all. You have founded here the throne for liberty of conscience as well
> as for true enlightenment. You support industry with the sacrifices of a
> noble disinterestedness. You encourage talents and arts, you see to it that
> science and letters serve the interest of nation and people. What is there
> that escapes your care, that your tireless activity does not watch and does
> not labor for? We harvest the fruits of all those cares, and when we, in
> the writings of foreigners, read your name, being mentioned as an ex-
> ample for the rulers, our hearts join in jubilantly, and we say to each
> other: as we love the king because of the fatherland, so do we love the
> fatherland because of the king.[41]

With the same spirit the Reformed Church placed full confidence in
the monarch. The renewed payment of salaries and the reinstatement
of theological faculties abundantly proved his royal good will toward the
church of his fathers.[42] But more than a show of good will was required
to include religion officially in the nation's restoration, and the government, not the church, was to make the opening move.

A Religious State

On December 21, 1813, King William called a committee of fifteen
members "to compose the constitutional laws for the State of The United
Netherlands."[43] Only two members pleaded for a complete return to the
former concept of the church and state relationship. The other thirteen
desired not to change the separation. The minority had some success: a
compromise was incorporated in the constitution of March 29, 1814.

The chapter "On Religion, Public Education and Poverty Administration" satisfied the minority primarily because of the inclusion of Article 133. It continued tradition by stating that "The Christian, Reformed
Religion is that of the Sovereign Ruler."[44] Article 134, on the other
hand, expressed the objective of the majority.

> All existing religions are given equal protection; the confessors of the
> same enjoy equal civil privileges and are equally entitled to occupy dig-
> nities, offices and functions.[45]

Both the majority and the minority agreed on Article 130, because it required the monarch to "exercise such control over all religious persuasions as will be found expedient in the interest of the state."[46]

The union with Belgium in 1815 necessitated amendments to the constitution. It provided for the separation of church and state, but did not mention the monarch's religion. The Belgians needed no Article 133 to be reminded that their sovereign was a Protestant. A new article, 190, was meant to assuage resentment against Protestant domination with the words: "The complete freedom of religious convictions is guaranteed for everyone."[47] Article 191 went on to assure believers that "all religious communions existing in the kingdom are given equal protection."[48] Nevertheless, restrictive steps could be taken if necessary under Article 193: "No public exercise of religion can be obstructed except in the case such exercise would disturb the public order or safety." Article 196 combined the disparate elements of complete freedom and government supervision without eliminating the disparity:

> The King takes care that no religion will be hindered in the freedom of its exercise guaranteed by the constitution. He takes care, too, that all religions keep themselves within the boundaries of obedience to the State's laws.[49]

Other articles regulated the continuous payment of funds to the several denominations.[50] Article 195 even opened the possibility of granting state subsidies to ministers and priests who could not claim such payments on the accepted rationale that they were made in lieu of the return of parish funds confiscated in the French period.

Church and state were separated, but only in the sense that the state did not endorse one particular denomination. All were held to be equal before the law. In his dissertation on H. P. Scholte, L. Oostendorp understood this to mean "that king and country continued in the basic principles of unbelief and revolution."[51] That judgment was only correct insofar as "revolution" meant "constitutional government," and insofar as "unbelief" meant the unwillingness to return to the church-state relationship which had prevailed prior to 1795. King William's government did not encourage unbelief in the literal sense of the word.

On March 1, 1815, the monarch signed the Sunday Observance bill. Its seven articles specified strict provisions:

> Since we, following in the footsteps of our God-fearing forefathers who always treasured this the most, took into consideration the necessity to guarantee the obligatory observance of the Lord's Day and other holy days of the public Christian Religion by uniform measures to be observed in all of the United Netherlands, we have heard the Council of State,

and have consulted with the States General of these lands, and have approved and understood . . . that on Sundays, and on such other holy days as are generally recognized and observed by the denominations of the Christian Religion in these lands, professional duties that may disturb Religion shall not be performed nor shall in general any public work take place except in cases of necessity for which the local government shall issue permission.[52]

Although theater performances, dancing, horse racing, and concerts could be permitted by the local authorities, this law superseded their jurisdiction by flatly forbidding engaging in such activities before religious services had been completed on Sunday mornings.[53] Stores had to close their doors and display windows. Local police were ordered to prevent excessive noise or other disturbances near church edifices when services were in progress. Thus the law went beyond the social provision of a day of rest and gave civil sanctification and enforcement to the observance of Sunday and other days of religious significance. The government frankly admitted this in the preamble of the law: "to guarantee the obligatory observation of the Lord's Day."

The Velvet Revolution had intended the opposite. The National Assembly of 1796 had dispensed with the Sunday laws of the *ancien régime* and left it to the individual to determine how he wished to spend the Lord's Day. Religion thus no longer enjoyed the protection by the state. The incorporation of the Dutch nation into Napoleon's Empire brought little change. The French law of *15 Germinal an X* made Sunday a day of rest for public servants, but only in the social sense. The law contained no religious provisions which favored the churches.[54]

State Administration of Religion

Civil support of the churches returned to The Netherlands after Napoleon's defeat, when liberated towns and villages reinstated the old Sunday laws. Local customs differed so widely, however, that King William sought to establish greater uniformity,[55] and this action ran contrary to a continuation of "the principles of unbelief and revolution." He continued the tradition of the old republic, unbroken by the revolution, that the state should be religious, and this explains why the king wished to concern himself and his government with the church. The state's religiosity was at issue, not belief or unbelief. King William and his advisors reinterpreted the separation of church and state by claiming for the government not only the *jus circa sacra*, as had recent administrations, but also the *jus in sacra*, although the latter was not appropriated as completely as it had been in the republic.[56] His government adopted no neutral position, but took the liberty to organize the denominations. Thus what was then known as the "king's fatherly care" affected every denomination, with the lone exception of the Mennonites.[57]

The Roman Catholic church in the new realm caused an intricate problem. Napoleon's concordat of 1801 continued for the Belgian part of the realm.[58] The North, however, where Napoleon had lacked the time to enforce his concordat, was still designated a mission territory supervised by the *Congregatio de Propaganda Fidei.*[59] The kingdom, however, primarily needed unity.[60] That could not be reached unless the religious situation was carefully handled.[61] King William demonstrated his good will, especially as a merchant-king, by liberally subsidizing the churches.[62] However, his personality lacked the warmth that would have put life into his efforts, and seventeen years of exile had taught him to rely on written reports rather than personal contact.[63] Thus he used the personnel of the ministry of public worship, a carryover from Louis Napoleon's administration, to implement the religious unity of his kingdom.[64] P. G. van Ghert, a Roman Catholic, and J. D. Janssen, a Protestant, had become experts in this field. By relying on these men to control the actions of the official cabinet ministers, King William "went to sleep in Bonaparte's bed."[65]

P. G. van Ghert admired Hegel's political ideals. For him the state was "the deity that was present" and thus exercised (as a matter of course) its right of control over the Roman Catholic church. Communications with Rome, the nomination of bishops, the training of priests— in short, anything of importance, was to be supervised by the state.[66] The ecclesiastical hierarchy in the South, already up in arms over the king's educational policies, was thus finally prompted to join the northern prelates. In 1825, Van Ghert finally succeeded in transferring part of the preparatory training for the priesthood from the minor seminaries, which had previously been closed by government order, to the state-controlled *Collegium Philosophicum* at Leuven.[67] Although the king personally tried to undo the strong resentment which arose because of this step by making a conciliatory concordat with Pope Pius VIII (August 17, 1827), the resentment did not subside. The Roman Catholics in the North successfully resisted on the ground that they never had and never would submit to a government that had a right of *placet* such as that provided by the new concordat.[68] Their counterparts in the South were much more accepting of the new provisions, but they resented the loss of former privileges which resulted from King William's oppressive policies. The church therefore found an unexpected ally in the Liberals, former archenemies, for they thought that King William's government was not democratic enough. This "monstrous alliance" proved strong enough to foment the revolt that brought independence to Belgium.[69]

J. D. Janssen scored an easier success.[70] The ministry's financial arrangements were very welcome to pastors, especially because arrears in salaries were being paid. A more critical attitude greeted the state's next major move, however, which was to impose government polities upon the denominations. Only the Mennonites were determined enough to succeed in their opposition.[71] The others, among them the Reformed Church, reluctantly acquiesced.

The State and the Polity of the Church

After the liberation, some provincial synods wished to revitalize the Reformed Church. The degree to which these synods were still thinking in terms of the former church-state relationship can best be seen, perhaps, in their request to King William that the government reimburse them for the cost of these reorganizational meetings.[72] Having been in exile for more than seventeen years, the monarch had to rely on the advice of his civil servants. H. van Stralen, his secretary of the interior, proposed on April 26, 1814, that a General Synod be called to accomplish what the provincial synods wanted to do.[73]

Van Stralen thus recommended the revolutionary step of convening the first General Synod since 1619. But his proposal to seat twenty-six ministers, eleven elders, and one advisory ecclesiastical professor contradicted the Dordtian church order that required delegates to be elected and instructed by the provincial bodies. On the other hand it must be admitted that only the province of Overijssel had officially committed itself to the church order of Dordrecht (July 30, 1619). Friesland operated under an order of 1586, Zeeland under another one of 1591, and Groningen under yet another one of 1595. Drenthe had drafted its very own in 1633.[74] Although these several polities did not differ in principle from the Dordtian order, until 1795 the Reformed Church in The Netherlands existed as a conglomerate of seven provincially organized churches. A General Synod could have been called during that period only if the provinces would agree to it politically as well as ecclesiastically.

The cumbersome structure of the more or less independent provinces came to an end during the French period and at that time the Reformed Church could have adopted a position independent of the state. She preferred instead the material advantages of an alliance with the new administration.[75] The Reformed Church responded in the same way when King William began his rule, for the provincial synods approached the new monarch for funds to meet the costs of their meetings. Again, the church encouraged close ties with the state. The petitioners thus accepted without protest his majesty's dictum to wait for a reply to their requests for funds. He wished to have the new provisions being readied by his department of worship in hand before he took action.[76]

Within the department, J. D. Janssen[77] preferred his own plan to that of Van Stralen's. Janssen wanted to call able ministers from each province to a consulting committee that would work out the proposals made in the plan of 1809.[78] Although Janssen was a minor officer in the department, his project survived because the Council of State rejected Van Stralen's proposal. This judicatory, the highest in the land, ruled against the state's interference with the church, unless complaints compelled the state to initiate such action. The council foresaw practical difficulties. Van Stralen's proposed General Synod could well be requested to spell out doctrinal purity which might disrupt the prevailing doctrinal moderation. Or, an orthodox party might reject the validity of a moderate synod and withdraw from the church.[79]

Conflicting evidence makes it hard to decide why Janssen's amended proposal won acceptance.[80] Knappert points out that on November 16, 1814, Van Stralen was replaced by O. Repelaer van Driel, while Janssen continued as secretary.[81] Although it is uncertain whether or not this change put Janssen in a stronger position, international complications urgently required governmental attention, especially those relating to the union with Belgium.[82] In that tense situation, the simpler plan might appeal to the government, and this may have been a deciding factor in favor of Janssen's proposal. At any rate, it was by a secret decree dated May 28, 1815, that the king appointed a "consulting committee of enlightened and esteemed ministers from the several Provinces."[83] The eleven members received Janssen's proposed church order by mail.[84] The exchange of opinions was channeled through the department and was thus under departmental control. There was some direct exchange when the committee met that same year (from October 25 to November 4), but differences were quickly ironed out and the king received the completed proposal on November 13, 1815.

Thereafter the Reformed Church was not consulted in an official capacity—classes and synods were not asked to discuss or vote on the proposed constitution. A royal decree of January 7, 1816, simply asserted that the "Concept of a General Order for the administration of the Reformed Church in the Kingdom of The Netherlands" would be put into operation.[85] To that end, the royal decree ordered "the Commissary-general of the Department of Education, Arts, and Sciences, in particular charged with the Affairs of the Reformed Church and other non-Roman Catholic religions" to take the following steps: dissolve the present classes and synods; submit names of pastors qualified for royal appointment to the new executive boards in each classis and provincial synod as well as to the new General Synod; and have the new church order in operation by the end of 1816.[86]

On February 6 the king approved the list of pastors proposed for royal appointment to positions in the new structure, and governors of the provinces received orders to convene the new synodical boards on the first Wednesday in March and install the appointees. The classical boards were required to meet on the last Wednesday of that month, and the appointees composing them were to be installed by the classis's representative on the board of the provincial synod.[87] The new constitution went into effect on April 1, and, consequently, the General Synod was to meet under the new provisions when called into session in June. Only the classes and provincial synods, which met earlier, were in a legal position to raise objections to the proposed chain of events. While thirty-six classes and eleven provincial synods accepted, or did not object to the new constitution, protests came from eight classes: Amsterdam, Delft, Delftland, Gorinchem, Haarlem, Tiel, Tielerwaard, and Utrecht.[88]

The government replied to the objections of the Amsterdam classis. The other protests were either not acknowledged or were responded to in the spirit of the official reply given to Amsterdam.[89] This classis deplored that the state, not the church, had taken the initiative; it viewed "with no small concern the indefiniteness of the influence allowed the ministerial department charged with the affairs of the Reformed"; it thought it conceivable that less favorable departmental influence might be exercised over doctrine and religious instruction, leading to a curtailment of religious freedom; it judged that ministerial membership in the General Synod was too small, and that the seating of delegates without binding mandate violated the principle of ministerial parity as expressed in Article 31 of the Belgic Confession.[90]

The classis delegated three ministers to personally deliver these objections to the king.[91] Receiving them in audience on March 7, 1916, the monarch promised careful consideration. Immediately following their audience with the king, the trio had a conference with the commissary-general. It was "a friendly dialogue" in which Repelaer van Driel assured them "that there was no intention to make a change in doctrine, but only in the manner of administration."[92]

Since the new constitution would be put in effect on April 1, 1816, any decisive action on the part of the church had to be taken prior to that date. The classis received the reply from the king's commissary-general on Friday, March 29.[93] Repelaer van Driel[94] pointed out how poorly the church had functioned under French domination, and that

the king had therefore done well to discontinue these chaotic conditions
by following the example of Louis Napoleon, who had also established
order in the church's external affairs. He reminded the classis of Protestantism's first principle: "a careful distinction between matter and
form, between Christianity and ecclesiastical administration . . . always
inseparably united by the Roman Catholics." He supported his point by
stating that other Reformed countries had adopted very different "external forms." Classes had not been originated by the apostles, but had
come about "as an accidental fruit of the circumstances in the 16th
century and of the political condition of these lands." Further, the classis
should not fear usurpation of power by the small number of delegates
to the proposed General Synod; the issues would be in the hands of the
ministers there present; the commissary-general's presence at the synod
was designed not to make that body dependent upon, but simply to
bring it into relation with the government through the department of
worship; a smaller number of synodical delegates probably ensured less
confusion and discord; the principle of a binding mandate had in the
past probably imposed more restrictions upon the church than it had
on the state; above all, the synod would not be called upon to decide
doctrine, but to govern the church; a multiplication of agreements made
binding by ministerial signature would not in itself guarantee the ministers' purity of doctrine, for such agreements had never prevented
ministers from doctrinal deviation. Repelaer van Driel did not miss the
opportunity to include in this letter the reply the king had promised
during the audience with the three representatives from Amsterdam:

> Thus far having acquainted the Classis of Amsterdam with the king's
> intention and the spirit of the appointed decree, I find myself further
> instructed by His Majesty to declare that His Highness never can, and
> even less intends to, encroach upon the Religious doctrine of a church
> to which His Majesty is wholeheartedly devoted; His Majesty expects
> and trusts that the petitioners, both as Teachers of Religion and as Sub-
> jects of the State, will present in their congregations [95] an example of
> confidence in the Sovereign, of obedience to the laws, and of esteem for
> those who are charged with their execution; and that the petitioners,
> now better informed about His Majesty's intentions and about the point
> from which the order of the Reformed Church's polity must be viewed,
> will not hesitate to behave in all respects in accordance with the same,
> and thus will cooperate to place the tottering administration of the Dutch
> Reformed Church on solid foundations, and under Divine Blessing to
> help contribute to her [i.e., the church's] welfare, and that of their par-
> ticular congregations, according to their ability and in the relations where
> they have been placed; while for the rest the petitioners are free and

unhampered to bring objections they might continue to hold before the next synod.[96]

The appeal to loyalty was not in vain. The Classis of Amsterdam agreed with the words of chairman W. Broes when he installed the new officers appointed by the king:

> And who of us, knowing his holy duties and desiring to be unswervingly loyal to them, would have decided to accept [royal appointment] unless in the conviction that the General Polity contains nothing that disagrees with the doctrine and privileges of our Reformed church, or in the conviction that, if anything of the sort had slipped in against the will of our righteous king, it will be taken out as soon as clearer seen.[97]

Polity and Doctrine

Neither the Classis of Amsterdam nor any other body of the Reformed Church carried its protests futher.[98] They acquiesced in a situation where church and state were separated in matters of doctrine, but joined in matters of polity. They, with the government, must have been convinced that such a policy was Reformed. Whether ecclesiastical polity belonged to the well-being (*bene esse*) of the church rather than to the being (*esse*) of the church was settled in favor of *bene esse*.[99] The doctrine of the Reformed Church in fact, however, opposes this interpretation. Article 30 of the Belgic Confession states: "We believe that this true church must be governed by the spiritual policy which our Lord has taught us in His Word." Article 31 adds: "We believe that the Ministers of God's Word, and the Elders and Deacons, ought to be chosen to their respective offices by a lawful election of the church, with calling upon the name of God, and in the order which the Word of God teacheth." Article 32 reads in part: "In the meantime we believe, though it is useful and beneficial that those who are rulers of the church institute and establish certain ordinances among themselves for maintaining the body of the Church; yet they ought studiously to take care that they do not depart from those things which Christ, our only master, hath instituted."[100] Yet, for the time being, no further opposition was raised.

The king appointed twenty persons to make up the first General Synod, which would meet on July 3, 1816: the twelve ministers who had served in the advisory commission; a permanent secretary chosen from among the ministers at The Hague; a permanent treasurer chosen from among the elders at Amsterdam; three pre-advisors from among the theology professors; one elder; and two commissaries politic.[101] Since the synod was to be convened according to the new polity, no questions were asked concerning the legitimacy of its foundations. President W. L. Krieger, a minister at The Hague, opened the session with a sermon. Repelaer van Driel then delivered an address, assuring the synod of its freedom to deliberate and act, as long as it obeyed Article 9 of the new polity. This article required the synod to maintain the Reformed position

> which honors no authority save Holy Writ, but which validates this authority, without condition or exception, as the perfect rule of faith and life . . . [and that] purity of that teaching be assured by the only sound guarantee: to establish arrangements fit to maintain and strengthen in the ministers and congregations true Christian spirit, namely by the increase of religious knowledge.[102]

The synod ended its first session on July 30, 1816. In the twenty-seven days of this session it had written and amended a great many regulations concerning the examination of candidates for the ministry, catechetical instruction, pastoral discipline and suspension, church visitation, vacancies, calling and dismissing ministers, and the costs of classical meetings.[103] The Reformed Church had become a collegiate body. Small gatherings, *collegia*, of state-approved officers governed the church, and the offices of deacon, elder, minister, and teacher were no longer allowed to exercise the supervisory functions which had formerly been their responsibility.

A clever compromise sought to establish a careful balance between a state-church, as Napoleon had wanted, and a church-state, as implied in Dordrecht's polity. The strict separation of doctrine and of polity (i.e., the constitution) had been used as a means toward that end, and decisive steps had been taken. It seemed that the state had succeeded in motivating the less than rebellious church to arrange its polity without touching upon doctrine. But was this not more than simply a molding of polity? The forces at work in the state were also at work in the church, and the state was affected in not only its form, but also in its basic governmental rationale. Could the church be different, could it be affected only in its form, and not in its doctrine?

The state obviously thought that it could. Change in form only was the core of the compromise. The government had issued strict provisions in Article 9 of the new polity:

> To care for the interests of both Christianity in general and in particular of the Reformed church; to maintain her doctrine; to increase religious knowledge; to improve Christian morals; to keep order and concord; to cultivate love for king and fatherland must always be the main goal of all who in their several functions are charged with ecclesiastical government.[104]

The order to "maintain her doctrine" simply transferred the problem out of the area common to both church and state and into the field that belonged exclusively to the church. The government desired this transfer because it adhered to the policy providing for the separation of church and state. But the state expected the church to follow the form which it had dictated, and doctrine was to be maintained—doctrine was to be rigid and unchanging, even though it was transferred into the field belonging exclusively to the church. Because the maintenance of doctrine was given to the church, Classis Amsterdam and the others ceased to protest. But could doctrine be frozen? Was it possible to neutralize doctrinal issues?

The church was expected to provide in her actions an affirmative answer to those questions, and from the beginning it was clear that it faced a dilemma. On the one hand, protests of the seven classes had been indicative of serious threats to unity, should the church fail in maintaining doctrine. On the other hand, unity would be gravely endangered if doctrine were maintained in its Dordtian form. Strict orders forbade the church to do anything but uphold doctrine, however. Compromise or development in the area of doctrine had been ruled out. The stage was set for conflict.

The elder Van Raalte and his consistory did not participate in church protests. Wanneperveen's minutes faithfully reflect directives from the synod and the governmental department at The Hague. Van Stralen's communication concerning the payment of back wages over the years 1811-13, for instance, was recorded without comment on January 29, 1814. Van Raalte received more than 570 guilders at a time when his annual salary amounted to 224 guilders. The minutes of September 4, 1816, recorded without comment the arrival of the new constitution.[105]

It is not suggested that Van Raalte's consent to the revised polity was bought with the payment of his back salary. If he or any other minister could have been bought at such a cheap price, it is hard to understand why he would have remained loyal to the church when in previous years he had at times received no payments on his salary. Nevertheless, a government that undertook payment of salaries owed by a foreign administration could be expected to gain the payee's confidence. The integrity of the ministers is really not in question. Pastors such as Van Raalte who had remained faithful to their flocks under the most strenuous circumstances could do little else but thank God for a monarch who wished to honor the Sabbath and bring order into the church. Besides, should Protestants object to the state's external control over their church and accept such control over the Roman Catholic denomination? After all, the powers were ordained of God, and the miraculous restoration of the Oranges to The Netherlands made it all the more certain that this particular authority was ordained of God. Royal assurance that doctrine would be maintained had settled the dispute. Wanneperveen's minutes testify therefore to the church's faithful continuation in its work. In retrospect, Albertus Christiaan correctly summarized:

> From the cradle my father inculcated in me obedience to the powers over me . . . obedience, if it did not debase me, must be rendered for God's sake, and . . . had therefore its limits where it would run contrary to his command.[106]

III

Dissatisfaction

REFORMED DOCTRINE:
ADMINISTRATION WITHOUT INTERPRETATION

As in earlier times, the Reformed Church had now accepted the state's tutelage. But the latter's promise that Reformed doctrine would be maintained required further interpretation. Should doctrine be equated with the three forms of unity: the Belgic Confession, the Heidelberg Catechism, and the Five Canons of Dordrecht? Or should it be equivalent to the Bible? Did current theology constitute the whole of doctrine? The General Synod was unable to deal directly with these questions. It was commissioned to administer but not interpret. And yet, through its acts of administration, doctrinal interpretation was unavoidably present.

Formula of Subscription

One of the synod's earliest accomplishments was to establish a formula for the admission of candidates into the Reformed Church's office of the ministry. A royal decree, signed July 30, 1816, made its use mandatory.[1] In Article 28, the synod spelled out the formula to be signed by the candidate:

> Having been examined, the candidates will be required to declare and affirm with their signature the following statements and promise: "We the undersigned, admitted to the public office of preaching in the Netherlands Reformed church by the executive of the provincial synod of _____, declare sincerely herewith that in teaching and practice we have very much at heart the interests of both Christianity in general and the Reformed denomination in particular; that we in good faith accept and sincerely believe the doctrine which, *according* to God's Holy Word, is contained in the *accepted* forms of unity of the Netherlands Reformed church; that we will diligently teach and uphold them, and that we will apply ourselves with all sedulity to the promotion of religious knowledge, Christian morals, order, and unity; binding ourselves with this our signature to all that is prescribed, and, should we be found to have acted against any part of this declaration and promise, to submit ourselves for that reason to the judgment of the competent ecclesiastical courts."[2]

Two phrases in this form became crucial: *"accepted* forms of unity" and *"according* to God's Holy Word."

"Accepted Forms of Unity"

Despite uncertainties, the synod never clarified what constituted the accepted forms. Of course, the Belgic Confession and the Heidelberg Catechism were generally acknowledged to be accepted forms. Although the other provinces included the Canons of Dordrecht, the Province of Friesland had always excluded them even though its ecclesiastical delegates to the Synod of Dordrecht had accepted these forms.[3] Therefore, one could argue that they did not properly belong to the forms generally accepted by the church as a whole. For unknown reasons, the Synodical Committee did not avail itself of this nearly perfect excuse. Instead, the committee stated its case against the canons much more directly in declaring that

> Examination in the Canons appears to us even more useless after the disputes which, in the course of more than two centuries, have come to naught; the diligence to defend the one or the other opinion has completely cooled off; and the denomination of the Remonstrants has declared that it neither adheres to those articles nor is willing that it be judged by them.[4]

However, the committee did not express itself in equally clear terms regarding what should be done about the situation which existed in the Classis of Walcheren. Since 1693, ministerial candidates had been required to sign the so-called Five Articles of Walcheren which condemned the teachings of Balthasar Bekker, H. A. Roell, and J. Vlak.[5] Signature to similar statements had been mandatory in other classes and synods,[6] and a case could be made that these time-honored requirements should be included in the accepted forms, together with the canons. This argument, however, surfaced too late to become very important.

"According to God's Holy Word"

The phrase "according to God's Holy Word" in Article 28 was in need of further definition and clarification. The so-called *quiatisten* understood it in the sense that the signing candidate concurred with the doctrine contained in the accepted forms of unity *quia,* that is, "because" they agreed with God's Word. The opposing *quatenussen* interpreted the candidate's signature to mean that he concurred *quatenus,* that is, "insofar as" they agreed with the Holy Word.[7] Hard-pressed by petitions and addresses, the synod successfully sidestepped choosing between the two.[8] (The unaltered form and declaration remained in effect until 1854, when a new formula with an equally ambiguous wording superseded them.[9]) Protests against the formula reached their highest pitch when in the decade following 1833 a large-scale secession began in the Reformed Church after the Belgian uprising had split The Netherlands. It is probable that protests came so late because the ambiguity in the formula allowed the individual minister a large degree of latitude. A *quatenus* had no difficulties following the more liberal trends in theology, while subscribing to the formula; a *quiatist* found latitude in the formula for his Dordtian orthodoxy. Besides, King William I commanded so much good will in the early part of his reign that few pastors felt moved to protest the church's new constitution.[10]

CONFLICTING INTERPRETATION

Since histories in the English language neglect these years, it sometimes appears as if the Secession of 1834 offered the first firm resistance to the newly-defined relation between church and state. Significant examples of dissatisfaction began to appear between 1816 and 1830 however. For followers of Mazereeuw and the *Zwijndrechtse Nieuwlichters*, the future was important and the past did not matter. Vijgeboom's Restored Church of Christ, on the other hand, insisted upon a return to classic Dordrecht. Neither of these movements gained a large following, but they attracted wide attention with their criticisms, some of which appeared in the Secession of 1834.

Jan Mazereeuw

Jan Mazereeuw's claim of being the second Elijah was governed by "purely religious considerations."[11] Greatly influenced by the writings of the Philadelphian mother, Jane Leade, Mazereeuw announced in the early 1820s that the world would soon come to an end.[12] His small following of sixty-five families adjusted itself to Christ's imminent return by divesting themselves of luxuries. Their children were withdrawn from the schools so that the parents might instruct them in the true religion, the only needful thing. But only the very first followers sold their farms in expectation of the impending glory. As a whole, the group was satisfied to do nothing more than wait. On Sunday morning, from eight until noon, Mazereeuw guided the faithful to a fuller understanding of biblical prophecy. Provisional forms of the perfect society to come were not tried, although the sacraments of baptism and the Lord's Supper were declared unnecessary.

The group did not constitute a threat to either church or state, however, since for more than twenty years Mazereeuw and his followers were one of the many conventicles in the Reformed Church. When they finally seceded in 1845, it was hardly more than the locking of a door that had long been closed. Neither the church nor the state took drastic actions against them.[13]

Zwijndrechtsche Nieuwlichters

The *Zwijndrechtse Nieuwlichters* attracted much more attention.[14] The principal founders of this group were skipper Stoffel Mulder, police captain Dirk Valk, and a domestic servant named Maria Leer.[15] They became best known by their nickname, *Zwijndrechtse Nieuwlichters*, but often referred to themselves as the Apostolic Brethren Association or the Communion of Saints. The location of their principal settlement was at Zijndrecht, situated near Dordrecht. *Nieuwlichters* literally translated means new-lighters. The name is a pun on the new light the group was spreading through selling their communally-made matches.

The *Nieuwlichters* did not fare so well in spreading their spiritual light, however. They did attract a following, but it consisted mostly of church members who were no longer content with their shadowy subexistence in the conventicles. What appealed to them was not the expectation of Christ's imminent return, but the immediate adoption of the Christian lifestyle as described in Acts 2.

In attempting to establish that lifestyle they rejected the social, ecclesiastical, and political order in the kingdom of William I. Repudiating civil marriage, registration of births, and especially conscription, they went so far as to abolish baptism and the Lord's Supper within the bounds of their religious communities. A worshipful spirit from day to day and the communion of goods became the mark of this truly renewed communion of saints.[16] Dissatisfied with a Sunday observance enforced by law, they hallowed every day as a day of the Lord.[17]

Unlike the followers of Mazereeuw, the *Zwijndrechtsche Nieuwlichters* collided with the government. What Van der Palm had called "the best of all nations" did not appreciate their criticism. Arrests took place and prison terms followed. But acquaintance with Professor H. W. Tydeman at Leiden saved the group. On intimate terms with King William, Tydeman assured the monarch that the group was only interested in the establishment of a kingdom of peace, and was therefore harmless.

When larger numbers began to join the group, however, many came less for the sake of the spiritual life than for the escape from poverty which the communal life offered.[18] Their presence threatened the group from within, a major part of the threat being their failure to attain the *Nieuwlichters'* high-minded attitude toward marriage. Embarrassed by reports of immorality, local authorities began to harry them to the extent that the *Nieuwlichters* were unable to maintain their disciplinary ideals. Their leaders were so often in prison that the baser element of their group could exercise influence. Thus, the *Nieuwlichters'* reformation of society and mankind[19] bogged down. The group formally disbanded in 1846, although a remnant of thirty members was influenced by Mormon teachings in 1863 and left for Utah. There they formed a colony that sympathized with, but kept itself distinct from, the Mormons.[20]

The Restored Church of Christ

Neither Mazereeuw nor the *Nieuwlichters* had challenged the Reformed Church because of her new constitution. This was first done by Jan Willem Vijgeboom.[21] Born in Germany in 1773, he came to The Netherlands in the nineties and soon became an *oefenaar* or lay-preacher. As such, he raised his voice in protest against the synodical organization of 1816, and despite several arrests and fines he refused to desist.[22] Vijgeboom's protest caused a secession from the Reformed Church in 1822, when a conventicle of dissatisfied church members at Axel, a small town in the Flemish part of the Province of Zeeland, engaged him as its *oefenaar*.[23] The group of approximately thirty members had ceased to attend services in the local Reformed Church, since in 1818 all but one of those who were serving on the consistory had been deposed because of their refusal to operate under the new polity of 1816.[24] The dissatisfied had nevertheless not relinquished their membership in the Reformed Church, for they hoped and prayed that she would restore the old order. But their status as a conventicle, an *ecclesiola in ecclesia*, changed soon after Vijgeboom's arrival. In August 1823 the group named itself the Restored Church of Christ. Formally seceding from the Reformed Church, it returned to the three forms of unity and the church order of Dordrecht.

Conflict with the State

Serious difficulties developed at this point. The government recognized as the Reformed Church only the one reconstituted in 1816. Anyone challenging her legitimacy would *ipso facto* challenge the legitimacy of what King William's government had done in that reconstitution. Thus the Restored Church of Christ in taking exception to the actions of 1816 came into conflict with not only the church but also with the state. The dissenting *Nieuwlichters* and Mazereeuwians had encountered far less opposition because they had not contested the ecclesiastical reorganization of 1816.

The Reformed Church could thus exercise an ecclesiastical discipline over the dissenters which was backed by civil authority. The civil authorities could hardly be expected not to defend what they had done in 1816. To concede to Vijgeboom and his group would mean that the Reformed Church as a whole would move back to the situation that had prevailed in the United Republic.

Nieuwlichters had been concerned about the present socio-religious condition, and the Mazereeuwians had been concerned about the future. Thus, both groups had readily given up the pattern of the past. But Vijgeboom's Restored Church of Christ saw an enduring validity in the Dordtian establishment. They pointed to that establishment in their appeal to King William I:

> [Our] doctrine . . . is that of the Dordtian Fathers; certainly not because we ascribe infallibility to the pronouncements of the Dordtian Synod, but because . . . [we] consider that doctrine . . . as being most and closest according to God's Holy Word: to err is, after all, human, perhaps [we] are in error; but so long as [we] are not convicted of error by the authority of Holy Scripture, so long must [we] be loyal to that doctrine which as far as [we] can see is the only true doctrine. Nobody will contradict that the church now called *Hervormd* does deviate from the forefathers' doctrine: nobody will therefore be able to reproach [us] for being apostate or schismatic, for we are undoubtedly those who in uprightness cling to the old Reformed church doctrine.[25]

Clearly, the Restored Church of Christ and its position on Dordrecht stood in opposition to the Reformed Church and Church Order of 1816. The state could not be neutral in the conflict, for it had assured the Reformed Church that the action of 1816 had represented an administrative step in which no doctrine was involved. Yet, the Restored Church of Christ had seceded on doctrinal grounds.

The Napoleonic Code

The government based its counterattack on Articles 291, 292, and 294 of the Code Penal, Napoleon's lawbook.[26] This lawbook had not been repealed in The Netherlands, and a decade later the government used these same articles against Van Raalte and the seceders of 1834. The articles are offered here in translation because the histories in English that touch upon the period do not reproduce them.[27]

> *Article 291:* No association of more than 20 persons, whose aim is to convene daily or on certain days in order to be engaged in matters of religion, literature, politics, or other subjects, may be organized except by approbation of the High Government and under such conditions as the public authority will impose upon the association. Those who live in the house where the association congregates shall not be included in the number of persons meant in this article.

> *Article 292:* Every association, as meant above, that has been organized without due authorization or that has violated the conditions imposed upon it when being authorized, shall be disbanded. The heads, directors, or administrators of such association shall be punished by a fine of 16 to 200 francs.

> *Article 294:* Everyone who without permission from the municipality permits or allows the use of his house or room, or a portion thereof, for the meeting of members of an association, even if authorized by the government, or for a religious exercise, shall be punished by a fine of 16 to 200 francs.[28]

Freedom of Worship—or Conscience?

Vijgeboom and his followers responded by referring to the constitutionally guaranteed freedom of worship.[29] But the minister of worship, F. W. F. T. Baron Van Pallandt van Keppel, distinguished between the freedom of conscience guaranteed in Article 190 of the constitution and the equal protection of Article 191 extended to . . . "all religious communions existing in the kingdom."[30] He contended that Vijgeboom's group was not in existence when the constitution had been adopted in 1815, and thus Article 191 did not apply to this new body. In fact, he counseled that all religious bodies not in existence in 1815 would require subsequent royal approval. Since the Restored Church of Christ had neither received nor applied for such approval, freedom of public worship would have to be denied them. Van Keppel went on to explain that although this body had seceded from the Reformed Church, it wanted to remain in the Reformed tradition and

> their intention is then of constituting a separate sect of an existing religion, and how dangerous that could become I hardly need to develop for your Majesty. The constitution, it should be added, knows only one existing Reformed Church with respect to this peculiar religious conviction; only this body may claim the protection and privileges allowed in

Article 191 and following; by separating themselves from the same, and by now joining themselves to another religious conviction in existence within the Kingdom, they lose every claim to protection and privileges in the religious sphere.[31]

The minister of justice, C. F. van Maanen, concurred in this view in his advice to the king:

> In my opinion, strict maintenance of the existing laws against all such fanatic seceders and new religious sects is the best means to counter them and to protect society against all confusion and irregularities which are otherwise to be expected therefrom.[32]

When the Restored Church of Christ appealed to the king again on May 10, 1824, they made it clear that they wanted to be understood as being the old Reformed Church.[33] The members pleaded that their public confession of faith should be honored as an oath of allegiance to the old Reformed Church and not to the reconstituted church of 1816. In addition, they raised objections that proved, in their opinion, the difference between the two. In the first place, they protested the singing of hymns in the worship services. They also expressed disagreement with the new practice of allowing non-Reformed Church members to participate in the Lord's Supper. Last, they lodged a protest against the liturgical novelty of asking the congregation four questions (as a preparation for the Lord's Supper) during the worship service. The same arguments reappeared not only in the Secession of 1834, but also in the secession that ruptured Van Raalte's Reformed Church in Michigan, U.S.A., in 1857. The setting of these three arguments is particularly worthy of note, because it will help to clarify why later the Reformed Church, together with the government, tried to oppose the seceders of 1834 with actions that had been successful against Vijgeboom's Restored Church of Christ.

The singing of hymns

The Restored Church of Christ had made a mistake in its first objection. The synod of 1816 could not be blamed for the 192 hymns that had been introduced into the Reformed Church in 1807,[34] since the provincial Synod of North Holland had initiated the move in 1796. It invited the other six provincial synods to appoint delegates authorized to compose a hymnbook extolling "the fulfilled gospel; the honor of the Savior and of the Holy Spirit; the atonement; and grace."[35] Response and acceptance were typically slow: the provincial Synod of Utrecht waited seven years before it appointed delegates in 1803. On September 4, 1805, the joint committee presented a collection of 192 hymns to Rutger Jan Schimmelpenninck, the acting head of the Batavian Republic.[36]

The hymnbook made its entry into the Reformed Church on January 1, 1807, but it scored no immediate success. Anticipating resistance, the committee had many hymns to the tunes of the Psalms. The effort was too obvious and missed the hard core of the objections, most of the resistance being inspired by loyalty to Article 69 of the church order of Dordrecht. This article directed the church to sing no other songs than David's Psalms in her worship services.[37] The committee was not unaware of Article 69, but it had banked heavily upon the more than forty revisions of the Psalms published in the seventeenth century as an indication that the Reformed Church might be ready to revise and perhaps enlarge the number of her songs to the Lord. But the committee failed to recognize the importance of the fact that none of these versions had managed to supersede the officially sanctioned version that Petrus Dathenus had translated from the French edition in 1566. This psalter, which came to be known as *Datheen*, was criticized for its alleged vulgar language, deficient rhyme, and faulty translation from the Hebrew. It weathered such criticisms until 1756, when the Reverend Andries Andriessen launched a decisive attack. He was able to convince the majority that *Datheen* should no longer be accepted as the genuine Psalms of David and as unchangeable as the Word of God itself.[38]

Within the framework of the United Republic, the Reformed Church could effect no major changes without the cooperation of the magistrate. And even though the States General decided in favor of a new Psalter on May 25, 1762, official action could not be completed until the seven delegates from the provincial synods met on January 12, 1773. However, the committee managed to complete its work in six months. Ordered to do no original work, the committee composed the new Psalter by selecting from three versions.[39] To make the Psalter more acceptable to the congregations, many melodies were uncritically borrowed from *Datheen*. But that precaution did not prevent widespread resistance when the Psalter was finally introduced on January 1, 1775.[40]

Many of the faithful treasured *Datheen* as the inspired Word of God, or at least as a very precious relic of The Netherlands' glorious struggle for freedom and true religion. They considered it to be sacrilegious to supplant it with something new. This was especially true for those who opposed the political changes at the end of the eighteenth century as a deviation from God's will. The orthodox insisted the more upon using the venerable *Datheen* because the Remonstrant Church used liturgically the Psalter of *Laus Deo Salus Populo*, from which fifty-eight psalms were taken for the new Reformed Psalter of 1775. Comrie and Holtius had already warned against *Tolerantie* as an unscrupulous scheme to reconcile old foes.[41] The orthodox feared that Dordtian truth would further dwindle into oblivion because the two denominations now held in common more than a third of their respective psalms.

Opposition to the combined forces of church and state could not win official victory, especially since the church order of Dordrecht had not been violated. Resistance thenceforth went underground, and *Datheen* was sung in numerous conventicles. Thus, the old Psalter was still being printed well into the nineteenth century.[42]

Against this setting, it may be seen that the appearance of hymns in public worship could readily be interpreted as a further deviation from ·Dordtian rule. When protests against the hymnbook were quelled by civil authorities, suspicions arose that the hymns were meant to foist *tolerantie* upon the church. France's tightening grip on the nation prevented a full-scale conflict, however, and no rebellion of any kind was allowed to take place. With such powerful backing the hymnbook could become firmly established in the church, and it proved to be doctrinally acceptable enough to take firm roots. In its introductory statement, the committee for the hymns could write with some justification that the hymns were ". . . to guard in our congregations the purity of doctrine in the midst of a stream of manifold dangerous modernities."[43]

King William's return brought no immediate change for the church. The Psalter and hymnbook were not affected when the new church order was introduced in 1816. Although violent objections did not occur at this time, the opposition had not died. It lacked, however, educated leaders determined enough to contend with the ecclesiastical and civil administrations. Vijgeboom's rambling publications failed to attract nationwide, solid support. Moreover, so many orthodox appreciated at least parts of the hymnbook that only a small minority could be aroused in support of the principle that hymns were un-Reformed and should therefore be banned from public worship.

On the other hand, not all the hymns embodied acceptable doctrine. Hymn 53 is illustrative:

> My God! what ever may be numb in me,
> Let me always believe in Thee.
> In virtue, and in eternal life;
> Then the feeling of my worthiness
> Will never leave my breast.
> However uneven my path here may be.[44]

Many more orthodox believers protested this optimistic faith. To them the question of hymns in the worship service was secondary to acceptable doctrine, and the establishment suppression of Vijgeboom's claims to have reestablished the Reformed Church of old and its Psalter did not deal with the underlying doctrinal issue. Therefore the question of the hymns cropped up again in the Secession of 1834, and many seceders objected to the hymns not so much as manmade additions to the Psalms, but as vehicles of false doctrine.[45]

The Lord's Supper

The second main protest of the Restored Church of Christ was directed against the participation of non-Reformed church members in the Lord's Supper.[46] They referred the king to the National Synods of 1578, 1581, and 1586, which required a personal confession of Reformed faith before the consistory prior to participation in the Supper.[47] It is strange, however, that they did not quote Article 61 of the Dordtian church order (1618-19), which demanded of participants in the Lord's Supper both "the confession of the Reformed religion" and the "testimony of a pious life."[48] Were they perhaps afraid that their opponents might remind them of the Anglican delegates from England who participated in the Lord's Supper at Dordrecht?[49]

The synod meeting in 1817 had made its desires explicit: on July 16, 1817, it ruled that

in order to prevent any confusion in the congregations, and also in order to create no discord between or suspicion on the part of other denominations, the Synod will instruct the Provincial Boards that members of other Protestant denominations who should so desire may be admitted to the Lord's Supper in our congregations, if in the consistory's judgment no contrary reasons exist and if they are of nonscandalous life and submit proof of ecclesiastical membership.[50]

That Vijgeboom's group stood practically alone in its protest against this is indicative of the lack of determined opposition within the Reformed Church. Hence, neither Vijgeboom nor the Secession of 1834 succeeded in their opposition.[51]

The Evangelical Lutheran Church cooperated with the Reformed Church and informed the synod about its decision to admit Protestant Christians "to the co-celebration of the Holy Supper."[52] That the open Supper failed to become a rallying point for more unity among Protestant denominations was probably a practical consequence of the prevailing theology, in which education, not the sacrament, was considered the vehicle of God's grace.[53]

New liturgical departures

The third main protest of the Restored Church of Christ was directed
against urging the congregations "to read four questions in the preparatory services prior to the Lord's Supper, to request those members
who plan to draw near to the Supper to rise and to answer said
questions."[54]
Although the synod's decision of July 11, 1817, first introduced these
four questions to the denomination as a whole, the liturgical custom
itself was not new. Congregations in the provinces of Groningen and
Friesland had prepared for the Lord's Supper according to this custom
at least since 1659,[55] and the synod adopted four questions closely re-
sembling those used in the northern provinces. They read:

> The members of the Christian congregation who desire to celebrate Holy
> Communion will please rise and in the presence of God who knows the
> heart will answer with me these four questions:
>
> I ask you first whether you believe heartily that the genuine and perfect
> doctrine of salvation revealed unto us by God is contained in the books
> of the Old and New Covenant? Those who believe this please join me
> in answering *yes*!
>
> Secondly, I ask you whether you believe heartily that you are deeply
> depraved and deserve before God punishment and whether you are dis-
> pleased with yourself in humility and contrition? Those who believe this
> please join me in answering *yes*!
>
> Thirdly, I ask you whether you believe heartily that God, in sheer grace,
> has given us his only begotten Son Jesus Christ as our only and perfect
> Savior, whose body was broken for us and whose blood was shed for us
> in forgiveness of sin; and whether with a believing heart you accept Him
> for yourself unto wisdom, justification, sanctification, and salvation? Those
> who believe this please join me in answering *yes*!
>
> Fourthly, I ask you whether in compliance with the obligation you have
> because of your baptism you sincerely resolve by the power of the Holy
> Spirit to persevere in this confession, to strengthen your faith, to improve
> your life, to live in true love and unity with your neighbor, and thus to
> render genuine thankfulness unto God for his grace. Those who are thus
> resolved please join me in answering *yes*![56]

There were very definite differences between the questions adopted
at the synod and those used in the northern province. The doctrine of
salvation as it was expressed in the first question was no longer equated
with Scripture, but was said to be contained in Scripture. Furthermore,
the doctrines of man's total depravity and the perseverance of the saints
were restated in less drastic terms.[57]

But the Restored Church of Christ made no mention of the doctrinal implications in the four questions. Rather, it held up this liturgical practice as being an example of the "several other actions" taken by the synod on July 11, 1817, against which it protested.[58] In these actions the synod had advised the congregations to set aside a preparatory Sunday prior to the celebration of the Lord's Supper. For the Lord's Supper itself the synod suggested that long tables be placed in the church, and that all participants should be seated about them so that the Supper could approximate being an actual meal. Differences in social standing were not to be recognized. Finally, the ministers were urged to say a brief meditation immediately prior to the passing of the bread and wine.[59]

The opposition did not object to the leveling effects the synod's proposals would have. They did express the fear, however, that in the new mode of the Supper, God and his Holy Spirit would be given less opportunity to operate in the mysterious ways of inwardly making the sinner a worthy partaker of the heavenly food. Man was now taking the initiative, and at the place and time of his own choosing.

This conflict over the liturgy of the Supper had deep roots. Although a more rationalistic and optimistic theology was gaining ascendancy in the Reformed Church, the synod's recommendation to adopt an ancient provincial custom indicated that the orthodox tradition had not altogether lost its relevancy. The Restored Church of Christ in its protest against a more inclusive participation in the Lord's Supper reflected but one side of that orthodox tradition. F. A. Lampe, 1683-1729, Jodocus van Lodenstein, 1620-77, and Bernard Smijtegeld, 1665-1739, had been among those early Reformed fathers who counseled that the true believer might partake of the bread and wine only if he could claim certain carefully described evidences of true belief.[60] The opposing view was represented, however, by equally orthodox fathers such as Petrus Immens[61] and Wilhelmus Brakel. These latter fathers specifically addressed those

who have not yet left the church entirely and declare that they are staying within the church: they attend the preaching of the Word, they fellowship with the saints in the church, but they abstain from using the Holy Supper, also because they see so many unconverted and scandalous members partake with whom they think to be in fellowship if they were to participate with them. To enlighten these—for we believe that most of them do this because of tenderheartedness and an erring conscience— we will put this question and treat it: *is a Christian permitted, yea is it his duty,* to abstain from the Holy Table of the Lord, although not seceding from the church, as long as the church is impure? We answer: absolutely not. . . .[62]

Suppression of the Restored Church of Christ

The Restored Church of Christ did not have the support of the orthodox members of the Reformed Church. In addition, those who held disparate views of the Supper found it unnecessary to transfer their membership to another church, for the conventicles offered them the opportunity to express their convictions without having to secede.

For most of them, however, the Lord's Table was so little used and held to be so holy that it had ceased to be a practical issue. Even in the town of Axel, Vijgeboom's home base, the greater number of those who no longer attended the Reformed Church did not formally join the Restored Church of Christ.[63]

Van Pallandt van Keppel, the government's minister of worship, exploited this situation by rearranging the finances of the Reformed Church at Axel so that the state would take over the three hundred guilders which was the congregation's share of the minister's salary of twelve hundred guilders.[64] Pastor N. Borsboom was then called to fill the existing vacancy.[65] Within three months he reported substantial progress: followers of Vijgeboom were returning to the Reformed Church.[66]

Meanwhile, the legal judgments against Vijgeboom and some of his principal followers were upheld. The Council of State, the highest judicatory in the country, reported to the king on November 22, 1824, that there were no grounds which would necessitate the reversal of the earlier judgments.[67] Also, the council's commission on the other Protestant churches upheld the restrictions of the *Code Napoleon* with respect to religious gatherings.[68] Thus, the committee could not recommend the rescinding of the judgments against the Restored Church of Christ on the basis of Article 19 of the constitution, although the committee did emphasize its concern for the principle of freedom of religion:

> . . . freedom of religion and conscience constitutes one of the state's foundations, and is constitutionally guaranteed to every citizen but would be of the opinion that one would very wrongly use this beneficent principle, like so many other good things, by exaggerating it and by applying it indiscriminately in all cases.[69]

In this particular case the committee argued as follows:

> . . . these memorialists—without adducing any legitimate ground that would justify their secession from the Reformed Congregation to which

they once belonged—could cause a schism through which perhaps in this Realm that unity now prevailing in the Protestant Church could be disturbed and therefore the regulating measures, effected by your Majesty and showing results thus far, might become less effective, through which further confusion might arise which could be of far-reaching consequences.[70]

This argument was not original. The committee stated frankly that it "could and must agree with . . . the joint report of the ministers of Worship and Justice." The two ministers had advised the king in August 1824 that the seceders' appeal for freedom of conscience "would have to be distinguished from the right to worship publicly under the protection of the state."[71] Only churches recognized by the government could claim the latter right. This being the prevailing judgment, the ministers argued against official recognition of the Restored Church of Christ:

. . . the memorialists' claim is especially strange because they—a few persons of lesser consequence desiring to value certain ideas and publicly seceding from the Reformed Church recognized by the state—now wish to claim that they must be considered to be Reformed, although they seek to inflict as much harm upon this church as they possibly can. Moreover, the direction of the spirit of these sectaries is designed to disturb as much as possible the now existing and steadily increasing brotherly harmony between Reformed and other Protestants; and their desire to appear in public seems inspired especially by the hope to succeed better in their goal to generate a new quarrel and discord. For that reason we believe that the interest of the State and of Religion certainly recommends: to decline and refuse the request submitted to the memorial returned herewith.[72]

Thus, the combined forces of church and state suppressed Vijgeboom and his group. The authorities, however, overestimated the persuasiveness of their actions. Local conditions at Axel were not conducive to further resistance, but not all seceders returned to the Reformed Church. Decisive battles were avoided. Governmental restraint was certainly an important factor in this situation, but other factors were also involved. The seceders' respect for the law, their love for the church, and their devotion to the House of Orange were great enough to make them reluctant to force a showdown. However, they were not totally lacking in resistive strength. In 1834, the conflict would no longer be avoided.

IV

The Dutch *Réveil:* Protest and Renewal

THE SIGNIFICANCE OF THE DUTCH *RÉVEIL*

The English-speaking authors mentioned earlier[1] have generally regarded the Secession of 1834 as a direct consequence of the *Réveil* or Awakening. The *Réveil* originated from the protest against the ecclesiastical and political persuasions which followed the restoration of the Kingdom of The Netherlands. The poet-philosopher Willem Bilderdijk became heavily involved in this protest, and consequently he has often been portrayed as a forerunner of the Secession of 1834. But the secession failed to attract Bilderdijk's disciples, and thus the *Réveil* flourished outside the Seceded Church. None of the authors mentioned above seems to have been aware of this problem, but it was clearly stated in a letter written by Isaac Da Costa, one of Bilderdijk's disciples, under the date of January 28, 1834:

> I shudder when I look back on my life's path and remember how our entire Bilderdijkian school had that tendency to hyper-spirituality and when I recall myself as a twenty-five year old who was the author of the Objections against everybody and everything. But the Lord has graciously preserved and will also further preserve those who for a moment through erroneous presumption have strayed away from the narrow and secure path in their eagerness that was not always holy.[2]

The protest against the new ecclesiastical and political realities in King William's restored kingdom clearly gave rise to both the *Réveil* and the Secession of 1834. But the Awakening did not automatically lead to a break with the Reformed Church.

The character of the Dutch *Réveil* makes it impossible to sketch it as a well-defined movement. Its best historian, Dr. M. Elisabeth Kluit, states that

> The *Réveil* can only be retold in the [biographies of] the participants. The *Réveil* took place in the inner man of which the external events were but a weak reflection. This produces peculiar difficulties for the historian. . . . a clear line of development is absent.[3]

In a later study Dr. Kluit defined this character of the *Réveil* even more clearly: "The *Réveil*-circle was no organized society but a small group of people who each in his own way fought against the superficiality, the stultification, and the deadness of the spirit of that time."[4]

To do justice to both the *Réveil* and the secession it is necessary to describe the way in which Bilderdijk became involved in the *Réveil* and what kind of protest he helped shape amid the general mood of complacence.

CONTENTMENT

The smaller secessions hardly disturbed the Reformed Church. The fact that they occurred, however, indicated that tensions were building. In the first years following 1816 all had seemed to go well for the Reformed Church, especially since the protests against the new church order had been so effectively suppressed.[5] An additional proof of the prevailing good will had come at the celebration of the Reformation's tercentenary in 1817. The many festivities often featured speeches by clergymen who modeled their addresses after the example of Isaac Johannes Dermout, permanent secretary of the Reformed Church's new synod.[6] In his opening speech to the synod on July 2, 1817, Dermout had stated that the church's "deep peace" was a consequence of the "mild spirit generated by the Reformation." Referring to 2 Timothy 1:7, he described how

> The Reformed Church in The Netherlands may, with thanksgiving to God, praise the present moment of her existence because of the peace among her confessing members; the brotherly love among her teachers; the light that is spreading from her schools unto all classes of men; and the improved organization of her institutional forms . . . it would dishonor us if we should lack in love—if we were to be bitterly zealous over against those who think differently—or if we were to arrogate to ourselves jurisdiction over everyone to whom the reasons for our convictions do not appear to be convincing at all. . . .[7]

Many Reformed congregations were inspired by this to adopt the following order for their celebrations: a history of the Reformation in the morning service, and the antiphonal singing of specially composed choral works in the evening service. Dermout's attitude was so successfully imitated by most ministers that even Roman Catholics were induced to attend these celebrations.[8]

Why the Reformed Church failed to plan similar festivities honoring the two hundredth year of the Synod of Dordrecht is not clear from the records. Did the Reformed Church not dare to reinterpret it in the same manner that the Reformation had been reinterpreted as a nine-teenth-century liberal movement? Or was the Reformed Church so con-fident of the canons' obsolescence that one could afford to ignore Dordrecht completely? Whatever were the reasons for the lack of a celebration, Dordrecht was not entirely forgotten.

SCHOTSMAN'S PROTEST

Nicolaas Schotsman, a minister of the Reformed Church at Leiden, raised a lone voice of protest. Born in 1754, Schotsman first worked as an apothecary and then took up studies for the ministry. He was or-dained in 1787. After having become a pastor at Leiden in 1793, he was deposed from that position in 1796 because of his support of the House of Orange. Under the general pardon of 1801 Schotsman was allowed to return to Leiden, and he resumed his pastoral duties. Although he rejoiced over Orange's return to The Netherlands, he expressed doubt about the new organization of the Reformed Church. But his main concern centered on the church's task to preach true doctrine. Knappert characterizes Schotsman as "exceedingly loyal to the confessions and exceedingly polemic."[9] It is only fair to add that Schotsman also was exceedingly loyal to the Reformed Church until his death in 1822.

Schotsman had never hidden his preference for the relation between church and state that had prevailed in the old republic. That preference led him to criticize even the House of Orange when King William I became the royal head of the expanded Kingdom of The Netherlands. Schotsman opposed the addition of Roman Catholic Belgium to The Netherlands, stating that King William, "the beloved Jehoshafat married into Ahab's house."[10] For Schotsman, as for many Dutchmen, the be-loved House of Orange was the God-appointed instrument by which it pleased him to govern his "Israel of the North."[11] To add millions of Roman Catholics as citizens of this chosen nation came close to a betrayal of the Dordtian fathers. Thus, Schotsman felt called upon to warn against the tendency to degrade the church's confessional past.

Recall to Dordt

In two evening services at Leiden, May 9 and 16, 1819, Schotsman memorialized the Synod of Dordt. The first sermon was based on Acts 20:30-31, while Revelation 16:15 formed the basis for the second.[12] They were soon published under the title: "Commemorative Column in honor of the National Synod held at Dordrecht two hundred years ago."[13] A devastating counterattack was unleashed, and Willem Bilderdijk was drawn into the battle. Schotsman's *Eerezuil*, Commemorative Pillar, was ridiculed as an *eeuwige schandzuil*, an eternal pillory.[14] This stirred up Bilderdijk, who wrote a strongly-worded introduction to the second edition of Schotsman's *Eerezuil*. In no uncertain terms, he identified which of the warring parties was truly battling for Jesus Christ. He encouraged Schotsman in a summarizing poem:

> Happy the man who at the decay of doctrine and morals
> Wipes the make-up off falsehood's face;
> Lays bare the cancer that chews away the church's heart
> And dares, to come under the eye—the shameless eye—
> Of the absurd spectre that under the guilded chandelier of conceited reason
> Shows on its Cain's forehead the visible mark of the curse.
>
> Yes, Schotsman, let us stand firm! Bowing at Jesus' cross;
> Let us despise the rancor of pagan and sophist
> Whose wisdom is vanity and craftily varnished lie
> And who fruitlessly try to wrest from us expiation in the Savior's blood.
> The hostile, wretched gang may march up in anger,
> But God on high himself laughs at their impotent effort:
> Prior to the world's creation itself He determined this battle's outcome.[15]

Schotsman stood firm. In his parsonage he received for private instruction in orthodox doctrine a few interested students who were enrolled at Leiden's theological faculty.[16]

Influence of the Swiss Réveil

Schotsman also widened the nation's horizon by encouraging his friend Cornelis Baron van Zuylen van Nijeveldt to translate for publication Ami Bost's French brochure: *Geneve Religieuse en mars 1819*.[17] Schotsman explained in the introduction that in calling attention to the Genevan *Réveil* he had no intention of inciting a similar secession in The Netherlands. Comparing the Dutch church to its Genevan counterpart, however, he did observe that the Genevan corruption there originated in principles that could also be clearly discerned in the Dutch situation. Opponents of true doctrine were infiltrating the Dutch church and were denying the validity of the confessional forms of unity. Hence there was every reason to be watchful. The Dutch church might fall asleep as had her Genevan sister, although the true believers in The Netherlands need not fear the oppression suffered in Geneva.[18] In his last publication, a translation of Ananias Asher's *The Falling Away from the Christian Church in our Days*, Schotsman repeated this thought and urged the Dutch church:

> Well then: take our confession again in hand;
> test it anew against God's word; peruse the close
> relationship between the dogmas of faith and wake
> up to the beauty and consistency of our confession;
> deplore, despise, and give up every aberration;
> and immediately discover, avoid, and escape the finest
> snares that the spirit of temptation is laying for us.[19]

BILDERDIJK JOINS THE BATTLE

Willem Bilderdijk and his pupils involved themselves openly in the defense of Schotsman, supporting his view of the relation of church and state. Through this defense the nascent Dutch *Réveil* became more and more a matter of public attention. Isaac Da Costa, one of Bilderdijk's Jewish converts, observed later, "The battle that Bilderdijk waged against Neology must be especially attributed to the vilification his friend [i.e., Schotsman] suffered for defending the truth."[20] Further, Da Costa wrote to his friend Willem van Hogendorp:

> Did you already read the second edition of Schotsman's *Eerezuil* with Bilderdijk's foreword? . . . and what did you say about it? Here one is furious at him [i.e., Bilderdijk] because of his writing, I hear. It is indeed forcefully written, but in that manner one must oppose those damned atheisms and conceited absurdities. . . . And my heart cheers enthusiastically the hero who dares to speak in the midst of a mad century and who dares to receive and preach the wisdom which God gives to him. I am sorry that as occasions arise, I am unable to make public pronouncements on the matter, but the subject is too delicate for one in my position to say much about it. You understand me and my feelings and therefore I can confide in you.[21]

Although in 1819 Da Costa was still a member of the Portuguese Jewish synagogue at Amsterdam, very intimate ties connected him with Bilderdijk. It is somewhat ironic that when Da Costa was fifteen years old, Mozes Lehmans, Da Costa's private instructor in Hebrew, introduced him to Bilderdijk.[22]

With the advent of the summer of 1813, Napoleon's grandeur was fading fast. Both Bilderdijk and Da Costa had admired the emperor, but had been disillusioned by his oppressive policies. In reaction both

Bilderdijk and Da Costa began to love The Netherlands more deeply.[23]
When Bilderdijk became Da Costa's private instructor in 1815, a profound friendship developed that was to last a lifetime. The classroom,
said Da Costa later, "gave occasion for many a confidential talk. There
a knot was tied for the duration of my life—and even more than that."[24]

Bilderdijk's Background

Bilderdijk was born in 1756.[25] In his youth a foot ailment kept him
in bed for more than twelve years. During those years, the developing
genius studied a broad variety of subjects, although his claim to have
learned Hebrew at the age of two must be discounted. He did graduate
from Leiden University's law school, however, and became a successful
lawyer in The Hague, often defending the underdog. He quickly advanced. As a fiery Orangist, he even had access to Prince William V.
When the new regime required an oath of allegiance in 1795, Bilderdijk
promptly refused to comply and was banished from the Batavian
Republic.[26]

In 1806, after eleven years of exile in England and Brunswick, Bilderdijk returned to what was then Louis Napoleon's Kingdom of Holland. Eager to win Orangists over to his side, the new monarch invited
Bilderdijk to teach him Dutch and appointed him as one of the executive
directors of his Netherlands Institute of Sciences. The suggestion has
been made that Bilderdijk conveniently forgot his love of Orange because of the handsome income he received from King Louis. But he did
not support the Napoleons for monetary gains, for cooperation was the
logical result of his firm belief in absolute monarchy. Explaining his
relationship to the emperor, Bilderdijk wrote,

> I saw immediately in him the man who was called to establish a new
> universal monarchy . . . the benefit of which would be that steps were
> taken against . . . the merchants, that refuse of humanity, with their rule
> Free Ship Free Goods, a rule that runs contrary to all good faith, and as
> a result of which Europe would have to face its complete ruin. If only a
> truly universal Monarch were to fasten them down in iron and unbreak-
> able schackles out of which neither the politics nor the strategem of that
> scum of hell would be able to sport their release.[27]

As Geyl has shown, Bilderdijk denied the democratic aspect of Dutch
history.[28] Instead, he emphasized the importance of the God-appointed
nobility whose duty it was to represent God in government. To attach
himself to the nobility, Bilderdijk created the legend that he was a
descendant of the noble family Teisterbant van Heusden, whose origins

went back to the mythical Knight of the Swan. That this noble family existed only in his imagination did not prevent him from describing it, and therefore himself, as the staunch defender of "oppressed innocence in hut or palace, for which this blood has flowed for a dozen centuries, devoted to God and honor; at one with itself; and invulnerable, however the storm may roar on the trembling earth."[29]

In contrast with this elevated self-perception, the shabby manner of Bilderdijk's second marriage is embodied in the unmentionable fact that he "married" without telling her that he was still legally married to his first wife. Bilderdijk's first wife had not followed her husband into exile (Germany), but at least he could have tried to be honorable about his foreign liaison. Bilderdijk claims that the exiled Prince William V (in England) dissolved his first marriage, but he did not produce documentary proof of that claim. One can imagine the howl that went up when Kollewijn, the biographer, published the letters Bilderdijk was writing to his first wife in The Netherlands while already sleeping with his "second" wife. It surely damaged his image as a Protestant saint and prophet!

In his reinterpretation of Dutch history, Bilderdijk created a reality of his own which he understood to be the God-directed course of events. This was his answer to Jan Wagenaar, whose account of Dutch history had made the democratic tradition of self-governing cities and provinces the backbone of the nation's past.[30] If Wagenaar had slighted Orange's part in that history, Bilderdijk defended its contribution so ferociously that he lost sight of historical accuracy. Bilderdijk's own pupil, Guillaume Groen van Prinsterer, the father of the Anti-Revolutionary Party, did not agree with his master's invectives against Wagenaar. Groen van Prinsterer defended the latter against Bilderdijk's charges of falsification, although he made it perfectly clear that he, too, had detected in Wagenaar too much of "the one-sidedness of a partyman who defended the regents of the province of Holland."[31]

Bilderdijk had little opportunity to make his insights known, but the impending appointment to the chair of Dutch language and literature at the Athenaeum Illustre at Amsterdam, later the Municipal University, would at last afford him the opportunity to make an impact. The government passed him over, however, and appointed J. P. van Capellen, a gifted mathematician but without literary qualifications. This obvious slight has often been interpreted as proof of narrow-mindedness and, perhaps, of conspiracy on the part of the supposedly liberal-minded authorities.[32] It would be easier to believe this charge if Amsterdam's magistrates had blocked Bilderdijk's professorate only on the basis of religious bias. However, Bilderdijk himself had caused serious doubt about his scholarly ability. As Geyl summarized:

> It is that self-righteousness, it is that unwillingness to build on what others have begun, coupled with his unrestricted fantasy, that made it impossible for Bilderdijk, with all his undeniable uncommonness and with all his indomitable energy, to assert himself in the scientific world. Jakob Grimm said very simply: "Bilderdijk would certainly accomplish more, if he did not rely so entirely upon himself."[33]

Bilderdijk's religious convictions were also a consideration. The prevailing theological mood ran contrary to his and probably prompted an unfair estimate of him. But this one aspect of the story must not be isolated from the others.

Lecturer at Leiden

Bilderdijk soon found a way to compensate for his disappointment. On the advice of Professor H. W. Tydeman, his friend at Leiden, Isaac Da Costa's father postponed his only child's enrollment at Leiden for one year and appointed Bilderdijk as tutor during the interim.[34] It was then that the deep friendship previously mentioned was born.[35] When Da Costa enrolled at Leiden in the fall of 1816, Bilderdijk followed him there within the year.[36] His friend Tydeman, who earlier supported his candidacy in Amsterdam, had already been urging that he come to Leiden to teach privately courses in Dutch history, "judicial, critical, diplomatic, and by an entirely new method."[37] Young Da Costa, too, had appealed to his teacher to join him in Leiden to provide "a good history of these Netherlands." Bilderdijk needed no further prodding, for Da Costa had written to him the following assurance:

> I can assure you that generally speaking Wagenaar is here differently appreciated than in Amsterdam; and that by far and away most young men of some refinement feel the necessity of other sources from which to draw the knowledge of such an important history as that of their country.[38]

Having arrived in May 1817, Bilderdijk began his lectures in late September. Six students attended the first course: Isaac Da Costa, Abraham Capadose, Willem and Dirk van Hogendorp (sons of Gijsbert Karel), Nicolaas Carbasius, and Johannes Tiberius Bodel Nijenhuis. Willem van Hogendorp and J. T. Bodel Nijenhuis were the only two who finished the course, which lasted until April 1819.[39] Although the empty places were soon occupied by others, the "young men of refinement" Da Costa had been speaking of did not flock to these lectures. During the ten years that Bilderdijk taught in Leiden, 1817-27, forty students in all heard him regularly.[40] Allard Pierson, the most sensitive observer of the *Réveil*, characterized Bilderdijk's work in these words:

> What Bilderdijk left behind, he bequeathed because of incapacity. Regular thinking, regular work, systematic exposition of his ideas to teach his nation—these he was unable to do. Nobody understood and deplored this incapacity more than he did. There lies the limit of this exceptional mind. That incapacity was the consequence of a lack of respect in his being; a lack of lasting sublimation; a lack of holding on to what he had grasped; a lack of working on the fruits of his intuition.[41]

What Bilderdijk lacked in formal procedure was compensated for by the effervescent, personal manner of his teaching. It fascinated the little band of students who heard him. For example, he had the habit of providing in his lectures medical detail for Capadose, the student of medicine, and would address Dirk and Willem van Hogendorp on the fine points of constitutional law as it applied to the situations of their father Gijsbert Karel and King William I. He gave each student his due. Moreover, the second Mrs. Bilderdijk and he were always available for any of the students who cared to drop in.[42]

Bilderdijk's Philosophy

Bilderdijk, sixty-one years old in 1817, made his viewpoints known with great urgency. The "lord of Teisterbant" saw himself in the midst of an apostate generation as the lone champion of the orthodox and only true understanding of Dutch history. His firm belief that the end of the world was close at hand made it all the more necessary that at least a few educated persons should continue as faithful witnesses to the corrupt nation.

In Bilderdijk's philosophy, matter is understood as a product of the immaterial which has its ultimate unity and reality in God. "All that God thinks outside himself exists *eo ipso.*"[43] But divine creation lost its harmony through man's fall brought about by man's insurrection. Afterwards, man's striving could accomplish no more than patchwork. "Only reunion with God can restore man, who fell from God in guilt."[44] It was Christ who came voluntarily from God to unite himself with man. Through him alone man can be reunited with God.

Therefore to study history was for Bilderdijk more than observing human affairs. "The way of God's providence with mankind . . . must be the object of our uninterrupted attention."[45] Through the study of history, man's soul, created by God to be in direct communication with him, discerns the Creator's ways. Man would completely misunderstand the world, argued Bilderdijk, if he were to ascribe to this world and its history a reality existing outside and independent of God and mankind. Nature and history have only relational value. Their true reality transcends both: it is only to be found in God. And since man's soul is the only organ with which he can know the Divine, man can never discern God's will and way except through his soul in relation to God.

> The Saviour relegated us to no principle taken from our rational understanding. It was the heart that He claimed. His ethics were not *think* and *do*, but *feel*. Love! Love with all your soul, with all your capacities and with the full scope of your susceptibilities. That is what he had prescribed for us as the only, the universal principle applicable always and in everything.[46]

Such a principle made it impossible for Bilderdijk to give reason a role in the area of faith. "One must feel, not think God. Feel Him, I say, through His revelation to the heart; through the heartfelt revelation of His operation . . . not think Him, for He cannot be thought."[47] Bilderdijk asserted that for faith the activity of the soul and the heart be given pre-eminence over reason. Only such faith could serve as the connecting link between man and God. Therefore he coined the epigrammatic saying: "The true 'autodidact' is 'theodidact.' "[48] Reason was for Bilderdijk a judge that could reliably make judgments concerning man's ultimate standards, but not form them.

These convictions put Bilderdijk on a collision course with most of those of his contemporaries who accepted reason as a legitimate and profitable means to know God. He considered them to be atheists, and lectures on Dutch history were given to prove that charge. This was clear from what he stated in his first session:

> Truth has no fatherland except with God; she and she alone is the aim of the historian, and as such the historian is neither Dutchman, nor Frenchman, nor Englishman. He is world-citizen, even citizen of heaven, who from above the world and without participation in it looks down on the agitation of the nations . . . He who accedes to the study of history places himself on the judgment seat of the Universe. . . .[49]

Not unwilling to admit that the human race was capable of some measure of peaceful coexistence despite its fall, Bilderdijk wanted to make the point that law and order did not originate in a manmade social contract. On the contrary, authority was delegated to man by God himself. The family, with the father as head, was proof of a God-given absolute authority that precluded arbitrariness. Since the state was a natural expansion of the family, according to Bilderdijk, the family possessed the authority of a father. Members of a family were of course not related on the basis of equality. The state could therefore not be considered to be the product of citizens contracting with each other on an equal basis. The concept of the people being the real sovereign of a nation was a monstrosity that resulted from atheistic thought.[50]

With such thinking, Bilderdijk reinterpreted Dutch history. In the insurrection against Spain, the beginning of Dutch national independence, Bilderdijk saw the work of God insofar as William the Silent led his people by faith. But in the midst of that struggle, on July 26, 1581, the States General had issued the *Acte van Verlatinghe*, the Act of Abandonment. In that document, King Philip II was reminded that "the ruler is appointed by God to be the head of his subjects . . . as is a shepherd to protect his sheep." Since Philip had failed to be such a shepherd, the States General declared him "*ipso jure* to be suspended from office."[51] Applying Bilderdijk's theory of the state to this situation, one would have to say that the children had deposed their father.[52]

And indeed Bilderdijk identified this act with *duivelen-leer*, devils' doctrine. In his eagerness to point out that the Oranges had always defended the rights of the common people against intrusions on the part of the minority, Bilderdijk denied the democratic tradition in Dutch history. In that tradition, polity had been constructed on the basis of a contract between governor and governed.

Nevertheless, Bilderdijk correctly criticized Wagenaar's history in stating that it had not done justice to the medieval contribution to the political system of The Netherlands. The medieval ruler, especially in the Province of Holland, had indeed protected the rising third class against feudal lords and usurping regents. Therefore Bilderdijk deserves the credit of having drawn attention to the fallibility of Wagenaar, "whose historical account was on the verge of becoming the fixed official truth."[53]

In his lectures Bilderdijk developed this theme to the point where the Oranges seemed to be the monarchs they should have been instead of the stadholders they actually were, and before long his pupils were defending theses at the University of Leiden that reflected these views.

Pupil-Disciples

The first pupil to defend Bilderdijk's thought in a thesis was Willem van Hogendorp, eldest son of Gijsbert Karel van Hogendorp.[54] At Leiden on May 27, 1819, he presented a dissertation entitled "William III and His Battle against France for Balance of Power in Europe." In this dissertation he tried to rehabilitate the stadholder, who became England's king, against Wagenaar's favorite, Johan de Witt, pensionary of the republic.[55] Similar thoughts were repeated two years later when on April 11, 1821, a student named Jacob Rau defended a thesis entitled: "On the Monarchy as the Best Form of Government."[56] Both studies revealed the impact Bilderdijk was making upon his students. The social contract as the source of authority in the state was denied.

If any doubts remained, Isaac Da Costa's literary doctorate delivered at Leiden two months later on June 21, 1821, removed them with some unmistakably clear theses. Thesis VIII asserted that history taught that the highest authority in the state could only be derived from God. Thesis IX carried the argument one step further: neither by the king's will nor by the demand of the people could royal power be limited. Thesis X concluded that contemporaneous efforts to limit this highest authority derived from God "exhibited the spectacle of an open war against God."[57]

Da Costa's raw absolutism so impressed Wiselius, Amsterdam's chief of police, that he reported it to the king.[58] William was displeased with this kind of support, and the more so because he wished to eliminate anything that might incite the Belgians against his government.[59] At Leiden, the faculty of law debated whether or not Bilderdijk should be allowed to continue his teaching. Drastic steps were not yet taken.

Instead, it was decided that the students should be given an antidote consisting of special discourses. Thus, Professor Kemper opened his autumn lectures with an oration entitled "De Liberali Disputatione." Urging the students to walk along the safe, middle road, he pointed out the advantages of unbiased research and debate. The next day, September 21, 1821, Professor Siegenbeek went a step further in his opening lecture, entitled "De laude Wagenarii," and defended the accuracy of Wagenaar's historical work.[60]

Bilderdijk's ideas, however, were not so easily neutralized. Dirk van Hogendorp, youngest son of Gijsbert Karel, proved himself a forceful disciple when on January 26, 1822, he presented his dissertation: "William the First's Right to the Sovereignty [of the Province] of Holland." Gijsbert Karel had only a vague idea of its contents, but surmised enough to be moved to write his son: "I only recommend to you not to reveal the obscurantism and despotism of Da Costa in his last three Theses."[61] Nevertheless, Dirk was prepared to defend the thesis that the authority of Holland's sovereign was not to be restricted by representative bodies. Thus, Dirk concluded that William the Silent did not need the approval of a representative body to accede to authority in

Holland. Bilderdijk was so pleased with the study that he supplied a poem to accompany it:

The coward may be silent, may adapt himself
Or may be in league with the country's traitors:
You remain attached to Nassau's [i.e., Orange's] house,
Attached to God, and to honor.[62]

On the day of Dirk's promotion he defended his views very successfully. His friends were disappointed, however, that Kemper and Siegenbeek did not launch the expected counterattack. Siegenbeek even spoke in warm praise of Dirk's moderation at the reception.[63] Was Bilderdijk's school to be ignored? Were the professors so certain of the success of their special lectures that they could afford to be generous?

Limitations

The outwardly united front of Bilderdijk's school lacked inner strength. When with apostolic enthusiasm Da Costa offered to translate Dirk's dissertation from the Latin into Dutch, the older Willem van Hogendorp counseled against it.[64] In spite of Bilderdijk's approval, Da Costa followed Willem's advice. Willem had earlier been very frank with Da Costa about Dirk's thesis: "Concerning those rights of the Prince [at the time of] the insurrection against Spain because of his status as stadholder: I am not so ready to admit them."[65] Here the student of history had reached the limit in supporting Bilderdijk. The master's personal charm failed to sway devotion to historical truth.

Nor was this the only respect in which Willem van Hogendorp expressed an awareness of Bilderdijk's limitations. The "lord of Teisterbant" was so firmly convinced of the imminent end of time that he prophesied about it to his disciples. Convinced of his fabled ancestors' greatness and godliness, Bilderdijk firmly believed what his great-grandmother had prophesied concerning him; he would see the last of days.[66] He reconciled this extra-biblical witness with the Word of God through John 16:12.[67] According to Bilderdijk, Jesus implied in this verb that Christians would be able to foretell the future, and Bilderdijk simply could not resist making predictions concerning the future and believing them with all his heart. Thus, he had spoken of 1819 as being a very crucial year. Willem van Hogendorp, graduated at this time, was so impressed with Bilderdijk's prediction that he could not decide upon a career for himself. He wrote to Da Costa:

As I review what our great man [i.e., Bilderdijk] always told us about the year 1819, and as I take a view of the amazing course of events around us. . . . [I wish] to think of nothing before at least this year 1819 has passed and I can somewhat calculate whether it is worth the effort to look out for some employment.[68]

Da Costa's reply reflects his lack of any desire to retire, even in the face of the end:

> This does not concern us except with respect to our religious principles. Let the events run their course, and let us run ours . . . *Et de la je conclus* that you with all your devotion to our blessed religious principles can have no reason for the sake of our earth's lot not to enter immediately upon the career to which you feel you are called.[69]

Willem van Hogendorp was unable to separate his religious convictions from his plans with respect to a career. Events proved Bilderdijk's prophecies wrong, however, and Van Hogendorp subsequently expressed his abandonment of this aspect of Bilderdijk's teachings in another letter to Da Costa:

> In 1818 and 1819, Bilderdijk told me at least twenty-five times that the world would perish in the course of that year. I no longer believe that he still thinks that way, and I am for myself convinced of the very opposite. . . . That chronology of Revelations: I am unable to understand it.[70]

Willem parted with Bilderdijk's teachings in another respect as well. The "lord of Teisterbant" was so convinced of mankind's impending doom that he abhorred the idea of improving the condition of man. Such efforts should be avoided by earnest Christians, he argued, because they would imitate the construction of Babel's tower. Beginning in 1821, however, Willem van Hogendorp enthusiastically worked as the secretary of the Commission to Study Poverty which was presided over by Prince Frederik, second son of King William.[71] He had a very high opinion of this work:

> As long as there is in our society one family that does not enjoy in sufficient degree at least the first necessities of life, so long can we expect a blessing neither upon that state nor upon its members. In that respect all of us are responsible or will experience the consequences.[72]

Willem van Hogendorp was fully aware that Bilderdijk did not rejoice in the social activities of his pupil. The young reformer complained to Da Costa:

> Bilderdijk hates so cordially whatever is called social improvement that the last time at Leiden it seemed to me that he had not been able to forgive me my position with Poverty Administration. In fact, he was as cold as ice.[73]

Bilderdijk refused to interfere in what he considered to be a process mysteriously directed by God. He was held firm in that view by the many disappointments of his own life,[74] and it agreed fully with his theological convictions concerning man's absolute dependency upon God:

> To be passive, totally passive in God's hand and like a leaf of a tree to be carried and driven by the wind where it may blow; thus without will and without cooperation to be carried by the Spirit of God is the only state of security and undisturbed calm that we can enjoy in this life.[75]

Willem van Hogendorp was prepared to alleviate the suffering of the poor, for he did not draw such theological links between suffering and godliness. Nor did he share Bilderdijk's sense of religious dependency in the economic aspect of man's existence. He shared Bilderdijk's desire to refrain from interference, but for other than theological reasons:

> I ask not a single protective step against poverty, but indeed the social body is at present gravely ill, and I admit the necessity of positive action against the poverty now present. But take away this present poverty which for a great part was born from the long wars and the hindrance of all industry; keep peace, do not tax heavier than is necessary, especially do not tax one industry at the expense of another, let all be free—and I say boldly with our forefathers: poverty, or to say it more correctly, the decline in one or other branch of industry will straighten itself out.[76]

Outwardly Bilderdijk's school seemed firmly united, for these differences did not come before the public eye. Besides, divergent views were obscured by the uproar in 1823 which arose when Da Costa published his brochure, "Objections to the Spirit of the Age." The public resentment against this brochure forced Bilderdijk's followers to forget for a time being their internal conflicts. By the time outside pressures had worn off, the pupils had altered their original emphasis. Religious issues became their major concern, although they never totally lost interest in politics, economy, and history.

BILDERDIJK, *RÉVEIL*, AND SECESSION

Neither Bilderdijk nor his disciples are treated fairly when lumped together as a strong, unified movement galvanized for action. Oostendorp characterized Da Costa's *Bezwaren tegen den Geest der Eeuw* with these words: "Here the Jewish convert had laid out his Mein Kampf." He summarized the significance of the "Objections" similarly:

With rare insight Da Costa had seen a "spirit" and in unmistakable language had identified the mark of his "beast" in the religious, social, and political life of Holland. This was a warfare "not with flesh and blood" but a struggle for right principles.[77]

Da Costa himself, however, in later life disclaimed such credit. In a careful analysis, Dr. Elisabeth Kluit has shown that Da Costa had freed himself from Bilderdijkian ties,[78] but she also emphasizes the fact that Bilderdijk remained for Da Costa the revered master who had guided his early steps. The national romanticism of Bilderdijk's school, however, changed through the person of Da Costa into a much more religion-oriented *Réveil*. Dr. Kluit answers her own question very clearly: "Must we understand the *Bezwaren* as a beginning, even as the beginning of the *Réveil*? No, definitely not."[79] Only part of Bilderdijk's thought lived on in the Secession of 1834, and not through the channels provided by Da Costa and the *Réveil*.

The first minister to secede, the Reverend Hendrik de Cock, had been converted to Bilderdijk's ideal not by Da Costa but by C. Baron van Zuylen van Nijeveldt.[80] When De Cock's secession took place in 1834, Da Costa and his *Réveil* circle no longer defended the form of Bilderdijkian teaching adopted by De Cock. They had moved away from the effort to implement in the present what Bilderdijk saw as the nation's true heritage and greatness.

The second seceding minister, the Reverend H. P. Scholte, adopted much more of Da Costa's later thinking. Oostendorp has correctly observed that "Da Costa was the real teacher of Scholte."[81] But while Da Costa and the *Réveil* solved inner conflicts by giving up the dream of a Netherlands restored according to Bilderdijk's specifications, De Cock and Scholte held to the dream and thus experienced these conflicts in the Seceded Church. Since Albertus C. Van Raalte mediated in that struggle, it will be necessary first to sketch in what manner Da Costa emerged from Bilderdijk's school as an independent leader.

V

Bilderdijk and the True Understanding of Dutch History

Bilderdijk believed with all his heart that the end of time was close at hand. He was equally convinced that the Dutch nation under the House of Orange would play a crucial role as history reached its end; he expected God to reveal the glorious role he intended for the Dutch Reformed Church. These convictions created, of course, certain attitudes toward the church and the Christian's involvement in the world. Thus, Bilderdijk was not at all an ardent member of the institutional church.

These attitudes created problems for Bilderdijk's two Jewish disciples, Da Costa and Capadose. They were young men, and Bilderdijk was already past sixty when they sat in his special lectures at Leiden. Da Costa especially struggled with the question of what he was to make of his life. Should he, a young man, refrain from seeking employment and give his life to a season of waiting until the Lord Jesus would return? What was to become of the precious fatherland, now so miraculously restored under God's special grace, if those who knew its true destiny were to do nothing but simply wait?

Bilderdijk's disciples had to cut this Gordian knot. Da Costa and Capadose, like the other disciples, modified their eschatological hopes so that they could involve themselves deeply in the life of the Dutch nation. But this very involvement meant that Bilderdijk's disciples failed to adhere to one of Bilderdijk's most fundamental tenets: Christ's immediate return. Nonetheless the disciples gained, quite literally, time for their own activities on behalf of the Lord in God's chosen nation. Although they did achieve the liberty of action, especially under the biblical instruction of Pastor Egeling at Leiden, neither Da Costa nor Capadose lost his deep respect for and gratitude to Bilderdijk.

A careful analysis of the relation between Bilderdijk and his two Jewish converts, Da Costa and Capadose, will help to clarify why the Dutch *Réveil* did not of itself lead to the secession. Nonetheless, for an adequate understanding of Albertus C. Van Raalte, and also of his fellow immigrant, H. P. Scholte, it is necessary to gain a full understanding of the *Réveil*. The Dutch migration to the United States which started in 1847 included many immigrants who were deeply affected by the spirit of the *Réveil*, and therefore theologically in agreement with Van Raalte and Scholte, but who had not taken the step of breaking with the Reformed Church. It has been too readily supposed that orthodox believers, especially those affected by the *Réveil*, left the Reformed Church, while the liberal element did not. Da Costa and Capadose offer clear proof that one could be a friend and admirer of Bilderdijk and an active leader in the *Réveil* while maintaining membership in the Reformed Church. Albertus C. Van Raalte was a witness to these facts and was even personally acquainted with some of the leaders in the *Réveil*. Some of the Dutch settlers in Michigan knew this and charged Van Raalte with the sin of judging that the Secession of 1834 had not really been necessary, and this became one of the reasons for the secession that took place in Michigan in 1857. What motivated the parties in that latter conflict was complex, but it certainly included convictions that had grown in the fertile soil of the Dutch *Réveil*. The following analysis of Bilderdijk and his two Jewish disciples will clarify some of those convictions.

ISAAC DA COSTA

As early as 1819, at the time of Bilderdijk's involvement with Schotsman's *Eerezuil*,[1] Da Costa had said, "in truth, I cannot stand the spirit of the age."[2] As a Jew, however, he did not feel free to enter the battle for orthodox Protestantism.[3] His heart yearned to join the fight, however: "Often I keep silent, but who is always able to do that? Especially when one has the opportunity to observe the smallness and mean frenzy of the general public."[4]

Bilderdijk's setting of yet another date for the world's end, now in the year 1820, plunged Da Costa into a state of "deep apathy and melancholy."[5] It is hard to say whether the lack of success Da Costa had in his new legal practice in Amsterdam resulted from this state or contributed to it.[6] At any rate, his gloom increased when the sister of his friend, Abraham Capadose, did not respond to his fervent love. The weight of all these pressures caused Da Costa to seek an escape, and he found it by identifying himself as a Jewish nobleman of Sephardic birth. Like Bilderdijk, Da Costa staked out a claim in the past of Jewish nobility.[7]

As the scion of a Sephardic family, Da Costa felt vastly superior to the Ashkenazim, the German and Eastern European Jews who spoke Yiddish. Thus he adhered to the tradition of the Sephardim, jealously guarding their favored position in the Dutch republic.

In 1796, however, the Sephardim accepted with reluctance the new emancipation act of the Batavian Republic. This legislation brought a new equality that ended their existence as a separate and officially recognized nation. The proletarian Ashkenazim were thus placed on a par with the Sephardim.[8]

Economic decline in The Netherlands during the latter part of the eighteenth century had also hurt the social position of Sephardic Jews, whose fortunes had been made in the now declining worldwide trade of the Dutch. The group was very sensitive about losing face, but it was too liberal to become politically conservative because of it. Thus, the Sephardim cooperated quite freely with the new Dutch and French administrators and sought to preserve its great heritage along different lines.

Isaac Da Costa's father, as well as the father of his friend, Abraham Capadose, were among the Sephardim who partially supported Napoleon's policy of Jewish assimilation. They declined, however, the emperor's invitation to attend the modern Sanhedrin which he convoked, and they did not compromise the practice of the Jewish religion.[9]

Appreciated Jewishness

In Bilderdijk, Isaac Da Costa found a teacher who respected the Jews. The members of the society, *Tot Nut en Beschaving*, consisting mainly of Jews determined to bring Jews and non-Jews closer together, had even recognized Bilderdijk in 1812 with an honorary membership.[10] Bilderdijk not only respected the Jews, but even boasted that in his Eastern appearance he resembled them. This resemblance had been a characteristic of the family, he claimed, for more than twelve centuries.[11] He objected strongly to the modern emancipation of the Jews, however, for in his thought such a scheme was contrary to God's manner of dealing with his chosen people. Their bondage had been necessary, he believed, because now the time was close at hand in which the Jews, the eldest sons of the covenant, would be emancipated by and glorify the returning Christ. They would do so more than the Christians, for such was their rightful calling and destination.[12]

Almost all of Da Costa's Christian biographers have tried to establish when Bilderdijk's influence produced the first Christian fruits in his pupil. Meijer, however, has given conclusive proof that Bilderdijk caused Da Costa to be first much more interested in his Jewish background than in the possibility of becoming a Christian.[13]

When Da Costa left Leiden in 1818, he was not a Christian. When he returned to Amsterdam, however, he found himself unable to fit harmoniously into its Jewish world. The promising and talented Da Costa thus became a lonely, disappointed young man, for he desired to bring about in the Jewish world what Bilderdijk was bringing about in the Christian world. In summarizing this period of Da Costa's life, Meijer describes him as becoming "the lord of the Jewish Teisterbant."[14]

Bilderdijk had located the roots of his existence in noble forefathers, the lords of Teisterbant. Da Costa, too, saw nobility when he began to investigate his Spanish-Portuguese ancestors. Bilderdijk prided himself in the fact that his fathers were not tainted by ignoble descent. Da Costa's patriarchs had similar purity, for they belonged to those direct descendants of David who had not returned to Palestine with the *vulgus* under Ezra, but had emigrated directly to Spain.[15] There they had been preserved as the tribe of Judah "from which the sceptre shall not depart." Da Costa did not hesitate to look for the fulfillment of the messianic prophecy of Genesis 49:10 in the glory and splendor of the Jews of Spain and Portugal. And just as Bilderdijk had made himself at home among his noble Dutch forefathers, Da Costa found a home among Jewish ancestors. But it was not among the common Jews of Palestine. As he explained to Willem van Hogendorp: "I belong to the Spanish Peninsula of the 17th century."[16]

Da Costa failed in attempts to interest his fellow synagogue members in their noble past. The Sephardim considered present emancipation to be more important than a glorious heritage. They could not understand Da Costa's infatuation with the days prior to 1795, and much less his refusal to accept for himself Dutch nationality. Unlike Bilderdijk, who had been able to form a school of at least a few disciples receptive to his ideas, Da Costa gained no hearing or understanding. Yet Da Costa was determined to fight the good fight. In a letter to Willem van Hogendorp he wrote of himself: "Easterner, Nobleman, Poet, and pupil of Bilderdijk: it is my intention to work in my circle according to my ability for the good cause."[17]

Conversion

Since the Sephardic world was not receptive to his ideas, Da Costa searched for another arena in which to fight. Bilderdijk had told him in a personal conversation late in 1820 that he would be one of the two witnesses mentioned in Revelation 11:3-12. Bilderdijk had also prophesied that the holy war against the beast from the abyss would be fought in Holland.[18] It was in Holland that Da Costa found his arena.

In 1819, Da Costa still felt restrained by the thought that: "The subject [namely, Schotsman's *Eerezuil*] is too delicate for me to say much about in my position."[19] He was aware of the distance separating him from the Christianity of Bilderdijk. Nevertheless, historical studies had made it easier for the Sephardic Da Costa to align himself closer with Bilderdijk. In these studies he had discovered that the Spanish Jews, unlike their Palestinian brethren, had not participated in Jesus' crucifixion. Moreover, many a noble Spanish Jew had accepted the New Testament as an accurate reflection of the Old Testament. Therefore it had been quite natural for many of the Sephardim to become Christians while at the same time clinging to their Jewish heritage.[20]

Thus, Da Costa the lawyer had found a precedent enabling him to be both a Jew and a Christian. Thus he strictly observed Jewish ritual when in July 1821 he married Hanna Belmonte, and again observed it on the occasion of his father's death in February 1822.

Eventually, however, Da Costa converted to Christianity. If the true Messiah had come, Da Costa felt he had to be able to profess it openly.[21] The Sephardic Jews could not be evangelized by way of oblique references to their ancestry. Because Da Costa felt called to join Bilderdijk's battle against the encroachments of the Devil, a public conversion to Christianity and an open engagement in the battle seemed necessary.

The implication that Da Costa's conversion to Christianity resulted solely from Bilderdijk's influence conjoined with his own frustration should be rejected. Meijer, who has analyzed his conversion with great care and understanding, does not draw this conclusion.[22] It is true that soon after his conversion Da Costa joined Bilderdijk's side when he published *Bezwaren tegen den Geest der Eeuw*, "Objections Against the Spirit of the Age."[23] But it is equally true that others besides Bilderdijk testified of their Christian beliefs to Da Costa. Furthermore, Da Costa continued earnestly and independently as a student of the Christian Bible. That would have been impossible if he had been drawing inspiration from Bilderdijk alone. Twelve years later, Da Costa described his move to independence from Bilderdijk in the words: "The Lord has graciously preserved. . . ."[24]

Da Costa's wife, Hanna Belmonte, raised no objections to her husband's conversion. Her parents had been baptized, and although she was not, she received instruction in the Heidelberg Catechism while attending school. Thus, she chose to share her husband's faith.[25]

Willem de Clercq, a dedicated Christian, became Da Costa's intimate friend in 1820[26] and their close relationship continued until De Clercq's death in 1844. Van Oosterwijk Bruyn summarizes the significance of this friendship in these words:

What Bilderdijk could not be for Da Costa because his personality lacked the elements capable of serving as examples worthy to imitate—since his family life in structure and conception showed in every respect the opposite of a quiet and well-ordered Christian family, that is what De Clercq and his faithful Caroline were able to do.[27]

The modest De Clercq and the exuberant Da Costa thus mutually strengthened each other in their Christian faith. Da Costa was also strengthened in the Christian faith through his study of the New Testament with Abraham Capadose, his friend and cousin. Together, they came to the conclusion that the Messiah promised in the Old Testament had appeared in the person of Jesus Christ.[28] Their joint Bible study enabled them to withstand the disapproval of their more orthodox Jewish relatives.[29]

Hard-pressed as they were, they sought and found a haven in Leiden. There they could be free from meddling relatives and be close to Bilderdijk. In September 1822 the Da Costas and Capadose took up temporary residence in Leiden, and Bilderdijk introduced them to the minister who was to catechize and baptize them.

Biblical Instruction

The Reverend Lucas Egeling's influence upon his three unusual catechumens has often been underestimated. Soon after their baptism, both Da Costa and Capadose published fiery pamphlets written strictly in the Bilderdijkian spirit. Since Egeling was not a follower of Bilderdijk, it would appear as if the pastor's service had accomplished little beyond the administration of the sacrament of baptism. Yet, Egeling shepherded the three converts in a manner that would eventually lead to a manifest departure from Bilderdijk's thought.

For all his religiosity, Bilderdijk had never formally joined the church,[30] and did not even attend church services regularly.[31] It is doubtful that he ever partook of the Lord's Supper.

Much has been made of the conventicle that Bilderdijk formed during his years in Amsterdam.[32] However, there was nothing unusual about forming a conventicle. During that time conventicles were often organized by interested persons.[33] Bilderdijk had a purpose different from secession in mind for his conventicle. On April 20, 1815, he wrote to his friend, Professor H. W. Tydeman, at Leiden:

> At the end of 1812 or in the beginning of 1813, it was that winter, I composed something dealing with Revelation and its application to Napoleon which is in the hands of a small conventicle that I for a few years now am leading in matters of Religion and Doctrine.[34]

The conventicle was more a sounding board for apocalyptics than a beginning secession.

There is no doubt, on the other hand that Bilderdijk on more than one occasion thought in terms of a division within the Reformed Church. He expressed that most clearly in 1810 through an address entitled *Aan de ware Hervormden in de Gemeente van Holland,* to the true Reformed [people] in the Congregation of Holland. The article was not published until Da Costa published it in 1833,[35] two years after Bilderdijk's death.

Seceded ministers argued later on the basis of this essay that "the professor [*sic*] Bilderdijk was entirely agreed with us in the same conviction concerning the Reformed Church and the believers' duty to leave her."[36] Rullmann, although pointing out that Bilderdijk did not adhere to secessionary thought, describes him nevertheless as one who, as a true seer, had "a premonition of the secession."[37] Oostendorp, too, leaves the impression that he considers Bilderdijk to be a "forerunner of the great separation from the State Church."[38]

It is not so easy, however, to make Bilderdijk a seceder. When Vijgeboom took action against the reconstituted Reformed Church of 1816, Bilderdijk did not join Vijgeboom's Restored Church of Christ. To be sure, he pointed out to Da Costa that he had prophesied such a secession, but he added these words:

> and I still see it as unavoidable . . . but I see yet too much orthodoxy in our church than that I could deem that secession profitable or necessary. . . . Then, it may be necessary locally although not generally.[39]

Bilderdijk had good reasons for taking a more optimistic attitude toward the Reformed Church than Vijgeboom, for he thought that his lectures in Leiden were yielding some fruit.[40] The small number of followers did not trouble him, for he had no confidence in manmade societies. "It is God," he argued, "who must do it through individual operation in the heart; but societies of men by men have always failed."[41] God was working in the hearts of his students, even though they be few in number.

Bilderdijk applied this principle of passivity[42] even more to the church, since he considered the last day to be imminent.[43] That day would climax the steadily worsening situation of the church, and Holland would play a central role.[44] Bilderdijk was not hoping for improvements before that time, as can be seen in the following:

> while the church is prospering, the Savior's visible acceptance of all dominion is not to be expected, but only when the church is dilapidated and in her dilapidation is groaning to God and is falling away from herself, [a church] which He alone knows and is able to gather, but no organization or power of man can.[45]

The visible church did not appeal to Bilderdijk and thus he did not join it. The only true church for Bilderdijk was the invisible church:

> We believe in Christ, not in the church; of the church we believe that she exists, namely over all the earth, and therefore that she is invisible and cannot be visible except in and at the time of the visible future of the Bridegroom.[46]

As Nauta has pointed out, because Bilderdijk used an unbiblical definition of the church he understood the only true church to be invisible. Thus he could counsel both loyalty to and separation from the Reformed Church,[47] because whether one left the visible church or remained loyal to it did not ultimately matter. It was only a matter of personal preference.

Thus Bilderdijk, who himself had no qualms at all about not formally joining the church, commended Mr. and Mrs. Da Costa and Capadose to the Reverend Lucas Egeling for catechetical instruction.[48] It is important to note that the Jewish converts found in Egeling a strictly biblical teacher. Oostendorp points out, however, that "Da Costa had spoken to Rev. Egeling about Revelation. It is a closed book, was the typical answer of this Reformed preacher."[49] Thus, Oostendorp leaves the impression that Egeling was not truly committed to the Bible. Undisputable evidence to the contrary comes from Capadose. Writing from Leiden to Willem de Clercq at Amsterdam, Capadose reported that he liked Egeling very much and agreed completely with his doctrine. The one complaint raised about Egeling was "that he is excessively determined to avail himself only of the Bible's very own words."[50]

Before his catechumens came to Leiden, Egeling wrote a kind letter of welcome to Da Costa:

> I write these few lines to inform you that upon your arrival in Leyden I will be completely at your service. . . . How glad will I be if, upon better acquaintance, we will get to know each other as those who in truth love the blessed Savior . . . hear with commiseration that Mr. Capadose because of his choice and intent experiences much opposition and difficulty, but if the heart is upright before God and the Savior, which I would so reluctantly doubt, then the beloved Bible will now be for him an open book.[51]

Emphasis on the Bible was characteristic for Egeling. His two-volume work, *The Way of Salvation According to Biblical Standards,* became very popular because of that emphasis.[52] The first volume, published in 1820, treated the church's dogmas. Egeling presented those doctrines by relating them strictly to the Bible itself, and his work could almost be characterized as a string of commentaries on Bible passages. He observed in the foreword to the second volume that he was engaged in "a very delicate undertaking, . . . here we meet Mysteries of God that we cannot understand and about which one can easily say too little and even more easily too much; [Mysteries] which our wisdom can quickly add to or take away from."[53]

Nevertheless, in his modest way Egeling criticized the three confessional standards, or forms of unity, of the Reformed Church. Although he praised the Heidelberg Catechism and the Belgic Confession for being "full of biblical education and Christian upbuilding," he insisted that these were dated documents and had to be understood "in the spirit and history of those times and in the circumstances the Reformed people then found themselves in."[54] He frankly acknowledged that for him these standards of unity had not absolute and binding authority such "as the Roman Church ascribes to the canons of the Council of Trent."[55] While Egeling had sympathy for the Belgic Confession and Heidelberg Catechism, he expressed his acute dislike of the canons in these words: "It would have been felicitious had these two standards never needed to be increased."[56] He blamed the two rival factions at that synod for this needless addition of Dordrecht. "Alas, they were unable to understand each other in the matter of the most delicate and holiest parts of doctrine; they quarreled about God's external and inscrutable counsel and how it is executed in the sinner's salvation by Jesus Christ."[57] It would have been much better, concluded Egeling, "if we had never had another Form of Unity than the Bible itself, as the first Christians knew, or sought no other [standard]."[58]

Egeling's view of the Scriptures was not literalistic, although he understood the Bible to be historically reliable. He considered it foolish in biblical scholarship to distinguish the historical setting and doctrine.[59] The two were inseparable. At the same time, however, he judged that "not all . . . that is written in the Bible is Divine Revelation; but all the Divine Revelation we need for our salvation is written in the Bible."[60] In a later publication, Egeling defended the view that the Bible has a certain human character along with its divine character:

> It is a book which, although from divine origin presenting divine things in the most divine manner, does not immediately come from God. It is not brought to us by an angel from heaven; but it came *by men*—and it has been written as much as possible *for human understanding.*—*By men the Bible has come to us*; through human beings we are here able to hear the words of God.[61]

For Egeling, reading the Bible should be undertaken with the following seven thoughts in mind: (1) it is a divine book and therefore requires the highest attentiveness; (2) it is a human book and must therefore be approached with simplicity; (3) since it is written for sinners, we must read it as sinners; (4) since it speaks to the heart and not primarily to our curiosity, it is the heart which must listen; (5) it is a book of the highest value and requires therefore our constant meditation as we slowly and carefully read it; (6) since various authors wrote the Bible, it is necessary for more complete understanding of it to compare Scripture with Scripture, especially Scripture of the same kind; (7) because natural man cannot, without the help of God, understand the Bible, we must constantly pray for guidance while reading it.[62]

Thus, it is clear why Egeling refused to join Da Costa and Capadose in Bilderdijkian speculations about Revelation. He stood firm despite the eschatological food that Bilderdijk provided abundantly for his Jewish converts. Da Costa reported enthusiastically to Willem van Hogendorp:

> Bilderdijk's house where we usually are is overflowing with health and joy. . . . Our conversation . . . is at present never dragging. Last Sunday he [Bilderdijk] read to us from his expositions on the Apocalypse. What amazing signs in the surrounding world did he by that reading call to our attention. We experience wonderful times.[63]

From the very first, Egeling impressed the three converts favorably. Da Costa wrote to Willem de Clercq: "Our discussions with Egeling began the night before last. They are indeed precious and beneficial. The man is a genuine Christian, not at all dogmatic, exactly as he should be."[64] Because of this favorable impression, Egeling was able to make an impact.[65] Da Costa could come to the conclusion: "Oh! how much there is yet to learn! How far I am still removed from that blessed Christianity that exists not in speculations but in the exercise of faith, love, and hope."[66]

Bilderdijk's fiery disciples submitted to Egeling's teaching for one reason: they recognized in their new spiritual guide a man of God.[67] For the first time in their lives, Capadose and the Da Costas were studying Scripture under the guidance of a conservative theologian. Unlike Bilderdijk, Egeling did not particularly emphasize Christ's imminent return. Rather, he concentrated on presenting a comprehensive view of the biblical witness. Although Bilderdijk's thought was not immediately displaced, Egeling's pupils advanced beyond the Bilderdijkian position. They learned to be more humble before Scripture, and became members of the Reformed Church. On October 20, 1822,[68] the Da Costas and Capadose knelt in the Pieterskerk at Leiden to receive baptism at Egeling's hands and be admitted to membership.[69]

Some time passed, however, before the difference between master Bilderdijk and his pupils would become more evident. Capadose and Da Costa continued to display Bilderdijkian colors. Filled with evangelistic fervor, the new converts defended the master's views in public.[70] They did not form a team, nor did they integrate their efforts, although they engaged in joint Bible study upon their return to Amsterdam after being baptized.[71] Their friendship was from time to time interrupted, however, because of vehement disagreements.[72] The graduates from Bilderdijk's "school" had their own respective ideas about interpreting and implementing the things which they had learned. Thus, they made their respective contributions individually.[73] Da Costa attacked the spirit of the age in the socio-political world. Capadose attacked the same spirit in the medical world. Da Costa later made some significant changes in his thought, but Capadose did not.

Eschatology and a Messianic Orange

Da Costa, unlike Willem van Hogendorp did not abandon Bilderdijk's eschatological expectations. Rather, he amended them. Bilderdijk foresaw nothing but a worsening of man's condition in the short time remaining before the Savior's return. Da Costa hoped with equal fervor for an immediate eschaton, but saw it preceded by "a short-lived victory of the good cause on earth under the government of the Prince of Orange [i.e., the later King William II, 1840-49]."[74]

Da Costa argued that the light would shine more gloriously as the darkness increased. He drew an analogy between the seemingly inevitable victories of the Pharisaism of Rome prior to the Reformation and of the current Sadduceeism of liberal thought. He could, therefore, assure Willem van Hogendorp that, "Liberalism will be an instrument to increase in limitless degree of intensity the radiance of our glorious faith."[75] Da Costa went on:

> . . . without fanaticism but rationally cool and in the calmness of a well-considered hope, I see the developing glory that we await. It is for me not a guess but a certainty, and when I think or write about it I am exalted above myself, as a poet, indeed as more than a poet. The pen is unable either to express or to follow the intensity of my feelings on this point. . . . My existence is as fused with those views. Without them I cannot live, and this great light, spreading already as the dawn before my eyes over the world, will arise from Holland. . . .[76]

Da Costa had learned from Bilderdijk to base this hope on his faith, and the Dutch nation under Orange was for him inseparably connected with that faith:

There is in Holland a beginning of life. We are admittedly, according to the opinion of the nations, in a state of inferiority compared to former times, but we possess the kernel of the Reformed Church; we have always enjoyed Providence's special protection, and there is no second royal family like ours in the history of the world.[77]

Thus, Da Costa discerned two evident signs of hope. First, he saw a messianic role for the House of Orange, and gave the following characterization of the status of the prince who would soon be King William II.

. . . a hero who in his physiognomy reminds one of the great and upright Maurice;[78] precisely now that the time is ripening for the great crisis in preparation for Europe, everything makes one mindful that this hero will then sit on his father's throne.[79]

This second messianic Orange would rise to glory in the closing era of man's history on earth.[80]

Second, Da Costa detected an almost invisible but growing circle of people, produced by Bilderdijk and his school, who longed for a government directly subject to "the pure and divine doctrine of the God-man [namely, Jesus]."[81] Da Costa spoke with confidence about that growing circle:

Bilderdijk and his school are one of those strange marks typical of Holland, as is the house of Orange, [both of] which will produce their fruits on the great day. On these is founded my expectation of a time of heavenly glory for our country, and in this manner I believe that the congregation of the faithful will form itself.[82]

This was the optimism which characterized Da Costa when he took on "the panoply of faith"[83] and began to prepare "a booklet in prose against the would-be enlightenment of the nineteenth century."[84] The brochure appeared in August 1823 under the title *Bezwaren tegen den Geest der Eeuw*. Its tone was sharp and almost bitter. In the final stage of writing the brochure, Da Costa had been angered by the triumphant spirit of the quadri-centennial celebration of Laurens Janszoon Koster's bookprinting invention.[85]

Bezwaren tegen den Geest der Eeuw

On July 10-11, 1823, festivities took place in Haarlem, where Koster had practiced his craft. Professor H. J. van der Palm had accepted the city's invitation to deliver the keynote address.[86] The selection of Van der Palm was not only due to his reputation of being "the most eloquent speaker in whose possession the fatherland may pride itself," but also due to his lack of reserve in giving Koster credit for the invention of printing.[87]

Bilderdijk refused to attend the festivities because the organizers had reminded the nation that Koster had lived prior to the Reformation, and should therefore be remembered in a spirit not of strife but of reconciliation.[88] In addition, Bilderdijk objected to the arrogant tone in which the nineteenth-century liberals who would be attending the festival praised their practice of tolerance. Most of all, however, Bilderdijk objected to the choice of Van der Palm as orator. The two had once been good friends, but by 1822 a growing coolness between them reached the freezing point.[89]

Since 1799, Van der Palm had been campaigning for a uniform spelling of the Dutch language. In 1804, as minister of education, he pushed the Dutch nation into adopting a system of spelling devised by Matthijs Siegenbeek, the first professor of the Dutch language at Leiden.[90]

In 1822, Bilderdijk expressed his long-simmering dissatisfaction with this system of spelling in a public attack on Siegenbeek. He then went on to blast his opponent's mild reply and incorporating morality, religion, and national safety into his argument.[91] He also inserted numerous barbs aimed at Van der Palm.

While tensions mounted, Van der Palm delivered his oration commemorating Koster. It had little to do with spelling. But in the view of Bilderdijk and his followers, the Van der Palm who was tampering with the Dutch language added insult to injury by praising a mere mortal in the hallowed Bavo Church of Haarlem. The orator glorified not God, but Koster for having "laid the foundation for mankind's enlightenment," thus loosing the bands of "human reason, the most divine [instrument] that is in us."[92]

Da Costa condemned the "pagan ceremonies" at Haarlem and reproached Van der Palm for his part in "that abominable idolatry."[93] In holy passion, he objected in his brochure to the "spirit of the age" that expected from man what it should expect from God.[94] Like a true evangelist, however, he aimed for a return to God on the part of his readers: Holland should not forget its special place in divine providence. Nor should the nation be led astray as the Jews had been, even the Sephardic Jews. Through Bilderdijk's tutoring and his own studies, Da Costa had become acquainted with the ways that led a nation to rebel against God. What had taken place in Haarlem in honor of Koster bore the mark of the beast; worse, God's nation cheered the false doctrine there proclaimed. Thoroughly alarmed, Da Costa sharpened his pen for a strong counterattack.[95] In the preface of *Bezwaren tegen den Geest der Eeuw,* Da Costa stated his thesis:

The booklet that you here open, modest Reader, is written to combat a prejudice generally accepted, defended, and cherished by the present generation, and practically everywhere and in everything most forcefully established as the principle how to think and act. It is [the prejudice] of the extreme superiority . . . in which the age we live in . . . does not cease to pride itself with a haughtiness equally ridiculous as unprecedented, equally unfounded as dangerous. It is ridiculous . . . that one dares to place oneself in such an impertinent manner above everything that former times thought right and true, and [that one dares] to look down upon that which the forefathers to whom we owe so very much handed down. But it is especially to the unfoundedness and the danger of this century's haughty attitude that we wish through this booklet to call attention (under the blessing of Almighty God against whom the Spirit of the Age through the system of vain wisdom and fraudulent enlightenment has caused the world to rebel).[96]

Da Costa explained how his thesis applied to ten different areas, devoting a chapter to each. Religion (1) and morality (2) came first, followed by tolerance of humanity (3), the arts (4), and sciences (5), the constitution (6), birth (7), public opinion (8), education (9), and freedom and enlightenment (10).

Da Costa noted that the doctrine of free grace, so vital to religion, was believed by only a small minority and therefore could not be an occasion for the present pride. Nor had morality progressed enough under Voltaire, Rousseau, Diderot, Lord Byron, etc., to warrant such pride. Tolerance was no more than a guise for wrongdoing, and it amounted to nothing more than vanity. The arts, originally meant to praise God, also fell victim to vanity and were practiced out of wantonness. With science man was now trying to resist God. The constitution had been devised by men blind to the fact that man cannot form a state, but is by Divine Providence born into one. Nor was birth so accidental as it was believed by those who were paradoxically so proud of man's worthiness and uniqueness. Education, which too often used the principle of competition to the detriment of children, sought to teach everything to everybody and thus meddled with the differences God had created between the classes. Freedom and enlightenment did not really exist in Holland insofar as they were a copying of French and German liberal thinkers, for the Dutch people were thus being enslaved to false gods.

Willem de Clercq had in vain asked his friend Da Costa to modify the sharp tone of his brochure. Da Costa had repeatedly read his manuscript to De Clercq. The listener asked: "Why do you wish to provoke the people? Can you not progressively bring them to your opinion?"

Da Costa replied that the Dutch nation could only be healed by punishment. He asked in return: "If they had eyes to see, would they not see everywhere the signs of their impending doom?"[97]

Willem van Hogendorp was in sympathy with these views of Da Costa, but remained objective enough to evaluate the brochure on the basis of its aims as well as its contents. He appreciated Da Costa's work as a manifesto for the like-minded, but he was not at all convinced that it could persuade either the opposition or the undecided. He warned Da Costa: "You can expect an angry counter-thrust, because your chapter on the constitution has stirred up against you all Jacobins in our country and even all the moderate liberals and constitutionalists."[98] Public opinion, taking the place of God's revealed will as man's guide, created nothing but disaster.

The chapter on the constitution had at the last moment even frightened the publisher, L. Herdingh. Taking the proof sheets with him, he called on Bilderdijk and requested that the master purge his pupil's text of any seditious statements. Bilderdijk saw no danger, however, and took the whole matter lightly.[99]

Bilderdijk was partially right in doing this, for criminal charges were not drawn up against Da Costa. But the government did take careful notice of his *Bezwaren*. Da Costa had sent a copy to the king. The minister of education advised his majesty to return it on the grounds that the brochure invited the king to ignore the constitution.[100] Van Maanen, the minister of justice, was less disturbed about the "silly and stupid writings of Bilderdijk's ape."[101] The latter's counsel not to react at all prevailed.

Reaction to Bezwaren

The country's press did not remain silent, however, and it became obstreperous in its counterattacks. Many articles and brochures decrying Da Costa's contentions were published. Da Costa's assault upon everything that his contemporaries understood as Christian progress incited the opposition to use any means it saw fit to defend itself.

Professor N. G. van Kampen was the most polite, charging that Da Costa had been so steeped in the Old Testament authoritarianism of his upbringing as a Jew that the New Testament had not yet set him free.[102] Other authors utilized Da Costa's Jewishness in much more vicious ways.

J. Roemer responded to Da Costa's theological argument against the abolition of slavery. Da Costa had argued as follows:

Even if on Cain's posterity is still resting the curse of that berated Patriarch, God's endless mercy has attached to that curse a blessing in order to soften it, and the Negro who according to the order ordained by God has been made subservient to the whites who far transcend the Negro in body and soul, does nevertheless enjoy in his state a safety and a prosperity that an endless number of free [people] lack in theirs [i.e., in their state]. . . . In the higher form of life to which our short sojourn on earth is but a preparation, we will one day justify the adorable wisdom that desired such great and manifold differentiation between Adam's children and we will detest and deplore the vain wisdom with which in our blindness we so often and yet so unavailingly tried to foil His inscrutable designs.[103]

Roemer's reply began with a question:

Why do you call Cain's posterity cursed? Has the curse not been pronounced over all the earth when Adam had sinned? Return from your delusion, O man! And do not boast in your superiority over the Negro because you are *white*. Because of the ill treatment you inflict upon him, he sees the devil—whom you imagine to be black—in your so highly praised color.[104]

So many descended in bitter attack upon Da Costa that Bilderdijk came to the aid of his pupil and published an explanation of Da Costa's *Bezwaren*.[105] Da Costa was unhappy when Bilderdijk sent him the galley proofs, but he later, after the master had modified his writing, thanked Bilderdijk for his "wonderful Explanation of my Objections."[106] Even in the revised edition, however, Bilderdijk used very strong language, telling the "barking dogs"[107] that they were doing the following:

extinguishing the holy Gospel-light, nailing the windows to shut out Divine grace, in order to substitute their stinking and asphyxiating lamplets of self-conceit, pagan delusion, and so-called critical mad philosophy. If one reads Da Costa's Bezwaren on this point, and if one re-reads them in a free and unbiased attitude searching for the truth, the result will be nothing else than the conviction of the God-provoking *pride of an age of slavery, of superstition, of false religion, of stupidity, and of darkness.* I make the admonitions in his *Conclusions* mine, and I refer all those still willing to listen to the Prophet who says *"For they are a rebellious people, lying (bastard) sons, sons who will not hear the instructions of the Lord, who say to the seers, 'see not,' and to the prophets, 'prophesy not to us what is right, speak to us smooth things, prophesy illusions, leave the way, turn aside from the path, let us hear no more of the Holy One of Israel.' "*[108]

Bilderdijk especially supported Da Costa's view that the king was not bound to his oath concerning the constitution. Thus, he told the "genuine supporters of [Olden] Barneveld," the "wretched philosophers,"[109] that the king as "Vicar of God on earth" was responsible only to his God.[110] The theory that government was a contract binding the people and their sovereign together was, according to Bilderdijk, nothing but a lie:

> [The king] who was deceived by the wolf [namely by the theory of a constitution], admitted him into the sheepfold, and under oath allowed him freedom, protection, and everything imaginable, [that] king is still not permitted to have the sheep entrusted to his care devoured or chased off the pasture.[111]

A host of other authors began to pounce upon the details of Da Costa's *Bezwaren*. The debate became very bitter as the opponents grew more and more contemptuous toward one another.

ABRAHAM CAPADOSE

Against Vaccination

Abraham Capadose entered the battle in November 1823 when he published a brochure against vaccination.[112] With Da Costa, Capadose objected to the Spirit of the Age particularly as it manifested itself in its pride over the accomplishments of vaccination. Just as Da Costa had used his pen in opposition to the glorification of Koster, Capadose used his in opposition to Edward Jenner, the English medical doctor who had started the practice of vaccination in 1795. Medical Professor F. van der Breggen delivered an address at Amsterdam on May 14, 1823, in honor of Jenner, calling May 14 a holy day on which "the physical rebirth of mankind" was to be celebrated:

> Thrice happy that mortal man [namely Jenner] who was generated by the Deity and becomes as His Vicar the means of His blissful benevolence . . . among his fellow men, and who as the hero of mankind, saving the lives of millions deserves to be praised. Thrice blessed Edward Jenner . . . for whom Antiquity would have built altars and for whom it would have instigated burnt offerings, to you we dedicate this day.[113]

Prior to his conversion, Capadose had not objected to vaccination. On the contrary, he even used it in his professional work.[114] Since his conversion, however, Capadose had come to believe that medical science had degenerated: "it has forgotten God and has adopted the principle that it should test all means . . . without first testing them against the principles of Religion."[115] Therefore Capadose chose Luke 5:31 as

a motto for the first chapter in his brochure: "Those who are well have
no need of a physician, but those who are sick."[116] In considering the
meaning of this text, he arrived at the conclusion that a healthy man
must not deliberately be made ill by vaccination.

Capadose believed that God had decreed the number of elect.[117]
Neither the minister nor the medical doctor could alter that number.
He did not conclude that therefore all preaching and healing should
cease, but he did consider all evangelistic and medical work which was
an attempt to interfere with God's ways to be blasphemous. Such
preaching and healing as was done rightly required great exactness and
devotion, because the minister and the doctor were serving God's precious elect.

For Capadose, it was no accident that vaccination had been discovered and used at the close of the eighteenth century:

> That period was branded with the seal of the curse by everyone who
> loved God and truth, a period that the Almighty seems to have destined
> to allow fallen man, driven by the spirit of darkness, a temporary but
> bitter victory over the true light, a period . . . prepared by a despicable
> Voltaire and his puny adherents.[118]

Capadose reminded the Dutch nation how God had blessed The
Netherlands, as in earlier days he had blessed Judea. Under Orange's
leadership, Holland had "through heavenly grace been used as a bul-
wark for true Religion." In view of "the terrible hour of Jehovah's flam-
ing wrath," he urged the Dutch:

> Let us no longer seek food for our hearts in that *France* where the
> detestable Voltaire and other murderers of the soul . . . had poisoned
> the air. . . . Let us no longer seek food for our reason from the fanatical
> German who presents us his philosophy, his magneticism, and other
> poisons instead of the true understanding given us by Almighty God.
> . . . Lastly, let us no longer seek the care for our physical existence from
> the reckless and crazy Englishman; here too we are given wormwood
> instead of honey, poison instead of medication.[119]

Capadose's *Vaccine* irritated the medical world, especially those doctors who were trying to break through the religious suspicion and resistance of the poor and less-educated people.[120] Among the best replies
to Capadose, the worthiest came from Dr. C. G. Ontijd in a brochure
entitled *The Value of Cow-Pox Vaccination Maintained.*[121]

Ontijd disagreed with Capadose's view that man's fall should be
understood as the source of all physical ailments, and that these could
never be taken away from man. In Ontijd's view, Adam's fall had caused
a moral decay that adversely affected man's physical nature. He found

support for his argument in the Bible. According to Romans 5:12, death itself, not illness, had resulted from the Fall. Was it not true that Adam had lived to the ripe age of 930 years? Capadose should have realized, argued Ontijd, that such an age could never have been attained if God had punished man through illness and disease. Vaccination was not an illegitimate escape from God, but "one of the greatest blessings ever bestowed upon mankind." Ontijd observed:

> Where man's help is vanity, there God can help; He who is all-good spoke, His spirit illumined Jenner's brain, and the vaccine was there to tame a plague under whose terrible wrath the human race in our part of the world had suffered for more than six centuries, costing it more victims than the bloodiest wars.[122]

Ontijd noted that Capadose was "an adept of Bilderdijk's sect," outside of which no light could, supposedly, exist:

> Father Bilderdijk and the two prophets who originated with him, the doctors Da Costa and Capadose, naturally excel as the shining stars among the bastard generation of this mad nineteenth century.[123]

Ontijd added the hope, however, that God might have given up "these two converted Israelites for a time, in order that their spirit might be saved in the day of the Lord Jesus."[124]

The host of opponents did not frighten Capadose in the least.[125] Into old age, he continued his battle against vaccination.[126] But he was bitterly disappointed that his close friends, first De Clercq and then Da Costa, "sacrificed their children to Moloch"[127] by having them vaccinated.[128]

De Clercq did not believe that vaccination was the sign of the beast, for he observed that God had allowed this means to be discovered in other countries "totally separated from any liberalism."[129] He concluded therefore that vaccination could be used so long as its use was accompanied with gratitude to God for the means which he had given to avoid disease. Da Costa came to the same conclusion in 1837, holding that the believer had to judge for himself whether or not vaccination served as a way to glorify God.[130]

Capadose deplored this. For him it was making a sinful act righteous by claiming to do it in faith. Da Costa rationalized his new position by explaining that he had given up his earlier "consequentism."[131] For him, vaccination had become a moral issue to be decided in faith by individual believers. Capadose disagreed, and charged that Da Costa lacked confidence in God. Three years after Da Costa's death, Capadose observed correctly that Da Costa "had never really belonged to the anti-vaccine men upon the strength of his own study."[132] Indeed, Da Costa's anti-vaccine position had been inspired by Bilderdijk. In the course of his independent Bible study, however, Da Costa discovered that the Christian faith did not require such opposition.[133]

Against Brasz

Da Costa and Capadose had earlier differed with respect to another fundamental issue. The difference centered around a Mr. H. Brasz, who in 1825 was to be ordained as an elder of the Reformed Church of Amsterdam.[134] Capadose had met the appointee at a church supper and found him to be a man who spoke flippantly about predestination and the Canons of Dordrecht. Complaining to the consistory, Capadose succeeded in generating a charge of heresy against Brasz and blocking his ordination despite a lack of conclusive evidence to support the charge. The lack of sufficient evidence prompted the consistory to issue a stern warning to Capadose about the dangers of bearing false witness. But Capadose interpreted the warning as proof that the consistory had not really wished to condemn the errors of Mr. Brasz. He made no effort to vindicate himself by appealing to the Classis of Amsterdam, the next highest judicatory. Rather than following this route of appeal as prescribed in the constitution of the Reformed Church, Capadose published a very extensive brochure which reviewed the issue from his view.[135] He even accused the consistory of bias against him because he was a Jewish convert, observing that enemies of the Lord would always express "their hate of the formerly chosen nation . . . with hate of the doctrines of election, free grace, and even of all orthodoxy."[136]

Bilderdijk agreed wholeheartedly with Capadose's views and reactions, but was critical of Da Costa's more independent views.[137] Da Costa in turn was critical of the views of Capadose.[138] Kalmijn believes that personal difficulties between the Capadose and Da Costa families added to the tension between the two converts.[139] In any case, Capadose expressed his remorse over this tension to Dirk van Hogendorp: "For several months since my affair with Brasz, the Evil One has been sowing between Da Costa and me a seed of discord that—alas!—I see growing and taking deeper root."[140] The break was such that Capadose no longer shared a daily meal with Da Costa, although they did try to spend at least Sundays and Wednesdays together.[141] Their friendship was finally restored,[142] but the cardinal difference between them was never resolved. That difference was the issue at stake in the affair with Brasz. Capadose, like Bilderdijk, expected that Christianity would not improve at all except through the purification of the Reformed Church. Da Costa refused to accept this view. Thus, he disapproved of Capadose's bitter attack against the alleged liberalism of Amsterdam's consistory.[143] Bilderdijk's school fell apart as its two most enthusiastic constituents developed differences in the interpretation of the master's teachings.

Capadose remained in many ways a Bilderdijkian conservative, and in manner and attitude he was so stern that even those of his friends who were Christian kept their distance.[144] Da Costa was much more open to change, provided such change was in accord with his interpretation of the Bible. Capadose clung tenaciously to the ideal of restoring the Reformed Church to what he thought to be its pure form, but in the long and fruitless struggle he lost all hope. In 1866, he withdrew his membership from the Reformed Church and never again affiliated with a denomination.[145] Da Costa, "once he was freed from Bilderdijkian ties, was a free man" and worked vigorously to save the Reformed Church.[146] Capadose tried to restore the Reformed Church by enforcing the confessional standards. Da Costa sought to reform the church through the medicinal use of the Bible.

Da Costa ceased to battle in the manner of Bilderdijk after 1826. Two years earlier, in 1824, he had initiated the custom of beginning every day with a worship service for his family and the servants.[147] The Reverend Mr. A. Chavannes, an exile from the Swiss Canton of Vaud, had been Da Costa's houseguest after a mutual acquaintance[148] introduced Chavannes to him. Learning from him how Bible studies were conducted in the land of Calvin, Da Costa resolved to use this method to the advantage of the Dutch church. Mrs. F. A. C. Koenen (nee Pauw), a good Christian friend of the Da Costas in Amsterdam, had already started something of a similar nature by inviting certain people to join her in a Sunday evening of Bible study.[149] Da Costa expanded this approach by opening his house to anyone who cared to come. Da Costa acted as a laypreacher for these meetings, and thus learned to exercise care in his study of the Bible.

RÉVEIL

Dr. Kluit has correctly pointed out that Da Costa's *oefeningen*, often called the *réunions*,[150] must be considered the starting point of the *Réveil*.[151] These gatherings were not radically new,[152] but they did signify the start of a renewal in faith and action.

Capadose was, in spite of his more conservative outlook, in this respect very much a part of the *Réveil*. When economic circumstances compelled him to leave Amsterdam in 1823, he wanted to find a village

"where many of God's precious people live."[153] Scherpenzeel was his
choice, and before long he conducted an *oefening* on Monday
evenings.[154]

Erosion of Bilderdijk's Influence

While Da Costa and Capadose rose to positions of leadership in their
respective *Réveil* circles, other men and women outside these circles
who were not, strictly speaking, Bilderdijk's students became leaders
in their own right. Most of them were personally sympathetic toward
Bilderdijk, but as a general rule they did not adopt as their own the
mission of spreading his ideas by way of the *oefeningen*.

A case in point was Dirk van Hogendorp, son of Gijsbert Karel van
Hogendorp. After completing his studies at Leiden, he had joined his
father in The Hague. He knew that *oefeningen* were being held, but
he did not join any of them. Dirk was suspicious of the *oefeningen* and
in a letter to Da Costa he complained that those who emphasized the
free grace of God to the extreme were merely pharisaic:

> and this is caused perhaps by the *oefeningen* they conduct among them-
> selves, where they report daily on what the Lord is doing in each of them
> as individuals. Those *oefeningen* where everyone is permitted to speak
> can only degenerate into schools of pride, jealousy, and pretense.[155]

Yet, Dirk participated without reluctance in the gatherings of his Christian friends, for he was one of the many orthodox Christians in and
around The Hague who sought to supplement their Sunday church
worship with further edification at social gatherings which studied the
Bible in depth and discussed contemporary spiritual subjects. The fact
that local, orthodox pastors like D. Molenaar of the Reformed Church
and J. C. I. Secretan of the Walloon Church often attended these gatherings prevented them from deteriorating into the kind of society Dirk
had told Da Costa he feared so much. Furthermore, the intellectual
quality of the gatherings remained high because they were small and
were seldom frequented by Christians belonging to socially and eco-
nomically lower classes. The *Réveil* did not start with an effort to solve
the social question of how Christians blessed with earthly goods were
to relate to Christians less blessed than they. But the *Réveil* did not
avoid the question when it was later to arise.

Eschatology

The lack of a break in social barriers can be readily understood in so
far as the *Réveil* was a movement which first spread among the upper

classes. But the Bible they so closely studied and applied to themselves taught that the lower classes also belonged to the Shepherd's flock. After 1830, concern centering upon this truth became public. Those who had been awakened to newness of faith and a consequent social concern became pioneers in many social activities. They often were ridiculed, especially by those who called themselves enlightened.[156] Yet, this development took place in spite of Bilderdijk, who had counseled that all activity to improve man's lot stood condemned because the last pages of history were being written. It was characteristic of those participating in the *Réveil*, however, that they not only intensified their acquaintance with the Bible but also sought to implement the will of God revealed there. Most of them understood this implementation to be, not withdrawal from the world in preparation for the end of time, but as a battle against the evil of the time which they were capable of winning.

Bilderdijk and his students had experienced differences with respect to the proper action to take in view of Christ's second coming, and the larger circles of the *Réveil* revealed a similar division. The Bilderdijkians and these larger circles were, however, very much in the minority. That Jesus would return, perhaps soon, was not disbelieved. In the interim, however, the majority did not want to remain idle. The clearest example was Da Costa, the student with whom Bilderdijk was most intimate. Da Costa could claim to be Bilderdijk's disciple;[157] but he also thanked God "who had graciously preserved" him through emancipation from Bilderdijk.[158]

Thus, the *Réveil* did not join Bilderdijk's premature move into the eschaton, but stayed within the flow of history. Insofar as it revived the *oefeningen*, it was an indigenous movement. That is not to say, however, that influences from abroad played no role. The Philadelphians and the Moravian Brethren, the Methodist revival, the *Deutsche Christentum Gesellschaft* in Basel, the revival in Geneva, and other similar influences contributed to the Dutch *Réveil*.[159] As the participants heard from abroad, through the *oefeningen*, they could not avoid thanking the Lord for the evidence of his grace.

These proofs of the continuing activity of the Holy Spirit, however, did not lend credence to Bilderdijk's prophecies of impending doom. On the contrary, the more individuals heard about successes abroad, the more they were willing to put into practice domestically what they believed in their hearts. Thus, Bilderdijk failed to significantly shape the *Réveil* with his convictions that contemporary history was near its end.

VI

Liberalism; The Groninger School; Secession

Bilderdijk and his school failed to attract the full support of the ministers in the Reformed Church. There were deeper causes than that Bilderdijk and his pupils were members of the laity, for the school's eschatological speculations made the theologians uneasy, and Bilderdijk and his school insisted on an understanding and experience of religion that most clergymen did not share. Da Costa charged that the theology prevailing among the ministers could not truly be called Christian:

> [They] try to take away the mysteries of the Truth and try to incapacitate the power of the written Word by their insipid inane word; they are for instance talking much about the Holy Spirit, but not as that person in the Godhead which is present in the heart to bring to faith and holiness, but merely as a general influence for the good; or they are boasting of Jesus Christ, the Crucified, but not as our Reconciler and Savior, but only as our Teacher and example while concealing His divine being and eternal truth; or again they speak of atonement and rebirth but they understand by these words only a partly moral partly religious improvement, not the real soul-changing meaning these words received from God. . . .[1]

In seeking to understand God's Word, Bilderdijk and his followers were not interested primarily in historical and scientific exactness. It is thus not surprising that they considered a critical attitude toward the history and the text of the Bible as completely unnecessary. "The Holy Spirit was their only professor."[2] While they excelled in extrabiblical, experiential knowledge,[3] their opponents concentrated on biblical, rational knowledge. That was for those active in the *Réveil* sufficient reason to refer to them as enemies. In the thought characteristic of the *Réveil*, God's truth was best defended by those who could unqualifiedly answer yes to Question 8 of the Heidelberg Catechism: "But are we so far depraved that we are wholly unapt to any good, and prone to all evil?"[4] Piety was piety of the heart. Rather than seeking after moral improvement, one had to be acutely aware in one's heart of both sin and forgiveness.

The *Réveil* did not fail to express its faith in practical forms, however. These actions introduced new dimensions of Christian charity into The

Netherlands.[5] Those whose religion had been revived in the pattern suggested by the Heidelberg Catechism as it was interpreted in the *Réveil* formed numerous charitable organizations to rescue fellow sinners. But even in this work the main premise was that these fellow sinners could be saved only by grace.

For the *Réveil* it was the *fides qua creditur* (the faith through which one believes, experientially) that defined the *fides quae creditur* (the faith-content one believes objectively and rationally). The Dutch world, however, was more interested in defining the *fides qua creditur* according to changes taking place in the *fides quae creditur*. What had been basic notions in the Christian faith were now being questioned. Scientific discovery contended with revelation. The authority of reason was replacing ecclesiastical authority. Thus, man's fall, redemption, and final judgment were being re-interpreted. Dr. Ontijd, for example, opposed Capadose's view that man's fall had produced incurable diseases. Thus, he did not consider vaccination to be an unchristian meddling with God's purpose.[6] While Bilderdijk and the early Da Costa understood scientific advance and constitutional government as dreadful signs of the end, Van Kampen and Roemer saw them to be signs of a new progressive era for mankind.[7]

Members of the *Réveil* tried to define as clearly as possible in which ways and to what extent the enemy was corrupting true faith. Those the enemy was supposedly corrupting, however, could not easily be fitted into definitive bounds. They differed in their respective degree of modernity and they did not understand themselves to be enemies of the true faith. They understood themselves to be engaged in the progressive and necessary corrections that would enable man to better serve God.

LIBERALISM

Van der Palm thus gave the following explanation to Theodor Fliedner, a visiting German theologian:

> German theologians who believe that God revealed himself usually place too much stress on the single dogmas of the Trinity, or Sin, or Regeneration. We Dutchmen do not deny them but in our sermons we place them more in the background, partly because they are incomprehensible and partly because the consequences and developments of these early dogmas in later time have become totally unbiblical. In contrast, we stress the doctrines of forgiveness of sin, of reconciliation, of the duty to give Christ the glory; and those doctrines we teach most frequently.[8]

To leave certain mysteries of the faith untouched was, in Van der Palm's view, in harmony with the nature of revelation. In one of his sermons, Van der Palm made the statement: "As the apostle John left this secret of Christ's divine nature unresolved for his pupils, so will I not try to lift for you this veil of mystery."[9] It was his conviction that it "ill behooved reason to probe the depths of the Divine Being."[10]

Philip Willem van Heusde

Philip Willem van Heusde, professor of philosophy at the University of Utrecht, 1804-39, taught a similar approach to mysteries of the faith.[11] However, he approached the subject more from the side of philosophy than theology, eclectically combining Platonic and Christian elements. Of his accomplishments he said: "If I have made any gains in grasping the character and spirit of Christianity, I owe it to the reading of our inspired records and further solely to Plato and the philosophy of the internal world."[12]

Jesus Christ was in Willem van Heusde's system the incarnate image of God, given to be the ideal goal of man's constant quest for what Plato had called the "likeness unto God."[13] Christianity was thus interpreted to be a method of self-perfection. Van Heusde admitted that man was morally incapable of achieving divine perfection. Through his study of the apostle Paul, however, Van Heusde came to believe that God had made men to be "reasonable and moral beings who as such must use our lofty powers of the soul to our improvement and to the salvation of our fellowman and society."[14] Christ could stir these dormant powers into action as men became motivated by observing his intercession with the Father on their behalf. In this respect, he was considered to be the true mediator between God and man, but he was taken to be the mediator in this respect alone.

Van Heusde had learned from his teacher Frans Hemsterhuis that man's best understanding occurs when he is able to feel intensely what he is being taught.[15] As professor at Utrecht, Van Heusde did his utmost in that manner to reach the many students who attended his lectures. No student could, in his opinion, become a true scholar without accepting the notion that mankind was in the process of becoming the incarnated image of God.[16]

The students were fascinated by Van Heusde's interpretation of the Middle Ages, not "the dark night of barbarism" but the "dawn of the later enlightenment."[17] In this interpretation Van Heusde digressed from his Platonism in favor of a philosophy of history that compared human history to the developmental stages of human growth. Greece represented boyhood, while adulthood was reached in medieval Germany. The present age should therefore be understood as the continuing fruition of the preceding ages. So many students accepted this view that Van Heusde became known as the *praeceptor Hollandiae*.

The teachings of men like Van der Palm and Van Heusde were generally accepted. Among the exceptions were Bilderdijk and his school, protesting in defense of the old orthodoxy. There was dissatisfaction in the ranks of the left, too, although it was not expressed in direct and open opposition to Van Heusde and Van der Palm. Often the left simply took steps to interpret modernity more radically in terms of its own theology. A typical example was Johan Melchior Kemper, professor of law at Leiden, who was not unkindly disposed toward Bilderdijk.[18] In 1818 he published a study of the Enlightenment, defending the following belief:

> faith and revelation may extend their hand in friendship to reason when the latter cannot climb higher; the divine authority can exalt reason's surmises into certainties; but a doctrine that would demand the sacrifice of our reason in the most important subjects of man's thought cannot be a doctrine originating with God because reason itself is a gift from the Godhead.[19]

It was not until 1840 that the left began to draw out the full consequences of this position.[20] With J. H. Scholten,[21] who occupied the chair of theology first at Franeker, 1840, and then at Leiden, 1843, there "began to rise a different type of spirit, the spirit of absolute antisupernaturalism of the German idealistic kind."[22] A full treatment of this new modernity would bring us beyond the scope of this study and will therefore not be undertaken here.

William I—An Erroneous Attribution of Liberalism

It is, however, necessary to make mention of the historical facts in order to correct English language publications touching upon this aspect of Dutch history. Almost all of them present incomplete if not erroneous interpretations of liberalism within the Reformed Church. Albert Hyma states that King William I and his advisers, in promulgating the ecclesiastical constitution of 1816

> permitted the preachers in the Reformed Church and the professors in the state universities to ignore the creed established by the international Church council of Calvinists known as the Synod of Dordrecht (1618-1619). No longer were they bound to adhere to the doctrines about original sin, predestination, the virgin birth of Christ, the doctrine of the divine in-

spiration of the Bible, the atonement. Many pastors and teachers suddenly drew the conclusion that the great minds of the seventeenth century, the men who made Holland a mighty nation, had been poor simpletons after all.[23]

L. Oostendorp asserts that under the organization of 1816 King William I and his "old clique who had been collaborationists" created a situation in which "Liberalism was encouraged, orthodoxy ridiculed."[24]

John Kromminga also places the blame for the rising liberalism in Holland on King William's church order of 1816.[25] A. J. Pieters also does so and adds that "the rationalism of the age had created a kind of comparative indifference to religion."[26]

Albertus Pieters, in his preparatory essay entitled "Historical Introduction,"[27] states erroneously that the synod created by William I took it upon itself to introduce the use of hymns in the liturgy.[28] He continued to be in error in his stating that this synod changed the formula signed by ministerial candidates, with the result that false doctrine could be preached with impunity.[29]

These authors have in common the view that the church constitution of 1816 was an open door through which liberalism entered the Reformed Church. It has been demonstrated above, however, that in 1816 liberalism, understood as non-Dordtian theology, was in large part indigenous.[30] The Reformed Church had for centuries been unable to force itself into the narrow orthodoxy spelled out by the Synod of Dordrecht, for Arminius's teachings were too biblical to be squelched by the synodical anathema. Since before the Reformation, biblical humanism had been rooted so deeply in Dutch hearts that the Synod of Dordrecht could not extirpate it. Therefore, the history of the Reformed Church in the Netherlands since 1619 abounds with conflicts and compromises between pro- and anti-Dordtians.

King William's church order of 1816 must not be understood as a breach in the conservative dyke. Liberalism had always been inside Holland. Nor did the king's intervention in 1816 in the affairs of the Reformed Church set a precedent for government involvement. The Synod of Dordrecht had been convened and financed by the highest civil authority in the Dutch republic, and its orthodox decrees had been decided upon under the benevolent eye of the state. Further, the Reformed Church succeeded in enforcing those decrees because the power of the civil government was at its disposal. The victorious party had at the time willingly paid the high price of state support in exchange for pure doctrine in the church. Since then, the state had enjoyed its *jus in sacra.*

It is historically incorrect to charge King William I and his advisers

with a heretical departure. Dutch history prior to 1816 abounded with
precedents in his majesty's favor. The cause of liberalism in the Reformed Church must therefore not be treated as a lapse on the part of
a king misguided by advisers collaborating with French oppressors.[31]
A. J. Pieters came closest to the real cause in her statement: "The rationalism of that age had created a mind of comparative indifference to
religion."[32]

Her judgment is correct if one identifies religion with Dordtian orthodoxy. There can be no doubt that in 1816 the Dutch nation as a
whole was as it had been in the many decades prior to that year, indifferent toward Dordtian decrees. Pieters's assertion is unwarranted,
however, if one understands religion in terms not exclusively Dordtian.
It is a historical fact that since 1618, the time of the Synod of Dordrecht,
the Protestant religion in The Netherlands had never been exclusively
Dordtian. On the contrary, Dutch religion at the beginning of the nineteenth century was still feeding upon the biblical humanism of both the
Brethren of the Common Life and Erasmus. It is no coincidence that
the so-called *Groninger School*, the branch of Dutch "liberalism" that
scored huge successes in the first half of the nineteenth century, presented itself as the legitimate heir of the Dutch pre-Reformation past.

THE GRONINGER SCHOOL

Petrus Hofstede de Groot

The *Groninger School* took its name from the University of Groningen in the northern part of The Netherlands. The nucleus consisted
of three professors. *Primus inter pares* was Petrus Hofstede de Groot,
1802-86, who came to his alma mater as professor in May of 1829.[33] A
few months earlier Van Heusde's student, J. F. van Oordt, 1794-1852,
had, on the occasion of his inauguration as professor of homiletics, given
an oration about the nature of holy eloquence.[34] The trio was complete
when L. G. Pareau, 1800-66, was called to the chair of church history
in 1830.[35] It should be noted, however, that the group steadfastly refused to be identified as the *Groninger School*. They did not wish to be
identified with a particular university, but with all of the nation and the
world, including all of the church and its history.[36]

The great significance of this group is that the members took particular care not to lose themselves in their own Latin-dominated academic
world.[37] They willingly opened their weekly evening meetings to local
pastors. Ministers outside the city of Groningen were equally wel-

come.[38] Vos, who is certainly no admirer of the theology of the *Groninger School*, gave credit to this circle of concerned pastors and theologians: "Especially the brotherly love and the feeling of solidarity, in spite of a difference that was revealed later, made the Groninger School a great power in the country."[39]

The spirit of this group is expressed well by Hofstede de Groot. Rejecting the name *Groninger School*, he preferred the designation *Groninger Theologen:*

> those friends who by way of this Periodical *Waarheid in Liefde* appear before the Public as *Theologians* and may be called *Groninger* theologians because most of them live in or near Groningen and the Periodical is printed there. Also, in this Periodical we prove ourselves as *Evangelical* and *Dutch* theologians. *Evangelical,* because we prefer to deduce everything from Holy Writ, especially from the New Covenant as the purest muniment of God's Revelation in Christ; *Dutch,* because we ally ourselves very closely with Wessel Gansfort, Erasmus, Lodensteijn, Hinlopen and Van Alphen, not to mention those who are living.[40]

Haitjema has made the point that the thought of Hofstede de Groot and his friends had its roots in the optimistic and rationalistic theology of the eighteenth century.[41] But he adds that the *Groningers* were a group in which the younger generation's dissatisfaction with the old rationalistic clichés was verbalized. They did not give up rationalism, but added to it the two notions of "heart" and "history" that came to overshadow the precious "good" of the previous century.

The Importance of the Heart

The *Groningers* followed Hofstede de Groot in the emphasis he placed upon the significance of the heart in the world of faith. Although the parallel with Schleiermacher is obvious, Haitjema is correct in stating that not Schleiermacher but the Frenchman, Constant, convinced Hofstede de Groot in 1824 of "the completely strange and novel" conception that religion has its source in man's religious heart and, stranger yet, that there *is* such a thing in man as religious feeling.[42] Hofstede did not make his acquaintance with Schleiermacher's *Der Christliche Glaube* until 1831, and he confesses that he did not understand the book until much later.[43]

For Schleiermacher, dogmatic theology was "the knowledge of the constellation of doctrines in a Christian church-communion at a given time."[44] This knowledge was derived by the use of only one instrument—namely man's feeling. Unlike Schleiermacher, however, the

Groningers did not rely exclusively on the heart. In their systematic theology they made use of "human nature with all its powers and needs."[45] When German followers of Schleiermacher like Ullman, Locke, and Nietzsche constructed their post-Schleiermacher *Vermittlungstheologie,* the net result was very similar to the theology developed by the *Groningers.* Both groups worked out a theology that was intended to prove the truth of Christianity through the Bible, history, and personal experience.[46] Through the applications of their respective theologies, both groups arrived at propositions which constituted what they believed to be authoritative doctrine. In that respect, the theologians of the heart did not differ much from the older rationalists. In the newer theology, however, man in his religious experience could make use of his heart as well as his reason. This became all the more significant because the approach to religion through the heart, in addition to reason, was sure to reach the common people.

Warm fellowship and heartfelt religion had not grown well on a pulpit-diet that consisted mainly of reason, virtue, and duty; and the need for a warmer and more experiential relation with the Deity had not died. Large numbers of the ministerial students trained at Groningen became pastors whose sermons spoke to the heart. Thus, the *Réveil's* insistence upon the personal experience of religion was matched by the ministers who belonged to the *Groninger School.*[47]

Revelation as History

Hofstede de Groot and his friends developed a deep interest in God's revelation as history. To be sure, the older, more rationalistic and supra-naturalistic theology had also been interested in the historical aspects of Christianity. One of its typical spokesmen had been Hermannus Muntinghe,[48] 1751-1824, professor of theology at Groningen, of whom Hofstede de Groot testified: "the grey but as yet forceful Muntinghe extricated me from most of my uncertainties and doubts."[49] Muntinghe had published a huge *History of mankind according to the Bible.*[50] In the eleven volumes of this work, Muntinghe investigated "what recorded history in the Bible is yielding with respect to the origin and step-by-step development of mankind's intellectual and moral civilization."[51] Understanding the stories in the Bible literally, Muntinghe came to the conclusion that "everything told in the Bible agrees with the simple process of nature."[52] Preaching along these lines, he became so famous that the farmers did not hesitate to walk seven miles one way to hear him "make God known from nature and history."[53]

In his view of history, Muntinghe believed that he did not have to go beyond the life of Jesus. For him the development of the human race stopped with the arrival of the God-man. It is at this point that Hofstede de Groot and his friends carried his thought further. Had not the revered Van Heusde taught that mankind was continually evolving under God's tutelage? The *Groninger Theologen* combined the respective historical methods of both Muntinghe and Van Heusde and applied the combination to the New Testament and the history of the church. They agreed in a basic presupposition as they made this application: "Most important in Christianity is the revelation and education given to us by God in Jesus Christ in order to make us more and more like God."[54]

The *Groninger Theologen* found both the orthodox and the earlier liberal doctrines of Christ wanting. In their opinion, the former was too exclusively concerned with Christ's satisfaction, while the latter only extracted from the living Christ a dry system of teachings and precepts. J. F. van Oordt summarized the *Groninger* approach in the words: "Not in teachings proposed by Jesus, but in Him, in His mission, in His person, in His history one can find the revelation of God."[55] According to Hofstede de Groot, "Revelation and education are one because education takes place through revelation and revelation serves education."[56]

For the *Groninger Theologen*, the process of mankind's education had not come to a halt with the birth of the Savior. Jesus Christ continued to reveal himself through the ages, and was thus still educating mankind. The *Groninger Theologen* were deeply interested in the culmination of the educative process that was to make man similar to God. They considered the contemporary world to be the harbinger of a glorious future, and displayed an intense interest in the history through which mankind had already evolved. As Hofstede de Groot put it: "History is really the essential thing in Christianity."[57]

Contrast Between De Groot and Bilderdijk

Bilderdijk and his school were also greatly interested in history. In their interpretation, however, God had assigned The Netherlands a unique place as the Israel of the North. The House of Orange was the messianic center of this Israel.[58] The *Groninger School*, on the other hand, considered The Netherlands to be one of the places in which God was educating part of mankind.

Bilderdijk expected the imminent holocaust of doomsday and interpreted the sufferings of his time as evidences that Holland, God's chosen nation, had left its true heritage. The *Groninger Theologen* read in the history of the church of all places and of all times abundant evidence of God's continuing education of mankind.[59] They were nationalistic only insofar as they brought to light what Dutch believers through the centuries had done to help actualize God's plan to ultimately deify man.

Bilderdijk and his school glorified the Synod of Dordrecht as the assembly in which the true, that is Dutch, religion reached its zenith. Hofstede de Groot, on the other hand, made the charge that Calvinistic and Lutheran thought had been unnecessarily imported into The Netherlands, since the Christian religion was already being peacefully reformed by Erasmus, Duifhuis, and others.[60]

While Bilderdijk issued his calls to prepare for the last judgment, Hofstede de Groot exhorted the Dutch to "join again our Dutch divines of old . . . who as Dutchmen understood the Gospel and applied it for Dutchmen."[61] The *Groninger Theologen* proudly asserted that they subscribed wholeheartedly to "the eternal Gospel, always and everywhere the same." But with equal pride they taught this Gospel "in that manner in which the Dutch people can best absorb its heavenly richness and divine power."[62]

Bilderdijk did not care to join the church because he viewed its actions as a meddling in the affairs of God. Hofstede de Groot stated his hope that the church would "in our lifetime expand and become catholic" through the process of divine education.[63]

Bilderdijk deplored the fact that the dividing lines between the true church and heretical bodies were disappearing. Hofstede de Groot was delighted to include his colleagues Pareau and Van Oordt within his social circle, even though Pareau was a Lutheran and Van Oordt was a Mennonite.[64]

Almost crushed by the avalanche of modern thinking, Bilderdijk and his friends expected the fruition of their labors to appear through miraculous acts of God. The *Groninger Theologen* were certain that through their labors God was ushering in the realization of mankind's ultimate triumph. As noted above, Hofstede de Groot and his friends had steadfastly refused to be identified as a school.[65] They did not consider themselves to be one among the many past and present schools, but the harbinger of the church of the future. They were certain that "the death of the papacy" was being hastened by the work of the Bible societies.[66] Hofstede de Groot frankly wondered "which reasonable theologian at this time could still be our opponent?"[67]

Groningen's supporters far outnumbered their opponents. Colleagues, ministers, and students accepted and advocated *Groninger Theologie* as did the citizenry at Groningen and elsewhere. Until approximately 1855, the *Groninger Theologen* continued to dominate the theology of the Reformed Church in general.[68] Nevertheless, there were influential opponents who refused to be made docile by the gracious but overbearing attitude of the *Groningers*.

Among them was Guillaume Groen van Prinsterer (best known by his shorter name Groen), one of Bilderdijk's first students at Leiden. It is curious that Bilderdijk, who was such a positive influence in the development of Da Costa's faith, was a negative influence upon Groen's faith. As Groen once wrote in a letter: Bilderdijk "has more frightened me away from unbelief than that he has brought me to faith."[69] He was admittedly one of Bilderdijk's most brilliant students, but his faith became more orthodox when he came under the care of Pastor J. Henri Merle d'Aubigne, the French-speaking minister of the Reformed Church in Brussels. But the greatest influence in Groen's spiritual development was his wife, Elisabeth M. M. vander Hoop.

Following the Belgian insurrection, King William's court settled permanently in The Hague, where Groen performed secretarial duties for the King's Cabinet. There Groen rose to a position of leadership in the *Réveil*, and six of its members joined him to form a group that in 1842 became known as the *Zeven Haagse Heren*. They were responsible for the Address to the General Synod of 1842 which demanded disciplinary action against "the theology of feeling which, having taken away the foundations of man's union with God, is now losing itself in idle speculations and dreams about a love without retributive punishment."[70] It must suffice to add that most of the members of the *Réveil* at Amsterdam, among them Da Costa, refused to sign this address.[71] The full tracing of this conflict will not be presented here because it would bring us beyond the scope of this study.[72]

Nor is it possible to do more than mention the theologians H. J. Rooyaards, J. I. Doedes, and A. des Amorie van der Hoeven, who attacked the unscientific way with which the *Groninger Theologen* so easily changed revelation into education.[73] These theologians were soon overshadowed, however, by a much more radical modernism.[74]

The opposition could not prevent the *Groninger Theologen* from reigning supreme till 1855-60, and in effect governing the Reformed Church.[75] Hofstede de Groot and his friends did not lose their nerve so long as their opponents stayed in the church. But their calm was disturbed, albeit momentarily, when in 1834 Hendrik de Cock, minister of the Reformed Church at Ulrum in the Province of Groningen, claimed that he was returning to the true Reformed Church and became the leader of a secession.[76]

SECESSION AND HENDRIK DE COCK

De Cock and De Groot

The irony of the situation was that Hendrik de Cock had been trained for the ministry at the University of Groningen at the same time as Hofstede de Groot. He also had belonged to the same circle of more advanced students.[77] Further, when Hofstede de Groot, serving as minister of the Reformed Church at Ulrum in the Province of Groningen, was invited to become a professor of theology at the University of Groningen,[78] he used his influence to cause De Cock to be called to fill the vacancy. When De Cock accepted, it was Hofstede de Groot who preached the sermon in De Cock's installation service on October 29, 1829.[79]

There were at first no theological differences between these two ministers. But while Hofstede de Groot was at the University of Groningen he came under influences which prompted him to go beyond Muntinghe,[80] and De Cock came under the influence of those of his parishioners at Ulrum who exhibited the remnants of the old-time Reformed piety as shaped by Voetius and Koelman.[81] While Hofstede de Groot was still the pastor at Ulrum, he had become fully aware of the make-up of his congregation:

> two elements which are long since present in the Netherlands Reformed Church: the old narrow particularism built upon the Synod of Dordrecht and the new free universalism arising from a more enlightened knowledge of the Bible and a sounder culture, a universalism that did not always respect the lines drawn by the Gospel.[82]

However, De Cock was little acquainted[83] with the "narrow particularism" that he met in one of the baptized non-communicant members by the name of Klaas Pieters Kuipenga.[84]

Hofstede de Groot had already been working with Kuipenga and others like him. As a very concerned pastor, he had urged De Cock to continue close pastoral shepherding of these peculiar sheep.[85] They had failed to respond to Hofstede de Groot's shepherd care. De Cock continued Kuipenga's private instruction but was unable to convince him that education was gradually making him perfect in God's sight. Kuipenga insisted: "Should I be required to contribute a mere whisper to my salvation, I would be forever lost."[86] Helenius de Cock states that his father often assured him how meaningless this confession of man's inability had been to him at the time.[87]

As a faithful pastor, De Cock was seriously searching for an answer that would overcome the lack of confidence in God displayed by Kuipenga and those who were like-minded. During this period, De Cock was not familiar with Calvin's *Institutes* nor the Canons of Dordrecht. His library even lacked a copy of the State Bible.[88] But help came when De Cock visited Wormnest, a fellow pastor at Warfhuizen. In the course of their conversation, Wormnest turned to Calvin's *Institutes* to prove a point. De Cock became so interested in the *Institutes* that he borrowed Wormnest's copy and took it home for further study. As a result of this study, De Cock began to see that Kuipenga was right—salvation must be understood as a work of grace in which man cannot meritoriously intervene.[89]

De Cock and C. Baron van Zuylen van Nijeveldt

As De Cock was becoming thus more and more interested in Reformed theology as it had developed in The Netherlands, he received a pamphlet that was to provide him with clearer insight into how this theology should function. The pamphlet was entitled *De Eenige Redding*, The Only Salvation, and had been authored by Cornelis Baron van Zuylen van Nijeveldt.[90] According to De Cock's son, this booklet "caused him *more than before* to see the relationship between doctrine and practice."[91]

In 1817 Cornelis Baron van Zuylen van Nijeveldt, 1777-1833, had become convinced that important events were soon to take place. He wanted to provide a refuge for the faithful, and therefore proposed the formation of the Society of True Friends of Christianity. Members were supposed to be able to strengthen one another in the faith by corresponding with one another. The effort had no significant success.[92]

The baron, who had served King Louis Napoleon as the secretary of the Dutch embassy at Moscow, had been chosen by King William I of Orange as the secretary-general for Foreign Affairs, 1815-16.[93] Poor health compelled the baron to resign, however. He became a close friend of D. Molenaar, a minister of the Reformed Church at The Hague, who in 1827 published anonymously an *Adres Aan Alle Mijne Hervormde Geloofsgenooten*, Address to All My Reformed Fellow Believers.[94]

The Rev. D. Molenaar

Molenaar accused the General Synod's committee of being woefully weak in enforcing the formula signed by candidates for the ministry. The *quatenus*, or "in so far," interpretation had allowed far more liberty than had been possible under the *quia,* or "because," interpretation.[95] Molenaar pressed his point home by charging that the formula "could be signed by a Christian of any persuasion, by the Roman Catholic, and even by the Jew."[96] He thus made a proposal:

> a general synod should be called to compose a calm and christian *Address to All Reformed Churchmembers* proposing to change the doctrines of the church, and seeing any who might not wish to do so, to proceed in simplicity and great calm to mutually divide the church and its properties.[97]

The reason why the government showed such a deep interest in Molenaar's pamphlet is intimately bound up with the grave problems besetting King William I's kingdom. Since 1815, the French and Dutch languages had been adopted as the official languages. Thus, while they were still annexed to France, the Flemish-speaking Belgians had been forbidden to use their native language in public affairs. King William had ordered in 1819 that Dutch be used in place of French in the public affairs of the southern provinces of East- and West-Flanders, Antwerp, and Limburg. Civil servants had to know or to learn the Dutch. At the three universities of Gent, Leuven, and Luik or Liege, the king created chairs of Dutch language and literature in addition to those of French.[98] But Flemish-Dutch had for so long been considered a crude dialect that this effort received no more than a lukewarm reception from the Flemish. The French-speaking Belgians gave it a very cool reception.[99]

King William's government encountered fierce resistance when it began a vigorous program to improve education at the elementary and secondary level. Authorities at the local level and especially in the church protested against the curtailment of their powers by charging that the government was using the schools to protestantize the Roman Catholic South. From the time the government had tried to improve secondary school training for priests,[100] it had encountered Catholic resistance.[101]

Under these circumstances, King William did not need a strong movement in the northern part of the empire demanding that the Reformed Church be returned to its former status. A Reformed Church restored to its former privileged position and the strict enforcement of the three forms of unity would undoubtedly lead to a more militant attitude in the membership. If the government were to give the slightest encouragement to such a development, the Belgian Roman Catholics would have even more reason to charge that Protestant heretics were trying to usurp power in the country. To keep his realm intact, King William had no choice but to avoid whatever could give the Belgians and their French supporters an excuse to agitate for a secession from the empire.[102] Hence, the government was compelled to prevent the return of a militant and aggressive spirit in the Reformed Church, because that spirit was intimately bound up with the battle the Dutch had fought for political and religious freedom. For instance, Da Costa spoke of the "firmer tie that must bind North and South together"—a tie that would have to be spelled out in terms of "the ancient covenant that William of Orange in Christian saving faith made with Almighty God and had sealed with his blood in surely bringing down more than Philip and Spain."[103]

Molenaar's *Adres* of 1827 came at a time when King William and his government were doing their utmost to come to terms with the Roman Catholic Church in Belgium.[104] Although the king and his ministers might personally have favored the mild over the strict wing in the Reformed Church, had they allowed the church to return to its earlier doctrinal position, the political consequences of such a move would have greatly endangered the precarious truce being worked out with the Roman Catholic hierarchy in Belgium and in Rome.[105] It is thus erroneous to understand the government's action against Molenaar solely in terms of a liberalistic enmity against orthodox doctrine, although that was a factor. Because the unity of the kingdom had to be preserved, the state could not allow the churches unrestricted freedom. All denominations therefore had to remain under some form of government control.

The Council of State, the highest judicatory in the realm, sent a report to King William noting that Molenaar in his *Adres* had strongly denied having associated with Bilderdijk's circle. But its Committee on Protestant Churches grouped Molenaar with Bilderdijk and Da Costa, on the basis of a letter Molenaar had written to J. H. den Ouden, the publisher of his brochure.[106] Molenaar's opening sentence read:

> Mr. Den Ouden! Knowing that you use your printing press in the true interest of the church of the Fatherland, I take the liberty to send to you the enclosed essay and to donate it to you as your property, requesting that you print it and distribute it as widely as possible.[107]

Since Da Costa, Bilderdijk, and C. Baron van Zuylen van Nijeveldt had made their insights known through this press, Molenaar's endorsement of it seemed incriminating.[108]

If the true interest of the fatherland would require the restoration of the Reformed Church to its former established position, the kingdom of The Netherlands could not be maintained in the form established by King William. In this predicament King William chose to ignore the counsel that urged stiff punishment for Molenaar. Instead he opted for

the more moderate course, and simply expressed his displeasure with
the pamphlet. He offered to accept Molenaar's apology "in the hope
that the petitioner Molenaar will refrain from everything that may disturb the peace of the Reformed Church and will conduct himself in
accordance with the laws and precepts."[109]

During this period, C. Baron van Zuylen van Nijeveldt befriended
Molenaar, assuming again his self-appointed, prophetic task of speaking
to the nation. In 1828, he published a brochure entitled *Het Liberalismus*, which declared that liberalism was man's effort to neutralize
God's free grace

> which is within God Himself that absolutely free decision by which He,
> without considering His creature at all, in His sovereign pleasure, chooses
> some men with His particular grace and brings them to Himself, while
> He leaves others in their destruction and justly condemns them.[110]

The baron identified this liberalism with the French revolution, and
believed that its principles were now corrupting The Netherlands.

The Belgian Revolt

It could not be denied that William I's kingdom was in trouble. On
August 25, 1830, a revolt broke out in Brussels. Republicans from France
who had escaped from King Louis Philippe's monarchy exploited existing dissatisfaction over unemployment and high prices to create an insurrection. They used the Belgian dissatisfaction to kindle the
revolutionary spirit that was to be used against the new regime in
France.[111] In addition, a large majority of the Roman Catholics were
inspired by Lamennais, and because of his influence wanted absolute
freedom for their parochial schools.[112]

King William's policies had not been wise enough to avoid the ag-
gravation of both Liberals and Roman Catholics to the point that they
forgot their differences and united in the so-called Monstrous Alliance.
The Liberals did not desire absolute freedom for Roman Catholic
schools.[113] Neither did the Roman Catholics desire absolute freedom
of the press and a parliamentary democracy. But both parties wanted
concessions from the king. By 1827, they had begun to unify their
respective protests. In this climate of unified protest it was possible to
stir up an insurrection, especially since King William did not immediately take strong, decisive action, but wavered between concession and
repression.[114]

The king's problems were complicated because Belgium had been
attached to The Netherlands at the orders of the Congress of Vienna.

Difficulties with Belgium could therefore always result in international complications, particularly with England and France.[115] Thus, when the insurrection at Brussels sparked other parts of the South into a more general revolt, King William was unable to treat it as a purely internal matter. It took nine long years of careful negotiations before England, France, Prussia, Austria, and Russia came to an agreement, with the result that Belgium and The Netherlands were divided into two independent states.[116]

During the nine years between the outbreak of the insurrection and the final separation, King William never lost the support of the North. It is true, however, that his support wore thin during the course of the long conflict.[117] The extremely heavy financial burdens required to keep the military forces equipped for battle finally prompted parliament to demand more controlling power. In the early stages of the conflict, however, the North rallied almost feverishly to William's support.

The orthodox element in the Reformed Church especially, although not exclusively, championed King William's cause, and did it in a characteristic manner. Groen van Prinsterer urged that a national day of prayer be ordered. "Let King and People humble themselves before God. One should not fear the mockery of the French and the French-minded. In our Piety, thanks to God, we have a preventative against French terror."[118] Willem de Clercq agreed with Da Costa that this Belgian uprising in 1830 was a continuation of The French Revolution of 1790. It was not a revolt against injustice and terror, but a rebellion against God.[119] Capadose rejoiced that the godless tie with Belgium was finally cut, for it had been manufactured by mere men. No longer connected to Belgium, The Netherlands was given the splendid opportunity to be itself and thus glorify God: "As soon as the cornerstone has been restored and the Reformed Church will again be the foundation for the entire State, the glory of God will be the principle of life."[120] God was using France and England to punish The Netherlands, his Israel of the North, for its former tie with Belgium—as in former days God had used Babylon and Assyria to punish his old Israel.[121]

But not all who were connected with the *Réveil* believed that the conflict should end with an unqualified restoration of the Reformed Church. H. J. Koenen, 1809-74, a lawyer and councilman of Amsterdam, attended Da Costa's private lectures on Dutch history and theology but did not always agree with his interpretations. He summed up the things which he objected to in what he called "Da Costanianism" in seven points: (1) the danger of the *oefeningen* causing a defamation of the church; (2) too many injunctive principles, for instance, against smallpox vaccination; (3) too much admiration for absolutistic political theories; (4) the deification of the House of Orange; (5) the bias against Remonstrants or Arminians; (6) an unfounded rejection of spiritual songs or *Gezangen*; and (7) too much emphasis on predestination.[122] But Koenen was quite alone in these criticisms.

National Infidelity to God and Dordt

The revolt in the South convinced C. Baron van Zuylen van Nijeveldt that God wanted to punish The Netherlands for having left the old ways which had made the country great.[123] Hence, he published in 1830 a brochure entitled *Uitboezeming aan mijne ware Hervormde Geloofsgenooten*,[124] Outpouring for My True Fellow Reformed Believers. In it he argued that the truly Reformed believers were those who shared the one sound principle that the public glorification of God had always constituted the strength of the nation. He therefore deplored the unification with Belgium, for union with Roman Catholic Belgium had made it impossible for the state to adopt the only true, that is Reformed, religion. The baron concluded therefore that God was now separating Belgium from the North. He urged the North to display true humiliation before God and a firm resolve to re-establish true doctrine in the land.

Since the nation showed few signs of making such a move, the baron continued to publish his view. In 1831 he wrote *De Eenige Redding*, The Only Salvation, followed in 1832 by *De Hervormde Leer*, The Reformed Doctrine.[125] Salvation could only be found in a restoration of the old Reformed religion: because its doctrine had glorified God and humbled man.[126]

Hendrik de Cock was deeply influenced by the baron's pamphlets. He agreed that the sufferings of The Netherlands were caused by the nation's departure from God's ways. De Cock saw the evidence of God's judgment in both the Belgian revolution and in the concurrent cholera epidemic which devastated The Netherlands.[127]

The highest authorities were alarmed at the appearance of Asiatic cholera in Germany. In 1831 the king dispatched medical doctors to Berlin and Hamburg to determine what preventive steps could be taken. He put strict quarantine laws into effect at both inland and coastal borders. Pamphlets were published warning against uncleanliness and the eating of overripe fruit. Characteristically, the royal exhortations ended with a fatherly admonition: "be calm, trust Providence, and do not forget that His Majesty gave orders to put these regulations into effect. Obey them therefore as loyal subjects."[128]

But the king did more. He proclaimed Sunday, December 2, 1832, as a national day of prayer. Hundreds of pamphlets containing sermons preached on that day flooded the market, and among them were some that accused the Jesuits of having introduced the cholera in Europe.[129] H. Nuse wrote a brochure entitled "The trumpet of the holy age, calling all sorts of men unto conversion and unto expectation of the true church of the New Covenant in order to be joined with her at the beginning of the millenium of peace."[130] The government impounded the booklet, however; nonetheless, many citizens saw the cholera as a punishment of God.[131]

Groningen, the wheat province, had prospered under the French regime.[132] Foreign imports of grain were greatly reduced when Napoleon began to enforce his Continental System, enabling the farmers of Groningen to sell their wheat at very high prices. When King William's government re-opened the country to foreign imports, the prices came down despite the fact that Groningen was able to export large quantities of wheat to Belgium. The poor harvests in the years 1828 through 1830 preceded the disastrous insurrection in the South. Losing Belgium as a market, the farmers were pressed even harder in the fall of 1830, as taxes had to be increased. Because of the tense international situation and the consequent necessity of keeping the troops ready, King William's government was unable to reduce taxation. Consequently, the revolutionary tendencies appearing in the Province of Groningen were met with force.[133] Additional troops were billeted in Groningen. An open conflict could thus be immediately and effectively dealt with. But agitation continued—especially when land taxes were increased in 1832. The situation became so tense that the authorities took very strong action against *De Ommelander,* a vocal paper of the opposition. Its publication ended when the editors were arrested and one of them, the medical doctor Middendorp, was publicly branded and given ten years in a penal institution.[134]

A Return to True Religion

Such were the times that caused De Cock to come to agree with C. Baron van Zuylen van Nijeveldt that these calamities were a divine punishment visited upon The Netherlands because it had forsaken its former inheritance. As a faithful pastor, De Cock was very concerned for the manner in which his flock would weather this punishment, reading Ezekiel 33:1-11 as if it were directly addressed to him. He therefore began to warn his congregation and all the nation,[135] writing a brochure entitled *Earnest and Hearty Address to My Fellow Citizens in These Precarious and Sad Days, Especially with Reference to Their Eternal*

Interests."[136] In it, De Cock identified with the views of C. Baron van Zuylen van Nijeveldt:

> Oh, that the treacherous scheme to attack the Reformed be discontinued, that is the true doctrine of godliness; oh, that one would act in honesty; that one would not conceal what needs to be said to awake, under God's blessing, man from his sleep of death; oh, that one would present to the congregation the whole counsel of God and not a half counsel, in order that it may be testified with Paul: "I am innocent of your blood"—oh, that everyone desirous to return to the errors of Roman superstition or Arminian, or Socinian, or Arian unbelief would do so openly and would not as a wolf in sheep's clothing destroy the flock of Christ.[137]

De Cock began to preach his weekly sermons in this spirit. In addition to the members of his congregation, many people from the Province of Groningen and elsewhere came to hear him. The people were ready for change.

In De Cock's area, the ultra-liberal reaction against the rather autocratic government of King William was as strong as elsewhere in the province. But dissatisfaction and frustration were shared by everyone—irrespective of political persuasion. When De Cock began to preach concerning what he considered to be The Netherlands' problems, the orthodox element flocked to Ulrum to hear the confirmation of what they had suspected for a long time.

Since religion never exists in a vacuum, it is necessary to place De Cock's phenomenal popularity against the background of the economic and social conditions of his time. That is the only way to do justice to De Cock, for he was convinced that the troubles which had beset his country were a result of false religion. While the liberal element sought to remedy the situation by further democratization of the government, De Cock advocated a return to true religion. In view of the opposition he faced, it is to De Cock's credit that he went about his task with an utter lack of fear.

P. Hofstede de Groot, after he had heard what was taking place in his former congregation, was among the first to oppose De Cock. To confirm what he had heard, he visited De Cock in the summer of 1832.[138] But his appeal to his successor "to walk again the way he had so peacefully walked before" was in vain.[139] As they parted, De Cock presented the professor with a copy of C. Baron van Zuylen van Nijeveldt's brochure *De Hervormde Leer.*[140] Hofstede de Groot promised to read it, and as a result several letters were exchanged between the two.[141]

The first letter received by De Cock made it clear that the brochure had not converted Hofstede de Groot. He replied:

DeCock! DeCock! Such a bitter and unchristian writing contains your confession of faith? How deep, deep have you fallen, and how dark is to me the counsel of God that such a doctrine is now being taught the congregation that once was mine. I have prayed to God many a time that He would grant me the spirit of moderation in order that I might exercise truth and love and avoid Van Zuylen's abusive tone.[142]

But De Cock was convinced that he did not "defend Van Zuylen van Nijeveldt but in him truth and piety."[143] He urged Hofstede de Groot therefore to read the Bible and John Calvin:

Yes, I pray that you read Calvin looking to God and praying for the guidance of his Spirit for Jesus' sake; the Lord will perhaps make you to see and to know the truth, and may let it be for you too as a blessed means of glorification of Himself and of your liberation from the fetters of the king of darkness.[144]

Hofstede de Groot pointed out that Van Zuylen van Nijeveldt was defending his doctrinal system, and was therefore blind to the biblical fact that God by the means of hope, love, and charity educates mankind to perfection.[145] For De Cock, however, the issue was simply a decision for or against the doctrinal position of Dordrecht. In his view the faith had always been and would always be the same, and therefore what Dordrecht taught sould be unqualifiedly taught and believed by all true believers.[146] To Hofstede de Groot such an opinion was the gravest possible sin. Fallible men like Augustine, Calvin, and the fathers of Dordrecht should not be placed on the pedestal as the end product of God's school of history.

Their conflict was rooted in their views concerning the proper manner in which to approach Scripture. De Cock was convinced that the doctrine of the trinity had been deliberately undermined by Arians. In former centuries, Arians had gone so far as to remove 1 John 5:7-8 from certain manuscripts. De Cock reminded Hofstede de Groot of the many learned church fathers who had accepted this passage in good faith and had shaped their faith accordingly.[147] Hofstede de Groot could not be convinced by what former generations had done, and wished to accept a more critical approach to the sacred text.[148] Thus, it becomes clear that these two friends had grown far apart. For De Cock, God's truth was eternally the same and therefore sinful man was in need of being converted from his fallen world to that eternal truth of God. Hofstede de Groot understood the divergencies of sinful man in the Bible and history as memorials of an educative process through which God was graciously perfecting mankind. Hofstede de Groot understood De Cock's conversion to the truth of a former age not as a liberation, but as a return to bondage. De Cock, in turn, was horrified that Hofstede de Groot dared to deviate from the final and complete doctrine which God had revealed to all saints of all ages. A reconciliation was not possible, and therefore their friendship ended.

In the course of theological reflection, De Cock perceived that heresy could be disguised in biblical arguments. Since these false doctrines constituted an insidious danger for God's nation, De Cock felt compelled to continue with even more intensity his task as a watchman "who saw the sword coming"—to blow the trumpet and to warn the people.[149] But Hofstede de Groot declined his request that they jointly publish their correspondence to that end.[150] For De Cock, the revolution in Belgium, the outbreak of cholera, and the rebellious spirit in the Province of Groningen were abundant evidence that the sword had come near. Thus, he plunged into the battle that would result in his deposition.

In 1833, De Cock published a pamphlet that included the Five Canons of Dordrecht. In the introduction, he presented the following urgent theme: "a return . . . to the true service of God . . . which had been forsaken by the majority of the population as it had turned to the idols of man's corrupted and darkened reason."[151]

In addition, De Cock took two additional steps that brought him into open conflict with church authorities.

Baptism in the True Religion

De Cock further displeased church authorities when he gave ear to those visitors in his crowded Sunday services who requested that he baptize their children. The parents were usually members of the Reformed Church, but invariably not at Ulrum. Since their own ministers did not satisfy them, they would come to hear De Cock voice his forceful warnings against false teachers. Under such preaching, parents began to wonder whether or not unfaithful pastors should be allowed to baptize their children.

De Cock was not certain how to respond to these requests. The board of elders did not deny the requests for baptism, but did not dare to grant them either. Consequently, they recommended that De Cock consult the Reverend D. Molenaar or C. Baron van Zuylen van Nijeveldt.[152]

In reply to De Cock's inquiry, Molenaar stated that "the worthy baron . . . my dear and precious friend . . . who was watching and praying for Zion," had very recently died.[153] Concerning the wakening stirring in the Reformed Church, he assured De Cock that this awakening among the orthodox should and could be sustained. In view of the possibility of realizing even greater gains if conflicts were held off, Molenaar advised Ulrum's pastor not to baptize children from parishes other than his own. He shared as his reason: "not because it is not permitted . . . but because especially under the present constitution of the church one must conduct oneself with care in relation to one's neighbors and colleagues (though they err) and one must avoid any appearance of evil."[154] In addition, Molenaar pointed out that "the parents are answering the questions in the baptismal liturgy so that their own interpretation of the form weighs far heavier than what some minister may make of it."[155] Molenaar also reasoned that the responsibility for the presenting of either true or false doctrine does not rest with the parents of children to be baptized, but with the pastor administering the sacrament. Molenaar admitted that "under the constitution of 1818-1819 (see my Address) pastors were allowed unrestricted freedom in preaching."[156] He saw enough signs of change in the church to give him hope for the future, and stated that this change was soon to come because God would "stand up in battle." Hence he urged De Cock: "Let us keep good courage. Let us be steadfast, unmovable, always abounding in the work of the Lord."[157]

De Cock was not satisfied with this answer, however. To be careful in one's relations with one's colleagues could equally well be either a sinful or a pious excuse. Nor was De Cock satisfied with the interpretation that the minister administering the sacrament was alone responsible for his own doctrine, as the parents of children to be baptized were responsible for their baptismal vows.[158] Thus the consistory at Ulrum decided on October 4, 1833, to baptize the children[159] of nonresident church members.

The reaction was immediate. Ministers around Ulrum were, of course, aware of the influence De Cock was exerting on parts of their membership. Through his preaching in congregations other than his own, De Cock had already begun to catechize all those who wanted to be instructed in what he considered to be the true religion. The next logical step was to grant the requests of those who asked him to baptize their children. That action, however, implied that Ulrum was responsible for a certain degree of discipline beyond its boundaries. However careful De Cock and his consistory may have been in their counseling with the parents, the pastor of Ulrum and the board of elders could not avoid giving an implicit endorsement to the parents' verdict about the orthodoxy of their home pastor.

Thus the Reverend A. P. A. du Cloux, pastor of the Reformed Church at Vierhuizen, turned to the Classis of Middelstum and protested De Cock's baptizing of children of his congregation. On November 18,

1833, the classis appointed a committee of three members to investigate the charge. One of the three members, Dr. A. Rutgers, pastor of the Reformed Church at Breede, went beyond his assigned task of investigating Du Cloux's charge. Corresponding with De Cock, Dr. Rutgers pointed out that Calvin (*Institutes* IV.3,5 and 15,16) spoke emphatically against the Donatists' error of linking the efficacy of the sacrament with the worthiness of the one who administered it.[160]

Nevertheless, De Cock remained unconvinced. In his opinion, Calvin's counsel applied only to the minister who, having left his congregation, administers the sacrament of baptism elsewhere. De Cock argued that this did not apply to him because believers were coming to *him* and requesting that their children be baptized. Thus, he did not feel that he could refuse them. Furthermore, he was unable to understand how the name Donatist could be applied to him. Both he and the parents expected the sacrament to be efficacious through the Holy Spirit, not sinful man. To bolster his case, De Cock appealed to Calvin's commentary on Matthew 28:19, to Articles 27, 28, and 29 of The Netherlands Confession of Faith, and to Ursinus. If these appeals were taken to be insufficient, De Cock made it known that he wished to be convinced of his error on the basis of God's Word and the laws of the church.[161]

An Attack on the "Wolves"

The Classis of Middelstum lacked the legal grounds for instituting proceedings against De Cock. There was no specific article in the church constitution forbidding a minister to baptize children from outside his congregation.[162] But the case took another twist when De Cock, while under classical investigation, published a pamphlet entitled *Defense of the True Reformed Doctrine and of the True Reformed Believers, Attacked and Exposed by Two So-called Reformed Teachers, or the Sheepfold of Christ Attacked by Two Wolves and Defended by H. DeCock, Reformed Teacher at Ulrum.*[163] The "two so-called Reformed teachers," or "wolves," were De Cock's colleagues L. Meijer Brouwer and G. Benthem Reddinghius, both of whom had authored pamphlets attacking the views and attitudes typical of De Cock.[164]

L. Meijer Brouwer warned against the teachings of those who tried to reduce the Savior to a mere high priest or sacrifice, and in so doing ignored him as a teacher and leader. The former doctrine should not be held to the exclusion of the rest of the doctrines arising from a comprehensive biblical faith. Man's expression of gratitude in leading a virtuous life which conformed to Christ's teaching and leadership would thus have to constitute a part in true faith.

In his *Brieven*, Benthem Reddinghiu answered the question: "What should be done with those who, because they were dissatisfied with their pastors, frequented the *oefeningen*?" The author admitted the religious earnestness of these seekers, but stated that it was an earnestness inspired by a stagnated theology. He therefore counseled that love and moderation be extended to those backward persons who believed that the Holy Spirit had ceased his work with the closing of the Synod of Dordrecht.

De Cock stated in his brochure that neither author was in agreement with the Three Forms of Unity. He therefore considered it his duty to expose these wolves in sheep's clothing. The language he used was so derogatory, however, that in its proceedings against De Cock the Classis of Middelstum forgot the baptism investigation and took him to task for what he had written about his two colleagues.

When De Cock appeared before the classis on December 20, 1833, the members were aware of the difficulties inherent in charging De Cock with having irregularly baptized non-resident children. President J. J. Damste, 1770-1855, minister of the Reformed Church in Uithuizermeden, had written to the Ministry in charge of the Reformed Church requesting its advice on how to proceed against De Cock. Damste had in vain searched the rules and regulations for an indication of what to do.[165]

The Ministry's secretary-adviser, J. D. Janssen,[166] informed Damste that De Cock was entitled "to enjoy as much freedom as any minister in our Church." Therefore, "every appearance of compulsion in matters of faith, every restriction of Protestant-Christian freedom with respect to the mystics must be avoided." But Janssen made it equally clear that "the slanderer . . . who busies himself in casting suspicion on the ministers, in agitating the congregations, in dividing and rending the churches, must be barred."[167]

The Classis of Middelstum had called De Cock before it to discuss "the complaints against him."[168] In this discussion, De Cock insisted that he be shown any indication in the constitution or the Word of God that he was at fault in administering baptism to children whose parents were not members of his congregation. As the discussion proceeded, De Cock freely admitted that he catechized whomever came to him for religious instruction. Also, he acknowledged that he had authored the *Verdediging*. He stated he would gladly discontinue such writing, however, if classis could prove to him that it was contrary to the Word of God. But the classis did not permit De Cock to explain the ways in which he believed his writings to be biblical.[169]

The Classis of Middelstum was in more than one respect out of order.

First, only five members of the required quorum of eight were present. Second, the only charge being investigated by the classis was that concerning baptism. According to ecclesiastical law, no questions should have been asked about De Cock's brochure until a committee of three had investigated and submitted a report.[170] Finally, the classis dismissed De Cock without hearing his defense. On the same day, the classis arrived at a verdict of guilty. In his report to the Ministry, Secretary W. Cost, 1766-1841, minister of the Reformed Church at Bedum, informed the Ministry that the classis had suspended De Cock

> in order to maintain law and order in the Reformed Church, to protect the name and honor of the ministers of the Gospel, and to prevent more disorders, divisions, and revolutions in several congregations in our Fatherland; . . . if preachers as DeCock were not halted in their reckless enterprise, this Board fears the worst.[171]

In its official verdict the classis charged that De Cock had slandered fellow ministers without having accused them before the proper judicatories, and was therefore guilty of causing dissension and mutiny. Consequently, he was suspended until he showed himself willing to confess his guilt before the classis. His salary, however, was not suspended.[172]

De Cock was unaware that this verdict was out of order and unlawful. Even so, he was resolved to submit to it for the sake of the Lord. Thus he discontinued all official ministerial acts while he appealed to the next highest judicatory. He viewed the process of appeal as an opportunity to air his cause before the highest judicatories.

Apparently, the classis had been too moderate, for the Provincial Synod of Groningen to which De Cock had appealed changed the terms of suspension. The synod stipulated that within two years the case was to be terminated either by submission or by deposition. During that time De Cock's salary was to be withheld.[173]

An Attack on Hymns

Just as both sides became entrenched, a new element entered the battle. At the Provincial Synod of Groningen De Cock was charged with having written the preface to a pamphlet against hymns[174] authored by J. Klok, a layman who was a dyer by trade.[175] De Cock indeed had written the preface, and in it had expressed his opposition to hymns. He expressed his desire to demonstrate that a layman as "the child taught by God stands far above the learned of this age in spiritual knowledge."[176]

In the preface De Cock charged that

> hymns were contrary to the Word of God; a clamor displeasing God; a
> patched up Koran in which out of blindness or perfidy the truth necessary
> to salvation is concealed; a collection of siren lovesongs fit to draw the
> Reformed believers away from the saving doctrine.[177]

As the Provincial Synod engaged in further investigation of him,
De Cock was given an opportunity to defend himself. But his defense
failed to convince the synod that the hymns had unlawfully been introduced into the church and/or were heretical. Subsequently, he was
deposed.[178]

The appeal to the General Synod brought some success for De Cock
in that the verdict of the Provincial Synod was repealed. However, the
General Synod ordered Groningen's synod to impose a suspension of
six months, before the expiration of which De Cock was to confess that
his preface to Klok's pamphlet had been harmful. He was to promise
that in the future he would strictly obey the order of the church.[179]

It took De Cock a few months before he finally succeeded in arrang-
ing a hearing before the now vindictive Provincial Synod. On October 2,
1834, he was given until January 16, 1835, to sign a statement drawn
up by the Provincial Synod, thereby acknowledging his error in publishing Klok's work and promising strict obedience to ecclesiastical
precepts.[180]

De Cock failed in his efforts to engage the members of the synod in
a discussion concerning the merits of his case in relation to the Word
of God. But he was still determined to seek vindication for his views.
Thus, to "be sure that he had tried everything possible,"[181] he appealed
to King William I and the General Synod.

The Rev. H. P. Scholte

The conflict resulted in a secession when H. P. Scholte, 1805-68,
minister of the Reformed Church at Doeveren since 1833, visited
De Cock on Wednesday evening, October 8, 1834.[182] Scholte had heard
about De Cock's troubles and had written him a letter of encouragement
on January 9, 1834.[183] In it Scholte spoke of the possibility that De Cock
might be deposed and asked whether De Cock's congregation

> would be willing to send in a protest against your deposition and to
> declare herself as independent of the Synodical Reformed Church and,
> if required, as a separate congregation to support her own shepherd and
> teacher as much as she is able to and thus to become a free refuge for
> all oppressed and hated children of Zion in the area.[184]

It is not easy to decide to what degree Scholte's visit was instrumental in changing De Cock's resolve not to secede. The historical facts are that Scholte attracted much attention when the rumor spread that he was to preach and baptize children at Ulrum on Friday evening, October 10. The Provincial Synod kept a close eye on De Cock, however, and word was sent to the classical supervisor of Ulrum, N. Smith, 1768-1845, minister of the Reformed Church at Leens, that no ministers were to preach at Ulrum unless approved by the supervisor.[185] When the request was made that Smith allow Scholte to preach, Smith refused and conducted the service himself.[186] As Smith left the building, an overflow crowd circled him and urged him to grant Scholte permission to preach in the afternoon. Smith reported that he steadfastly refused, and was subsequently kicked and beaten. De Cock as well as Scholte denied this, but two men were later arrested and sentenced to eighteen months in jail, having been charged with these assaults.[187].

The situation that Sunday was so tense that the police found it necessary to close the church in order to prevent violence.[188] But so many had come to hear Scholte that a service was held outdoors. That night, Scholte left Ulrum.[189]

Secession

De Cock announced to his consistory on the following Monday that he had decided to postpone a secession no longer. Helenius de Cock, his son and biographer, insists that "a decision to secede was not taken during the four days of Scholte's stay." But he adds that during the preceding months his father had been thinking more and more about secession. However, he had "not concerned himself about the manner in which it should take place. To that end especially served the discussion between father, and consistory, and Scholte."[190]

Scholte states that he discussed the secession, but had no part at all in drawing up specific plans.[191] However, his biographer, Oostendorp, states that it was characteristic for Scholte not to present the whole picture.[192] If this is true, Oostendorp may be correct in claiming that Scholte "was no doubt both the occasion for and inspiration of this action."[193] This statement would agree with De Cock's statement that "the arrival of Scholte gave a totally different turn" to his plan not to secede: "everything now fitted together for me as if it were an indication of the Lord what I had to do and which way I had to go."[194] But two years later, in 1836, De Cock emphatically stated:

Scholte is certainly not the cause of the secession, as has been slandered; the reason for his visit at that time was for him equally unexpected as for us, caused namely by the illness of one of his relatives. That the secession took place at that time was solely caused by the fact that in ecclesiastical and civil respect everything came together and all means had been exhausted, since the Provincial Synod had rejected all fair reasons and demanded an absolute rejection of truth and Christ.[195]

In any case, De Cock decided to discontinue his appeal to the General Synod and the king. His defense of true doctrine in the Reformed Church thus came to an abrupt end, and De Cock and his consistory invited the congregation on Tuesday, October 14, 1834, to sign the Instrument of Secession and Return.[196] It was a secession insofar as the congregation seceded from what they considered to be a false church, and it was a return insofar as the congregation returned to the old forms of the Reformed Church. De Cock and his followers thus adopted the Three Forms of Unity and the Church Order of Dordrecht as infallible guides. The Instrument stated that communion with the present Reformed Church was not to be reinstated until she return to the true service of God. Because De Cock judged the Reformed Church so harshly, many orthodox believers refused to follow him. This did not deter him. The secession was for him a true reformation of the church.

VII

Van Raalte Leaves the Reformed Church

Van Raalte enrolled as a student in theology at the University of Leiden where he joined the so-called "Scholte club," which Anthony Brummelkamp, Simon van Velzen, G. F. Gezelle Meerburg, and L. Bahler had formed in conjunction with H. P. Scholte.[1] A complete account of how these men fared in the Secession of 1834 is beyond the scope of this study. It must suffice to deal briefly only with those who were closest to Van Raalte.

On October 29, 1834, H. P. Scholte was suspended by the Classis of Heusden because of the charge that he had preached in a congregation other than his own without the consent of the classical supervisor. Unlike De Cock, Scholte did not appeal his suspension. The day after he was informed of his suspension, he drew up an Act of Secession. Unlike De Cock, Scholte did not incorporate a "return" to the church of old into the rationale for his secession.[2]

Scholte had enrolled as a student of theology at the University of Leiden in 1829, when he was twenty-four years old. While there, he assumed the leadership of a group of younger students that came to be known as the "Scholte club." Scholte's influence was considerable, but it was not so strong that his younger friends merely copied him. On the contrary, as evidenced by the actions of Brummelkamp, Van Velzen, and Van Raalte, each of them went his own way.

Anthony Brummelkamp, 1811-88, became the minister of the Reformed Church at Hattem on October 19, 1834.[3] A conflict soon broke out because Brummelkamp refused to sing hymns. He also refused to baptize children whose parents were not confessing members of his congregation or did not have witnesses present who were members in good and regular standing of his congregation. Furthermore, he sent an Address to the General Synod demanding that the old liturgical forms be adhered to. Because Brummelkamp added that he could recognize ecclesiastical laws only insofar as he judged them to agree with the Word of God, he was accused of having broken his recent, solemn vows of ordination in which he had promised to obey the church order. Thus, the Provincial Synod of Gelderland suspended him on October 7, 1835. He made no effort to appeal, and on October 22 withdrew from the Reformed Church.[4]

Simon van Velzen, 1809-96, became the minister of the Reformed Church at Drogeham on October 9, 1834.[5] In consultation with Brummelkamp, his brother-in-law, Van Velzen also sent an Address to the General Synod. Although his address was not identical with that of Brummelkamp, it was similar in intent. On July 6, 1835, Van Velzen demanded that the General Synod exclude all ministers who rejected the Three Forms of Unity from serving the Reformed Church. Further, he decided not to grieve those among his membership who refused to sing hymns. Although he himself was not against the singing of hymns, he conducted the worship services without them. He also refused to submit to the church order unless in his judgment it agreed with the Word of God and the Three Forms of Unity. When the Classis of Dokkum consequently suspended Van Velzen for a period of six weeks, he replied on December 11, 1835, that because he considered the Reformed Church to be a false church he was withdrawing from it.[6]

Le Féburé's Oefenaar

Albertus Christiaan Van Raalte, 1810-76, graduated from the University of Leiden in 1835.[7] Like Brummelkamp and Van Velzen, his brothers-in-law, he had been trained for the ministry. With them and the other members of the "Scholte club," he had frequented conventicle-type meetings conducted by Johannes Le Féburé, 1776-1843, owner of a washing establishment for textiles in Leiden.[8] It seems quite likely that, at these meetings, Van Raalte met Christina Johanna de Moen, who was to become his wife.[9] It is also likely that Brummelkamp and Van Velzen met Christina's two sisters at this *oefenaar*. Brummelkamp married Catharina Wilhelmina de Moen, the oldest of the three sisters, and Van Velzen was united in marriage with the youngest, Johanna Christina.

For more than thirty years, Le Féburé's *oefeningen* had been held weekly on Sunday and Monday evenings.[10] In 1831 he began an additional meeting on Thursday evenings. Because of the cholera epidemic many people had become concerned for their souls, and the Thursday meeting was meant to handle the resultant sharp increase in attendance. Le Féburé was well acquainted with C. Baron van Zuylen van Nijeveldt and had gone so far as to publicly defend Molenaar's *Adres*.[11] The spirit in which Le Féburé must have conducted his *oefeningen* is therefore clear.

One may legitimately ask to what extent Le Féburé's *oefeningen* were instrumental in Van Raalte's entering into the ministry. Van Raalte tells no more than that his "young life was very aimless and for the most part was directed by the respect I felt for my father and by the desire to please him. Goal and sincerity were born only briefly before and after that first time of cholera."[12] The first cholera epidemic broke out in 1832, at which time Le Féburé reported a great increase in attendance. It seems, therefore, logical to assume that the cholera was a motivating factor. On the other hand, Van Raalte states very clearly that "from that time no worldly ambition but the service of the Gospel became my aspiration. I desired nothing but to spend my life in preaching. The form and the government of the church were rather dead notions to me."[13] This statement would indicate that Le Féburé did not instill in Van Raalte the desire for a restoration of the Reformed Church evident in his support of Molenaar's *Adres*.

It is quite possible that Le Féburé's influence upon Van Raalte was not very decisive. His father had brought his son, Albertus Christiaan, to Leiden and had personally recommended him to Professor J. Clarisse.[14] All his life Albertus Christiaan remained thankful to this friend of his father, Clarisse,[15] who taught exegesis, preaching, natural theology, ethics, and encyclopedia, and was known as an excellent teacher whose enthusiasm made him even more popular than Van der Palm, his great colleague.[16]

Synodical Examination

Van Raalte completed his academic studies for the ministry in 1835. In order to be admitted to the ministry of the Reformed Church, he had to be examined by the synod of the province in which he resided. Thus, Van Raalte appeared before the Synod of Zuid-Holland on May 6, 1835.[17]

The candidate H. G. van Nouhuijs was examined with Van Raalte. The eight members of the Synodical Board took their time, and consequently the examination lasted "four full hours." Van Nouhuijs received six favorable votes, and was therefore "admitted to the office of preaching."[18]

The Minutes of the Board report on Van Raalte:

> Mr. Van Raalte would have been admitted in the same manner, if after the examination he would not have repeatedly stated that he was to some extent acquainted with the existing ordinances but had not sufficiently examined them to be able to judge how far they agreed with the reformed Doctrine, and that he, in the usual signing of the candidate's Statement and promise by which one commits oneself to submit to the judgments of the proper judicatories of the church, therefore wanted to reserve for himself the right to that end to make himself better acquainted with

them by further examination if in the future he would have the time and
the desire to do so; and if he would meet therein aberrations from or
contradictions to that doctrine that he would either protest or send in
his objections in order to resign from office in case his conscience should
not be sufficiently satisfied;—and also to do this in case ordinances of
similar nature would be added or made mandatory. The Board has found
no sufficient justification to fail Van Raalte either on the basis of insufficient proficiency or because of unsatisfactory convictions with respect to
revealed Religion, but the Board did not feel free as yet to submit to him
the regular candidate's Statement and Promise in order by his signature
to admit him to the office of preaching in the Netherlands Reformed
Church, and the Board decided to give him time and opportunity to
study sufficiently an issue upon the outcome of which in his opinion he
wished to act in accordance with his findings and conviction. The Board
wants to await his further statement on this matter in the meeting of next
August or so much later as he wishes. This decision was then orally
communicated to Mr. Van Raalte by the President.[19]

Other minutes of the synod make it very clear that the decision on
Van Raalte was not a rare exception. On the same day, two other candidates were examined. They were found wanting, and were ordered
to engage in further study and return for re-examination.[20] What the
synod did to Van Raalte was technically not out of the ordinary.

Van Raalte's recollections do not agree with the record in the minutes.[21] The latter create the impression that he was not questioned
about his difficulties with respect to the regulations in the constitution,
but simply volunteered uncertainties. Van Raalte states, however, that
President G. van Kooten asked him whether he felt free to promise by
his signature that he would obey these ordinances. According to Van
Raalte, his reply was that he, like any other candidate, did not know all
these ordinances by heart and had simply supposed that they would
contain nothing, of course, that disagreed with the Forms of Unity.
According to his account, he also stated that should he come to believe
that the ordinances did disagree with the Forms of Unity, he would
resign from office.

Van Raalte recollects that Pastor Pluigers of Leiden had asked him
whether or not he, like Scholte, planned to create a disturbance in the
church.[22] Van Raalte replied that he desired nothing so much as "to
bring people to faith in Jesus Christ." He was convinced that "only this
faith makes it possible for man to return to God and is the only means
of salvation."[23]

While Van Raalte insisted that no candidate was familiar with all of
the regulations, the board maintained that he could not be admitted
into the ministry unless he had acquainted himself with them. Van

Raalte replied that if the board would assure him that the ordinances agreed with the Word of God, he should be allowed to sign. He added that he wished to acknowledge by his signature his acceptance of the ordinances *because* and *not insofar as* they agreed with God's Word.[24] But the board avoided a discussion on that matter, placing the burden again on Van Raalte by insisting that he should know the degree of agreement of the ordinances with the Word of God on the basis of his own study.

Van Raalte felt that the board was creating a precedent by making such an issue of the regulations. The board, however, told him that no candidates had heretofore professed to *not* know the ordinances.

Van Raalte may have felt that he was so exceptionally treated because of his relationship with the "Scholte club" and Le Fébure's *oefeningen*. But the board assured him that "according to the nature of love it could not but think well of him."[25]

Requests for Approval

Since the Provincial Synod had obviously won out, Van Raalte could do little but comply. He did try to use what little leverage he had, however, and thus turned to his beloved professor at Leiden. Clarisse was upset enough to write a note on behalf of Van Raalte to the president of the General Synod, H. H. Donker Curtius, 1778-1839, requesting that the candidate be as yet permitted to sign. Van Raalte made the trip to The Hague to deliver the note, and later stated that Donker Curtius more or less excused the Provincial Synod "because I was known as having belonged to the club which having formed itself at the University threw everything into commotion as soon as they had entered the Church."[26] Van Raalte added that he would never forget Donker Curtius's statement: "Preach what you want, and allow us also to preach what we want, but obey the regulations."[27]

Surprisingly, Donker Curtius did accept Van Raalte's claim that he should not be barred from signing the Statement and Promise. He thus sent Van Raalte to the secretary of the General Synod, J. Sluiter. Pastor Sluiter explained that he could not proceed without violating the constitution, and therefore simply urged Van Raalte to study and examine the ordinances.

Van Raalte wrote, "I looked into that great stack of regulations in my father's library, but to me those books had neither soul nor life. I did not live in that atmosphere."[28] Now the time had come for him to look into them with great care and attention. In the process, he became convinced that he would never agree with all of them.

Van Raalte must also have heard adverse comments from his two brothers-in-law, who were both preparing to argue with church officials over the same issue that concerned Van Raalte. Furthermore, Van Raalte was greatly influenced in the development of his objections by Abraham Capadose's booklet, *Earnest and Prayerful Word*.[29] On the one hand, Capadose denied the necessity to secede from the Reformed Church. Although the Reformed Church was sick, it had not yet become a false church, for one could still preach the pure gospel from its pulpits. On the other hand, Capadose recalled with a sympathetic tone the protests that several classes had raised against King William's reorganization of the Reformed Church. On the basis of these protests, he strongly urged that a much-needed restoration of the Reformed Church be undertaken by undoing the original interference on the part of the state.

Van Raalte again appeared before the Provincial Synod of Zuid-Holland on August 5, 1835. He pointed out that there were regulations with which he could never agree, and as an example he quoted a regulation stating that consistory was not allowed to hire a layman over thirty years old to instruct catechumens. Van Raalte protested that he would never exclude a good man who was over thirty from teaching and instruction. In addition, he objected to intercommunion with the *Remonstranten*, the Arminians, on the ground that this practice "refuted what our Forefathers had accomplished."[30]

The laconic minutes simply report:

> Van Raalte declared . . . that he had found regulations and ordinances that could not be brought into harmony with his view and conviction; also that the entire spirit of the ecclesiastical polity did not at all agree with the Doctrine of the Synod of Dordrecht, and that he therefore would not be able to sign the said Statement and Promises in an upright spirit. The Board thereupon permitted Mr. Van Raalte to leave without getting into a further exchange of opinions.[31]

The minutes agree with Van Raalte's account insofar as they report that a discussion was avoided. Van Raalte adds the detail that he tried to argue his case theologically, but the board refused to hear his arguments.

Van Raalte did not give up however. On October 3, 1835, he requested in a letter to the Provincial Synod of Zuid-Holland that he be allowed to sign the Statement and Promise because he

> is with all his heart dedicated to the doctrine of our Church, as founded upon the Word of God, and is able and willing to sign in good faith the normal Statement and to submit himself thereby to a Reformed administration and their Reformed ordinances.[32]

But the catch was in the word normal. For Van Raalte normal was conformity to what had been established by the Synod of Dordrecht. Anticipating a negative response and unwilling to compromise, he asked the board "to give him a statement that the cause for his exclusion was not lack of knowledge, theological convictions, or moral misconduct."[33]

The Provincial Synod replied on October 15, 1835, that it had compared Van Raalte's letter with its records and had found no reason to modify its decision. Nevertheless, the board

> did not wish to refuse the statement that the Board in its meeting of May had not excluded him on the basis of incompetence nor because of religious convictions manifested by him during his examination, so that he would have been admitted to the office of preaching by majority vote, if there had been no reasons not to submit the normal Statement and Promise for his signature. Mr. Van Raalte will be notified of the Board's decision by a copy of this part of the Minutes to be sent by the Secretary.[34]

Two months later, Van Raalte again wrote to the Provincial Synod. This time he had no requests. He informed the board:

> The voice of my conscience and the infallible sayings of the Holy Scriptures compelled me some time ago to break all ecclesiastical union with you, and to join those who by word and deed prove their desire to live according to God's ordinances, the opposite of which is taking place in the Reformed Denomination.[35]

Almost thirty years later, in April of 1862, Van Raalte wrote from Holland, Michigan, to his brother-in-law Van Velzen. In this communication he gave a review of his past which was later published in book form.[36] He frankly acknowledged that for him it was "the most painful sacrifice to give up the preaching so fervently desired."[37] He had done all he could to avoid an open break, for he hated "no longer to be able to occupy the pulpits of my father, to become a shame unto my relatives and to my mother."[38]

The Netherlands Reformed Church lost a loyal, capable son.

Epilogue

After his secession in 1835, Albertus Christiaan Van Raalte served the Christian Seceded Church as a pastor for eleven years at Genemuiden-Mastenbroek, 1835-36; at Ommen, 1836-44; and at Velp-Arnhem, 1844-46. In addition, at Ommen he instituted what became the best seminary training available to candidates for the ministry in the Christian Seceded Church. In 1844, moving to Velp-Arnhem, he fused this school with the one under the direction of his brother-in-law and fellow pastor, Anthony Brummelkamp.

When the potato blight caused starvation conditions in 1846, many destitute members of the Seceded Church made efforts to leave for the United States of America. With Brummelkamp, Van Raalte engaged in aiding a party of prospective emigrants in their preparations. At the hour of their departure, the decision was born in Van Raalte's pastoral heart to accompany these sheep who were without a shepherd. Guiding them on their long journey, he led this first wave of immigrants to the forests of Michigan where they settled on the shores of Lake Macatawa. From 1847 on, other settlers came who helped to carve out an existence as they created the town of Holland and cultivated the surrounding lands. Van Raalte here reached the zenith of his ministerial career.

The immigrants profited in America from the business experience Van Raalte had gained in The Netherlands. The economic and social crises of the 1830s in The Netherlands had caused Van Raalte to engage in the developments of virgin land and of industry. He opposed free "handouts" to the destitute and advocated instead economic and social reform. Characteristically, he practiced what he preached. It is difficult to understand how Van Raalte, without these valuable experiences, could have provided the leadership necessary for the survival of stubborn Dutchmen in an area of Michigan not well-suited for immediate development.[1]

Not all colonists appreciated Van Raalte and his work. Antagonism among a small portion of the growing number of settlers reached a peak in 1857. The *Ware Hollandsche Gereformeerde Kerk,* or True Dutch Reformed Church, broke away from Van Raalte's Reformed Church.

Van Raalte continued to be the pastor of the First Reformed Church of Holland, Michigan, until his voluntary resignation in 1867. Failing health made it impossible for him to spend the energy necessary to succeed in his new venture: to establish Dutch colonies in Virginia.

Although supported by the brethren in Michigan, the new settlements ended in failure by 1877.[2]

Van Raalte had returned earlier to Holland, Michigan, where his children cared for him. On November 7, 1876, he died. As he had requested prior to his death, those who attended his funeral—and they were very many—sang the first stanza of Psalm 116 in the Dutch language:

> God heb ik lief, want die getrouwe Heer
> hoort mijne stem, mijn smekingen, mijn klagen.
> Hij neigt zijn oor, 'k roep tot Hem al mijn dagen.
> Hij schenkt mij hulp, Hij redt mij keer op keer.
>
> God do I love, for this faithful Lord
> hears my voice, my supplication, my complaint.
> He lends his ear, I call on him all my days
> He grants me succor, He saves me again and again.

Endnotes

CHAPTER I

1. According to Dutch custom, the name is spelled with a small *v* if the Christian names or initials precede it; with a capital V if they are absent. In this study, however, the V in Van Raalte will be capitalized without exception.
2. A map of this *departement* appears in P. J. Blok, *Geschiedenis van het Neder-landsche Volk* (vier delen, 2ᵉ druk; Leiden: A. W. Sijthoff, 1915), IV:589-90. Henceforth: Blok, *Geschiedenis*.
3. Blok, *Geschiedenis*, III:584ff. Cf. Jan en Annie Romein, *De Lage Landen bij de Zee* (vier delen, 4ᵉ druk; Antwerpen, Brussel, Gent, Leuven, Zeist: Uitgevers-maatschappij W. de Haan N. V. en N. V. Standaard Boekhandel, 1961), III:7-33. Henceforth: Romein, *Lage Landen*. Cf. P. Geyl, *Geschiedenis van de Nederlandse Stam* (zes delen; Amsterdam-Antwerpen: Wereldbibliotheek, 1952), V:1306. Henceforth: Geyl, *Geschiedenis*. The Dutch word *Patriotten* will be used in the text in reference to this movement.
4. W. Verkade, "Eigengereidheid en Samenwerking," in J. S. Bartstra en W. Banning, eds., *Nederland tussen de Natiën* (twee delen; Amsterdam: Uitgeverij Ploegsma, 1946), I:32. Henceforth: Bartstra-Banning, *Nederland*.
5. Johan Huizinga, "De Beteekenis van 1813 voor Nederland's Geestelijke Beschav-ing," in his *Verzamelde Werken* (negen delen; Haarlem: H. D. Tjeenk Willink en Zoon, 1948-53), II:536.
6. William V had married the Prussian princess in 1767. Blok, *Geschiedenis*, III:508.
7. Romein, *Lage Landen*, III:27.
8. Ibid., 28; cf. Geyl, *Geschiedenis*, V:1352, where the English-Prussian agreement at Berlin is mentioned. Cf. Blok, *Geschiedenis*, III:630.
9. Geyl, *Geschiedenis*, V:1355; cf. Romein, *Lage Landen*, III:28-29.
10. Geyl, *Geschiedenis*, V:1368-69; Blok, *Geschiedenis*, III:630, 645.
11. Henriette L. T. de Beaufort, *Gijsbert Karel van Hogendorp* (Rotterdam-Antwer-pen: Ad. Donker, 1948), 127-28. Henceforth: De Beaufort, *G. K. van Hogendorp*. Cf. Jan en Annie Romein, *Erflaters van onze beschaving* (8ste druk; Amsterdam-Antwerpen: Em. Querido's Uitgeversmaatschappij en Wereldbibliotheek, 1959), 601-02. Henceforth: Romein, *Erflaters*.
12. Romein, *Lage Landen*, III:29-30; cf. especially P. Geyl, *Nederlandse Figuren* (twee delen; Amsterdam-Antwerpen: Wereldbibliotheek, 1962), I:55-56.
13. Geyl, *Geschiedenis*, V:1370-71.
14. Friedrich Ehlert presents a lucid account of the United States' involvement in *The Dutch Republic and the American Revolution* (Johns Hopkins University Studies in Historical and Political Science, Series XXIX, No. 2; Baltimore: Johns Hopkins Press, 1911).
15. Blok, *Geschiedenis*, III:616-18. Geyl, *Geschiedenis*, VI:1497, reports a deliberate effort on the part of the French ambassador to gain the support of the Orange party at Rijswijk.

16. See H. T. Colenbrander, *De Bataafsche Republiek* (Amsterdam: Meulenhoff, 1909), and J. Postmus, *Oud-Holland en de Revolutie* (Kampen: Kok, 1910). Very revealing is J. J. Hangelbroek's article *"Patriotten,"* in volume IV of the *Christelijke Encyclopaedie voor het Nederlandsche Volk* (zes delen; Kampen: Kok, 1925-31). "[The *Patriotten* were] the party favoring the French, originating in the second half of the eighteenth century, a party opposed to the stadholder form of government concepts, they sought a good relation with France, the cradle of atheistic concepts, over against the stadholder who thought an alliance with England advisable in the face of increasing unrest on the continent of Europe. Their activity led to the revolution that exploded in 1795."

17. Geyl, *Geschiedenis*; Romein, *Lage Landen* and *Erflaters*.

18. Geyl, *Geschiedenis*, VI:1498 and 1505.

19. Ibid., 1497. Geyl quotes Stadholder William V expressing an unwillingness to yield to democratic ideas among what the prince called "Orange-zealots."

20. Blok, *Geschiedenis*, III:669.

21. Geyl, *Geschiedenis*, VI:1505-06, 1511, and 1539.

22. Ibid., 1517; cf. Blok, *Geschiedenis*, III:675-76.

23. Geyl, *Geschiedenis*, VI:1524; cf. 1541-42.

24. The treaty was concluded on May 16, 1795. Blok, *Geschiedenis*, IV:13-15; Geyl, *Geschiedenis*, VI:1563-64; Romein, *Lage Landen*, III:48-49.

25. Romein, *Lage Landen*, III:50; Geyl, *Geschiedenis*, VI:1573-74.

26. Quoted from an unknown source by Romein, *Lage Landen*, III.

27. See note 23 above.

28. Geyl, *Geschiedenis*, VI:1730-32; Blok, *Geschiedenis*, IV:44-45.

29. Daendels's coup took place on June 12, 1798.

30. Romein, *Lage Landen*, III:48.

31. Ibid., 54-55; Blok *Geschiedenis*, IV:56-58.

32. Geyl, *Geschiedenis*, VI:1573-75.

33. Blok, *Geschiedenis*, IV:72-80.

34. Ibid., 92.

35. His letter to that effect was dated December 26, 1801; Romein, *Lage Landen*, III:55-56; Blok, *Geschiedenis*, IV:88.

36. Dutch representative Schimmelpenninck signed the treaty on March 27, 1802.

37. Blok, *Geschiedenis*, IV:88; Romein, *Lage Landen*, III:55.

38. Romein, *Lage Landen*, III:55-56; Blok, *Geschiedenis*, IV:93; cf. pp. 95-96 for efforts by this coalition to win Anglo-Prussian support for neutrality on the part of the Dutch.

39. The war began in May 1803.

40. Blok, *Geschiedenis*, IV:102; Romein, *Lage Landen*, III:56, oversimplifies Napoleon's demands.

41. Blok, *Geschiedenis*, IV:113-15; Romein, *Lage Landen*, III:57.

42. Blok, *Geschiedenis*, IV:114-15 gives the details of this "Comédie Triste."

43. Ibid., 115-21: This is a good account of increasing alienation between Napoleon and his brother.

44. His teacher was the fiery Orangist Willem Bilderdijk. After Napoleon's fall, Bilderdijk again supported the House of Orange. With him originated in part the Dutch *Réveil*. How Bilderdijk's involvement was treated by diverse historians is superbly reviewed by P. Geyl in an essay, "Een eeuw strijd om Bilderdijk," published in P. Geyl, *Van Bilderdijk tot Huizinga: Historische Toetsingen* (Antwerpen-Utrecht: Het Spectrum, 1963), 7-81. Henceforth: Geyl, *Bilderdijk-Huizinga*.

45. Blok, *Geschiedenis*, IV:123.

46. J. Presser, *Napoleon, Historie en legende* (twee delen; 4ᵉ druk; Amsterdam-Brussel: Elsevier, 1958), I:530-31. Napoleon provided the legal basis for this drastic step in the Decree of Rambouillet. Article I contained the phrase: "la Hollande est réunie à l'Empire."
47. For a full coverage of this period see Johanna W. A. Naber, *Geschiedenis der inlijving bij Frankrijk* (Haarlem: Tjeenk Willink, 1905); also H. T. Colenbrander, *Inlijving en Opstand* (Amsterdam: Meulenhoff, 1913).
48. Blok, *Geschiedenis*, IV:1603-13. See, for a vivid description of this visit, Colenbrander, *Inlijving en Opstand*, 127-50.
49. See Bilderdijk's poem "De Alleenheerscher," written in 1783, a glorification of Denmark's absolute monarchy, quoted in Geyl, *Bilderdijk-Huizinga*, 63-64. Dutch authors opposing Napoleon at this time are treated by G. N. de Vooys, "Nederlandse letterkundigen tegenover de Franse overheersing," in his *Verzamelde Letterkundige Opstellen* (Antwerpen: N. V. Uitgeversmij. Kosmos; Amsterdam: De Sikkel, 1946), 269-85.
50. "Ode aan Napoleon," R. A. Kollewijn, *Poezie van Willem Bilderdijk* (Zwolle: Tjeenk Willink, n.d.), 13-14. Opposition to Bilderdijk and his thought in the reconstituted Kingdom of the Netherlands cannot be understood without reference to this period. James Hutton Mackey, *Religious Thought in Holland during the 19th Century* (London, New York, Toronto: Hodder and Staughton, 1911) does not mention this period and is therefore inadequate.
51. "Gijsbert Karel van Hogendorp" by Romein, *Erflaters*, 592-618; cf. De Beaufort, *G. K. van Hogendorp*, especially chapter viii, 226-51; cf. Dr. A. J. Teychine Stakenburg, *Gijsbert Karel van Hogendorp, Wegwijzer naar Nieuwe Tijden* (Rotterdam-Den Haag: Nijgh en van Ditmar, 1963), 43-78.
52. Members of the committee were F. D. de Jonge, L. van der Duyn, and A. F. J. van Limburg Stirum.
53. The attitude of Van Hogendorp and his committee is very evident in their official proclamation to the nation that began "Orange Above-Holland is Free!" Key sentences are "What has been suffered is forgiven and forgotten—men of consequence and consideration return to administrative authority. . . . The people are to have a day of rejoicing at the public expense, without being allowed to plunder and commit any excess. . . . Old times are returned." The proclamation is reproduced in Romein, *Lage Landen*, III:61. Reproduction of the official English translation may be found in *Tentoonstelling Oranje Boven!*, a special edition of the *Maandblad's-Gravenhage*, 18ᵉ jaargang, no. 11, November 1963, 16. It should be noted that this English translation is not entirely accurate.
54. Romein, *Erflaters*, 636-38. Romein explains William's reluctance to accept the title of king and his preference for the title Sovereign Ruler as evidence that he wanted to avoid a constitution, for it would undoubtedly define and limit his royal power. Only after the hurried union with Belgium following Napoleon's escape from Elba did William take the title of king.
55. "De Eenheid Nederland-Oranje," J. Huizinga, *Nieuwsblad van het Noorden*, February 1, 1938, 13-14, and reprinted in J. Huizinga, *Verzamelde Werken* (negen delen; Haarlem: H. D. Tjeenk Willink en Zoon, 1948-53), VIII:563-70.
56. H. Graaf van Hogendorp, *Brieven en Gedenkschriften van G. K. van Hogendorp* (acht delen; Den Haag: Martinus Nijhoff, 1866-1902). Van Hogendorp's observation is corroborated by B. G. Niebuhr, Prussian delegate in Amsterdam at the time, who remarks that "man ist nicht im geringsten neugierig wie der Entwurf [i.e., the constitution] laute," Blok, *Geschiedenis*, IV:203.

57. De Beaufort, *G. K. van Hogendorp*, 250. Cf. Colenbrander, *Inlijving en Opstand*, 309-320.

58. Quoted by Romein, *Lage Landen*, III:64. Romein does not indicate the source of this quotation. Nor does he offer additional comments on this aspect in his *Erflaters*, 592-647, where he treats of both Van Hogendorp and King William I. However, a similar observation was made by the contemporary B. G. Niebuhr: ". . . eine absolute Monarchie . . . unter Formen die dem Leser auf den Blick einbilden dass constitutionelle Freiheit existiere." Blok, *Geschiedenis*, IV:203. For a good review of the many contrasting evaluations of William I, see L. J. Rogier's article "Willem I" which was added to the second, posthumous, publication of L. G. J. Verberne, *Geschiedenis van Nederland in de Jaren 1813-50* (twee delen; Utrecht-Antwerpen: Het Spectrum, 1958), I:10-31. Verberne's work was first published as volume VII of *Geschiedenis van Nederland*, edited by by H. Brugmans (Amsterdam, 1937).

59. Rudolf Steinmetz, *England's Anteil an der Trennung der Niederlande 1830* (Den Haag: Nijhoff, 1930), 35-36. Steinmetz also reviews William's own desires and efforts to unite Belgium with "his" Netherlands, 31-32. Henceforth: Steinmetz, *England's Anteil*.

60. A summary of the involved diplomatic exchanges appears in Blok, *Geschiedenis*, IV:204-12. P. Geyl, in a series of spirited essays entitled *Noord en Zuid, Eenheid en Tweeheid in de Lage Landen* (Utrecht, Antwerpen: Het Spectrum, 1960), 90-149 and 177-93, has disproved the account of this period offered by Henri Pirenne in *Histoire de Belgique*. Henceforth: Geyl, *Noord-Zuid*.

61. For a detailed account, somewhat favoring the Arminians, see J. Reitsma, *Geschiedenis van de Hervorming en de Hervormde Kerk der Nederlanden* (vijfde, herziene druk door J. Lindeboom; Den Haag: Martinus Nijhoff, 1949), Chapters IX and X, 236-84. Henceforth: Reitsma, *Hervorming*.

62. Exiled Arminian preachers, e.g., began to return after Prince Maurice of Orange died in 1625. Dordrecht's *anathema* could not be enforced and by April 1630, the Arminians held their first synod in The Netherlands at Rotterdam. They opened their own seminary at Amsterdam in 1634.

63. J. Huizinga, "Nederland's beschaving in de zeventiende eeuw. Een schets," *Verzamelde Werken*, II:449-63.

64. B. ter Haar, "Nederland de steun en het toevlugtsoord der vervolgden," B. ter Haar en E. Moll, *Geschiedenis der Christelijke Kerk in Tafereelen* (twee delen; Amsterdam: G. Portielje en Zoon, 1864-69), II:432-57. Henceforth: Ter Haar-Moll, *Geschiedenis CKN*. Cf. L. Knappert, *Geschiedenis der Nederlandsche Hervormde Kerk gedurende de 18e en 19e eeuw* (Amsterdam: Meulenhoff en Co., 1912), 45-67. Knappert's earlier volume covered *16e en 17e eeuw* and was published by the same firm in 1911. Henceforth: Knappert, *Geschiedenis NHK*.

65. For a review of this development see Th. L. Haitjema, *De nieuwere geschiedenis van Neerlands Kerk der Hervorming: van Gereformeerde Kerkstaat tot Christusbelijdende Volkskerk* (Den Haag: Boekencentrum, 1964), 18-74. Henceforth: Haitjema, *G.K.N.* This portion relies on Ter Haar-Moll, *Geschiedenis CKN*, II:183-87, 322-38; and Knappert, *Geschiedenis NHK*, I:232-72; K. Dijk, *De Strijd over Infra- en Supra-lapsarisme in de Gereformeerde Kerken van Nederland* (Kampen: Kok, 1912).

66. Haitjema, *G.K.N.*, 124-25.

67. Cf. Voetius, *Exercitatio de prognosticis commentarum*, 1664.

68. Cf. Balthasar Bekker, *Ondersoek van de betekeninge der kometen . . .* (Leeuwarden: Nauta, 1683). Superstitions regarding comets persisted long and as late as 1832. P. G. Witsen Geysbeek wrote a book, *Geruststelling voor minkundigen*

zakelijk samengetrokken uit het onderzoek over de kometen van Balthasar Bekker, to calm the hysteria over two comets which made an appearance that year.

69. In 1668 Bekker had published his *De Philosophia Cartesiana admonitio candida et sincera.* See W. P. C. Knuttel, *Balthasar Bekker, de Bestrijder van het bijgeloof* ('s-Gravenhage: M. Nijhoff, 1906), 323.

70. This work was published in four volumes: the first two by Nauta in Leeuwarden, 1691, and the complete work by Van den Dalen in Amsterdam, 1693.

71. Reitsma, *Hervorming,* 348-52; Knappert, *Geschiedenis NHK,* I:278-84; Ter Haar-Moll, *Geschiedenis CKN,* II:415-31.

72. Heinrich Heppe claims in his *Geschichte des Pietismus,* 319, that De Labadie had a following of more than 50,000 at Amsterdam. Reitsma, *Hervorming,* 349, refers to a study by Professor T. Cannegieter which refutes this claim.

73. No remnants of this group survived. Even those who migrated to America in 1683, settling on the Labadie Tract in Maryland, dissolved their community in 1730. See Henry S. Lucas, *Netherlanders in America: Dutch Immigration to the United States and Canada* (Ann Arbor: University of Michigan Press; London: Oxford University Press, 1955), 12-13. Henceforth: Lucas, *Netherlanders.*

74. See for Koelman: Reitsma, *Hervorming,* 314-16; also A. G. Weiler, O. J. de Jong, L. J. Rogier, and C. W. Mönnich, *Geschiedenis van de Kerk in Nederland* (Utrecht-Antwerpen: Het Spectrum, 1962), 143-46. Henceforth: *GKN.* In addition, Cornelia W. Roldanus, *Zeventiende eeuwse geestesbloei* (Herziene 2ᵉ druk; Utrecht, Antwerpen: Het Spectrum, 1961), 78-99. Henceforth: Roldanus, *Geestesbloei.*

75. This point of similarity in every age since the Reformation in Holland, as well as elsewhere, has been demonstrated by M. J. A. de Vrijer, *Schortinghuis en zijn analogieen* (Amsterdam: H. J. Spruyt's Uitgeversmaatschappij, 1942).

76. Ter Haar-Moll, *Geschiedenis NHK,* II:337.

77. K. Groot, *Die Erweckungsbewegung in Deutschland und ihr literarischer Niederschlag als Gegenstück zu dem Holländischen Reveil* (Wageningen: Veenman en Zonen, 1932), 21 and passim.

78. J. C. Kromsigt, *Wilhelmus Schortinghuis, Eene bladzijde uit de geschiedenis van het pietisme in de Gereformeerde Kerk van Nederland* (Groningen: J. B. Wolters, 1904), Chapter VI, "Strijd over de conventikels," 112-40. Henceforth: Kromsigt, *Schortinghuis.*

79. It should be observed that the subject in the Five Canons of Dordrecht is not so much predestination as fallen man. Thus the *gratia infusa in hominem* could become of greater concern than the author of that grace; God and his church had to yield first place to man and his church.

80. Koelman's influence extended even into the twentieth century. His writings were still being printed as late as 1928. Roldanus, *Geestesbloei,* 82.

81. Blok, *Geschiedenis,* III:298; Reitsma, *Hervorming,* 33-35.

82. See for this Erasmian characteristic, 10.

83. Supra, 16.

84. Translation of this title: *Eubulus or Good Advice.* The book appeared a year after the author's death. Reitsma, *Hervorming,* 336-37.

85. *GKN,* 154.

86. The loose structure that joined the provinces into the one republic and the intricacies of each provincial constitution made it possible for such an ecclesiastical situation to develop.

87. The Dutch word *tolerantie* means tolerance.

88. The spelling of his name has been adapted to the form used in this study because of its familiarity among the Dutch in America.

89. Honig had taught dogmatics since 1903. He was rector for the academic year 1933-34. The address was published as a brochure by Kok, Kampen, 1934. Translation of the title: *From Comrie to De Cock, or: The Credo of the Secession.*
90. Ibid., 26-27.
91. Ibid., 29.
92. The capitalization is Honig's.
93. Ibid., 8.
94. Ibid.
95. Ibid.
96. Holtius was born in 1693 and graduated at Leiden in 1716; Comrie was born in Scotland in 1706, and prior to his graduation at Leiden in 1734, he had been in business.
97. Knappert, *Geschiedenis NHK*, II:88-92; Reitsma, *Hervorming*, 381-83; S. Blaupot ten Cate, *Geschiedenis der Doopsgezinden in Friesland van derzelver onstaan tot deze tijd uit oorspronkelijke stukken en echte berichten* (Leeuwarden: W. Eekhoff, 1839), 215-16.
98. Reitsma, *Hervorming*, 384.
99. The full title is, in translation, "Examination of the design for Toleration to unite the doctrine established at the Synod of Dordrecht in 1619 with the condemned doctrine of the Remonstrants."
100. Knappert, *Geschiedenis NHK*, II:92, leaves the impression that Holtius and Comrie were thoroughly silenced. Honig points out that Comrie as late as 1763 prefaced a reissue of a publication by Voetius with the warning that *Tolerantie* would mean the union of the "two opposing important families of Protestants," 6-7.
101. Knappert, *Geschiedenis NHK*, II:90.
102. Ibid., 158.
103. Ernst Troeltsch, *Protestantism and Progress: A Historical Study of the Relation of Protestantism to the Modern World*, trans. W. Montgomery (2d ed.; Boston: Beacon Press, 1958), 199.
104. Ibid., 125.
105. This point is well made by J. Huizinga, "Nederland's beschaving in de zeventiende eeuw," in *Verzamelde Werken*, II:459-61. He also points out that the University of Leiden, since its foundation in 1575, had been intended as a "steadfast preserver . . . of freedom . . . not only in religious questions, but also in matters pertaining to the common civil condition or well-being." Knappert, *Geschiedenis NHK*, II:144-55, traces this development in fuller detail. Typical of this attitude was Professor Harm Venema at Franeker who applied a rational approach to exegesis, church history, and systematic theology. Venema held the chair at Franeker from 1724 until 1774.
106. This optimism is treated by J. Huizinga, "Natuurbeeld en historiebeeld in de 18e eeuw," *Verzamelde Werken*, IV:341-59.
107. The process is too optimistically understood by J. Hartog, *Geschiedenis van de Predikkunde in de Protestansche Kerk van Nederland* (tweede verbeterde en vermeerderde druk; Utrecht: Kemink en Zoon, 1887), 124ff. Henceforth: Hartog, *Predikkunde*.
108. This paragraph and what follows in this chapter depend for factual information upon Knappert, *Geschiedenis NHK*, 183-250; Reitsma, *Hervorming*, 152-56, 399-516; Ter Haar-Moll, *Geschiedenis CKN*, 610-25.
109. The expression "velvet revolution" is an accurate description of the religious as well as the political aspect.
110. The session opened on March 1, 1796. See Knappert, *Geschiedenis NHK*, II:186.

111. Deposition took place in June 1796. The deposed ministers accepted Pastor J. Hamelau's offer of a temporary spiritual home in his Restored-Evangelical Lutheran Church at Amsterdam. Knappert, *Geschiedenis NHK*, II:201.
112. See Geyl, *Geschiedenis*, VI:1680-84.
113. Supra, 5-6.
114. Toleration was in those days not entirely an empty word: the Lutherans at Amsterdam and the Jews at Groningen declined the government's offer to select for their worship services a Reformed Church edifice which would then become their property. Knappert, *Geschiedenis NHK*, II:200-01.
115. Quoted by Th. L. Haitjema, *De nieuwere geschiedenis van Neerlands Kerk der Hervorming: van Gereformeerde Kerkstaat tot Christus-belijdende Volkskerk* (Den Haag: Boekencentrum, 1964), 87. Henceforth: Haitjema, *NGN*.
116. Supra, 19.
117. Supra, 7.
118. Haitjema, *NGN*, 88.
119. Haitjema, *NGN*, 90-91.
120. This church had its beginnings in The Netherlands with Petrus Codde, apostolic vicar for the United Republic, who refused to sign Alexander VII's condemnation of the Jansenists. Codde was deposed in 1704 but, aided by the States General and governed by the church's Utrecht chapter, the church of the Old Diocesan Chapter led an independent life. To this church came the Old Catholics of 1870 for fellowship and guidance, beginning a formal union in 1889. For a history of this church see B. A. van Kleef, *Geschiedenis van de oud-Katholieke Kerk van Nederland* (Rotterdam: Nijgh, 1937). A second edition was published in 1955.
121. Knappert, *Geschiedenis NHK*, II:196-97. Reitsma, *Hervorming*, 407-08, states that the invitation was addressed to the Protestant ministers.
122. Knappert, *Geschiedenis NHK*, II:196-97.
123. Ter Haar-Moll, *Geschiedenis CKN*, 404-14.
124. The oldest member in 1797 was 31 years of age.
125. E. F. Kruijf, *Geschiedenis van het Nederlandsch Zendelinggenootschap en zijne zendingsposten* (Groningen: J. B. Wolters, 1894). Henceforth: Kruijf, *GNZ*.
126. J. van den Berg, *Constrained by Jesus' Love* (Kampen: Kok, 1956), 128-31.
127. The complete translated title of the address is: "Address by the Missionary's Association at Rotterdam, founded on December 19, 1797, to all genuine worshippers of our Lord Jesus Christ in The Netherlands who have an interest in the Extension of His Kingdom." Kruijf, *GNZ*, 20.
128. Ibid., 21.
129. Ibid.
130. Ibid., 41-42.
131. Supra, 16-19.
132. A. Pierson, *Oudere Tijdgenooten* (tweede druk; Amsterdam: P. N. van Kampen en Zoon, 1904), 16-17. Henceforth: Pierson, *O.T.*
133. A. de Groot, *Leven en arbeid van J. H. van der Palm* (Wageningen: H. Veenman en Zonen, n.d.). Henceforth: De Groot, *Van der Palm*.
134. Ibid., 153.
135. Ibid., 251.

CHAPTER II

1. This epistle was included in an edition of documents and papers relevant to the Secession of 1834, first published in 1863. I used the second edition: *Kompleete*

Uitgave van de officeele stukken betreffende den Uitgang uit het Nederl. Herv. Kerkgenootschap van de leeraren H. P. Scholte, A. Brummelkamp, S. Van Velzen, G. F. Gezelle Meerburg, en Dr. A. C. van Raalte, tweede druk (Kampen: G. Ph. Zalsman, 1886). Henceforth: *K.U.*

2. Ibid., 534-35. The reference to the hymns will be dealt with later. Hymns had been introduced into the Reformed Church when Albertus Christiaan was five years old (1806). They remained controversial, and became a major issue in the Secession of 1834. Disagreement about the singing of hymns during services of worship was also a factor in the secession in Michigan in 1857.

3. These minutes were thought to be lost, but by persistent research I brought them to light. Through the kindness of the pastor at Wanneperveen, the Reverend F. C. Roosa, a microfilm copy was made which is now available in the Netherlands Museum, Holland, Michigan.

4. Mr. A. T. Naudin ten Cate, former archivist of the Netherlands Reformed Church, kindly helped to compose the record of the Reverend A. Van Raalte's ministerial service: 1794-1811, Renswoude; 1811-20, Wanneperveen; 1820-22, 's-Heer Abts-en Sinoutskerke; 1822-25, Rijsoord; 1825-28, Scherpenisse; 1828-33, Fijnaard.

5. The mayor of Wanneperveen, A. W. Acker, wanted these schools to be under the control of the municipality. The church appealed to P. Hofstede, prefect of the department of the Yssel-Estuary. He affirmed the church's rights and ordered the mayor to seek "a reasonable arrangement with the church." Minutes from October 4, 1811, to November 26, 1812. The quotation appears in the latter.

6. Blok, *Geschiedenis*, IV:159.

7. De Groot, *Van der Palm*, 63-74, 81-92. Van der Palm was one of the law's main architects.

8. J. Kuiper, *Geschiedenis der wording en ontwikkeling van het Christelijk Lager Onderwijs in Nederland* (Den Haag: C. Blommendaal, 1897), 60. Henceforth: Kuiper, *Onderwijs*. King William signed the decree March 20, 1814, and applied the same law to Belgium when it was added to The Netherlands.

9. De Groot, *Van der Palm*, 82-83.

10. Kuiper, *Onderwijs*, 50. Schools owned and operated by a schoolmaster were usually financed by tuition charges.

11. L. G. J. Verberne, *Geschiedenis van Nederland in de Jaren 1813-50* (twee delen; Utrecht-Antwerpen: Het Spectrum, 1958), I:192-93, quotes the royal report on poverty of 1816 as listing the eleventh part of the population as paupers. Henceforth: Verberne, *G.N.*

12. See Kuiper, *Onderwijs*, 51.

13. P. Oosterlee, *Geschiedenis van het Christelijk Onderwijs* (Haarlem: Erven F. Bohn, 1929), 3-5. Henceforth: Oosterlee, *Geschiedenis Onderwijs*. L. Oostendorp's statement that "Religion was banished from the state schools" is completely misleading. L. Oostendorp, *H. P. Scholte, Leader of the Secession of 1834 and Founder of Pella* (Franeker: T. Wever, 1964), 34. Henceforth: Oostendorp, *Scholte*.

14. Oosterlee, *Geschiedenis Onderwijs*, 5. Cf. Kuiper, *Onderwijs*, 46; De Groot, *Van der Palm*, 87.

15. Kuiper, *Onderwijs*, 12.

16. Examples of provincial regulations are quoted by Kuiper, *Onderwijs*, 17-19. Emphasis was laid upon the removal of "papal superstitions," because at that time the battle against the combined forces of Spain and Rome was still in full swing.

17. Ibid., 59. The Province of Gelderland, for instance, issued a decree in 1681 requiring the schools to teach the catechism only to children of Reformed parents.

18. Quoted from *The Reformed Standards of Unity* (Grand Rapids: Society for Reformed Publications, 1952), 42. Henceforth: *Reformed Standards*.
19. Ph. J. Idenburg, "Machten en krachten in het Nederlandsche Schoolwezen," Bartstra-Banning, *Nederland*, I:153-54.
20. Kuiper, *Onderwijs*, 59; cf. p. 21.
21. Quoted from a government report in 1799. De Groot, *Van der Palm*, 62.
22. Ibid.
23. Ibid., 65.
24. Ibid.
25. Kuiper, *Onderwijs*, 60-61.
26. Verberne, *G.N.*, II:40-44. In France, Lamennais had defended the rights of Roman Catholic schools by arguing that education is by nature a right of the parents. Bartstra-Banning, *Nederland*, I:162.
27. Non-seceding Protestants, and since 1864 the Roman Catholics, bore the brunt of the battle against state-enforced religion in the public schools. The struggle lasted until 1917, when school pacification brought complete equality for both public and private schools with the government financing both. This pacification was made possible because of the principle that since the commonwealth taxes for education the state should subsidize private and parochial schools because all citizens are entitled to a fair return on their taxes. Oosterlee, *Geschiedenis Onderwijs*, 277.
28. The new constitution of 1848 established the principle of the separation of church and state so clearly that the hierarchy could afford to swing its support away from the liberals. A complete break occurred after Pius IX's encyclical *Quanta Cura*. Since 1864 the Roman Catholics joined the orthodox Protestants' drive for a complete equality of public and private schools based on state financing of both. For this development see *GKN*, 322-23. Oosterlee observes that Roman Catholics in the North met with less opposition to their drive for the equality of private and public schools than did the Protestants. *Geschiedenis Onderwijs*, 44-45.
29. These objections were at first almost incidental. Oosterlee successfully defends the thesis that Protestant opposition was organized only after 1840. *Geschiedenis Onderwijs*, 1-90.
30. *K.U.*, 533.
31. Romein, *Erflaters*, 638.
32. The nation's political laxity has previously been noted, supra, 18-20.
33. Knappert, *Geschiedenis NHK*, II:230-31. In 1811 ministers were paid only a third of their salaries, and in 1813 nothing at all. The French police began to warn Napoleon about the seditious tendencies which were arising among the pastors because of the growing misery of their flocks. In 1813 the tax on an income of 2,000 guilders amounted to 900 guilders. L. Knappert, *Het jaar 1813 en zijne glorie, Rede uitgesproken te Haarlem, 24 November 1913* (Leiden, G. F. Theonville, 1914), 12. Henceforth: Knappert, *Het jaar 1813*.
34. J. C. Rullmann, *Een Nagel in de heilige Plaats. De Reformatie der Kerk in de 19e eeuw. Reveil en Afscheiding* (Amsterdam: W. Kirchner, 1912), 44-45. Henceforth: Rullmann, *Een Nagel*.
35. Ibid., 45. Knappert states that the decree was based upon the regulations of 1810. *Geschiedenis NHK*, II:252-53.
36. Huizinga, *Verzamelde Werken*, II:537.
37. Knappert, *Het jaar 1813*, 19.
38. De Groot, *Van der Palm*, 106.
39. Ibid., 108. Van der Palm lost his academic preaching position under the new law of 1815 but was reinstated in 1821. He preached his last sermon for the university

in 1836. His complete sermons were posthumously published in 16 volumes. Cf. pp. 173-76 where De Groot compares Van der Palm with his contemporaries.

40. Ibid., 127-28.
41. Quoted by G. J. Vos, *Groen van Prinsterer en zijn Tijd, Studieën en Schetsen op het gebied der Vaderlansche Kerkgeschiedenis*, Vol. I: *1800-1857* (Dordrecht: P. Revers, 1886), 26. Henceforth: Vos, *Groen.* The second volume covers the period 1857-76 and was published by the same firm in 1891. In the 1830s Guillaume Groen van Prinsterer became a leader in the *Réveil* and originated the Anti-Revolutionary party of Parliament in opposition to the ideas of the French revolution. He became the father of the Christian school, although his ideal of confessional public schools for Protestants, Roman Catholics, and Jews was abandoned by his disciples. Prior to those developments Groen was very much in agreement with the sentiment expressed above by Van der Palm. Vos quotes Groen's reaction to this speech: "Not a flattering panegyric. No! As a testimony affirmed by almost every listener as narration of history, as the basis of salutary prophecy. . . ." Ibid.
42. The reinstatement of the theological faculties at the universities by William I should not be understood to mean that they had been' completely inoperative under French domination. They were reopened in 1801, albeit in modified form. Cf. the excellent study of Otto J. De Jong, *De Theologische Faculteiten en de Bataafse Revolutie* (Nijkerk: Callenbach, 1969).
43. Haitjema, *NGN*, 92. The words describing the realm are significant. The term republic is avoided and the term state is used instead. However, the designation United Netherlands connects very clearly with the situation prior to 1795.
44. J. B. Bomans, *De Kerkelijke Politiewetten* (Hilversum: Paul Brand, 1923), 7. Henceforth: Bomans, *Politiewetten.*
45. Haitjema, *NGN*, 92.
46. Bomans, *Politiewetten*, 7. It should be noted that this provision has undergone no significant change for more than a century, although the text was shortened in 1848.
47. F. L. Bos, *Archiefstukken betreffende de Afscheiding van 1834* (vier delen; Kampen: Kok, 1939-46), I:xii. Henceforth: *Archiefstukken.*
48. *Archiefstukken*, I:xii. There is a translation problem with the word "communion." The Dutch reads *gezindheid,* which should be translated "conviction" or "persuasion." The translation in the text is based on the original French wording: "Protection égale est accordée à toutes les communions religieuses qui existent dans le Royaume."
49. Ibid.
50. Haitjema, *NGN*, 92-93.
51. Oostendorp, *Scholte*, 34.
52. Bomans, *Politiewetten*, 9.
53. Ibid., 10. The reference is to Article 5.
54. Ibid., 15.
55. In the framework of the United Republic, each province could more or less regulate its own affairs. The country did not return to that situation in 1813. A new polity was therefore required.
56. Knappert differs, since he defines the king's actions as falling within the bounds of the *jus circa sacra. Geschiedenis NHK*, II:257.
57. The Mennonites successfully rejected interference by the state. Blok, *Geschiedenis*, IV:243.
58. *GKN*, 301-03.

59. Ibid., 311. This mission status came to an end when the hierarchy was restored in 1853.
60. Verberne stresses the king's concern for unity. *G.N.*, I:127. J. H. J. M. Witlox states that "the king practically was the only enthusiastic and convinced supporter of the unity." J. H. J. M. Witlox, *Varia Historica* ('s-Hertogenbosch: Teuling's Uitgevers Maatschaapij, 1936), 52. Henceforth: Witlox, *Varia*.
61. The new realm consisted of 3,000,000 Belgians and 2,000,000 Dutchmen, according to Verberne, *G.N.*, II:18. Blok estimates that of the Dutchmen 1.5 million were Protestants and 0.5 million were liberal Roman Catholics. *Geschiedenis*, IV:242.
62. Verberne, *G.N.*, I:127. William also saw it as his God-given task to supervise, regulate, and aid the churches. Ibid., 106. William died behind his desk. In front of him lay an open French copy of Thomas a Kempis's *Imitatio*. It was his habit to read a chapter of this work every day as his morning devotion. Ibid., 31.
63. Witlox, *Varia*, 54, states that the king in personal relationships "gave little love and therefore received little."
64. Haitjema, *N.G.N.*, 89-90; cf. Knappert, *Geschiedenis NHK*, II:220.
65. L. J. Rogier, *GKN*, 305. Romein characterizes William as "a Dutch Napoleon with the same will of steel and the same broad insight, but set in another surrounding and therefore with another goal and with another failure." Romein, *Erflaters*, 640.
66. *GKN*, 302-03; cf. Verberne, *G.N.*, I:128-29. This attitude coincided very well with the old liberalism, which believed in the truth of its convictions strongly enough to enforce them through the state. Ibid., II:45.
67. Romein states that this step galled the Roman Catholics the more because the *Collegium* was housed in the same building that Joseph II had used as his school for priests, Romein, *Lage Landen*, III:66. Verberne states that this step was not completely unwarranted because of the poor facilities provided by the minor seminaries. Equipped for 1,200 students, the *Collegium* attracted 551 in all, 550 of whom were given full scholarships. With the Belgian uprising in the year 1830, Van Ghert's creation automatically came to an end. Verberne, *G.N.*, II:48-50. Ibid., 62.
68. *GKN*, 307.
69. H. T. Colenbrander, *De Afscheiding van Belgie*, Vol. XXI of *Nederlandsche Historische Bibliotheck onder leiding van H. Brugmann* (Amsterdam: J. H. Meulenhoff, 1936). Henceforth: Colenbrander, *Afscheiding*.
70. C. W. Pape, *Het leven en werken van J. D. Janssen* ('s-Hertogenbosch: Gebroeders Muller, 1855). Henceforth: Pape, *Janssen*.
71. Blok, *Geschiedenis*, IV:243.
72. A. Goslinga, "Het einde der Classis Amsterdam," *Christendom en Historie, Lustrumbundel 1930, uitgegeven vanwege het Gezelschap van Christelijke Historici in Nederland* (Kampen: Kok, 1931), 171. The essay, one of seven, is printed on pp. 170-91. Henceforth: Goslinga, "Classis Amsterdam."
73. Haitjema, *NGN*, 99. Hendrik van Stralen was an old-time Orangist placed in charge of the interior during the French period, Blok, *Geschiedenis*, IV:93, 104, 123, and passim. Since December 2, 1813, he had been King William's Commissary for the Interior. Knappert, *Geschiedenis NHK*, II:252.
74. H. Bouwman, *Gereformeerd Kerkrecht* (Kampen: Kok, 1928), 311.
75. Reitsma, *Hervorming*, 402.
76. Goslinga quotes this as the essence of the king's reply given during an audience he granted North Holland's provincial synod deputies on April 14, 1814. Goslinga, "Classis Amsterdam," 173.

77. Janssen became Van Stralen's deputy on March 8, 1814, Pape, *Janssen*, 10.
78. Haitjema, *NGN*, 99. Cf. for the plan of 1809: supra, 22.
79. Reitsma, *Hervorming*, 421; Goslinga, "Classis Amsterdam," 173-74. For a detailed account, see J. C. A. van Loon, *Het algemeen reglement van 1816* (Wageningen: H. Veenman en Zonen, 1942), 71-153. Henceforth: Van Loon, *Algemeen Reglement.*
80. Goslinga, "Classis Amsterdam," 174.
81. Knappert, *Geschiedenis NHK,* II:253.
82. This is the point made by Haitjema, *NGN*, 99-100.
83. Van Loon, *Algemeen Reglement,* 80.
84. Knappert mentions their names and gives a few additional details, Knappert, *Geschiedenis NHK,* II:253. Oostendorp makes the unwarranted statement: "Under influence of men like Janssen and Van der Palm, the king reorganized the whole Hervormde Kerk without so much as consulting the church itself." In the footnote from which the quote is taken he makes reference to Reitsma, *Hervorming,* but to the 4th edition (1933) rather than to the 5th (1949). The footnote makes mention of "the French record" of Janssen and Van der Palm, but fails to prove the latter's involvement in the development of the new church order. It is perhaps significant that Oostendorp mentions collaboration with the French on the part of these two men, but fails to state that Bilderdijk, whom he calls "the father of the Dutch Réveil" (p. 29), was an enthusiastic supporter of both Louis Napoleon and the Emperor himself. Oostendorp, *Scholte,* 34.
85. The king had consulted only three members of the Council of State and accepted their suggestions with respect to what minor changes should be made in the proposal submitted by Janssen and his committee. For the details: W. Volger, *De leer der Nederlandsche Hervormde Kerk* (tweede druk; Franeker: T. Wever, 1946), 18-19. Henceforth: Volger, *Leer.*
86. Goslinga, "Classis Amsterdam," 175.
87. *Volledige Verzameling van alle Wetten, Reglementen, en Besluiten het Kerkelijke en den Eeredienst, bijzonder bij de Hervormden, betreffende, van het laatst van 1813 tot op heden* (twee delen; Zutphen: M. C. A. Thieme, 1817-20), passim, I:66-85. Henceforth: *Volledige Verzameling.* The total number of classes was reduced to forty-three, largely because of the realignment which came with the new constitution.
88. Van Loon, *Algemeen Reglement,* 154-83. Appendixes, pp. 236-71. An additional protest came from the Walloon (French-speaking Reformed) Church at Dordrecht.
89. Volger, *Leer,* 33.
90. The pertinent sentence reads: "As for the Ministers of God's Word, they have equally the same power and authority wheresoever they are, as they are all Ministers of Christ, the only universal Bishop, and the only Head of the Church." *Reformed Standards,* 85.
91. According to Goslinga, the three ministers were Visch, Van Rossem, and Sweighold. Visch was one of the eighteen ministers deposed because of their loyalty to the House of Orange. Goslinga, "Classis Amsterdam," 179-80.
92. Goslinga, "Classis Amsterdam," 181.
93. *Volledige Verzameling,* I:85-101.
94. Knappert states that Janssen replied. Knappert, *Geschiedenis NHK,* II:254. Van Loon corrects this in pointing out that the draft of the reply is in Janssen's handwriting. Van Loon, *Algemeen Reglement,* 159.
95. The Dutch word is *gemeenten,* the plural form of *gemeente.* It is ambiguous because of its dual meaning: (1) ecclesiastically, congregation; and (2) politically, municipality.

96. *Volledige Verzameling*, I:101.
97. R. Dijkstra, *Boek van rijke Herinnering aan de Reformatie der Kerk te Amsterdam, aangevangen op 24 Mei 1578 en voortgezet tot op dezen dag* (Amsterdam: J. R. Vrolijk, 1928), 118. Henceforth: Dijkstra, *Rijke Herinnering*.
98. Volger, *Leer*, 30-33.
99. This solution is described as the state's *jus circa sacra* by those who agree with the implicit presupposition. If one understands polity as belonging to the essence of the church, the state is exercising *jus in sacra*.
100. *Reformed Standards*, 85-86.
101. Reitsma, *Hervorming*, 422-23. According to Knappert, the provinces took turns in yearly sending a "synodical elder" to the General Synod, Knappert, *Geschiedenis NHK*, II:255. In 1827 a General Synod committee was established to deal with synodical matters when the synod itself was not in session. Its members were chosen by the king from a double slate submitted by the provincial synods, ibid., 256.
102. Volger, *Leer*, 33.
103. Because of insufficient time, this session did not take up the agenda item dealing with regulations for consistories and liturgy. The same day the first session came to its close on July 30, four of the synod's documents received royal approval after they had been passed by the Council of State. The king signed the remaining documents on November 30, 1816.
104. Van Loon gives the final text as well as the several drafts preceding it. Van Loon, *Algemeen Reglement*, 77-90. Cf. Volger, *Leer*, 23-26.
105. Detailed information about these minutes has previously been noted, supra, 25, 28-29.
106. Supra, 25.

CHAPTER III

1. Volger, *Leer*, 38.
2. Ibid., 41, italics mine. Knappert, *Geschiedenis NHK*, II:269, refers to it as Article 38 because the synod of 1831 revised the form and changed the numbering of the articles; its contents remained the same. Haitjema, *NGN*, 105, reproduces the earlier statement required by the Synod of Dordrecht and formulated in its 164th session. For comparison: "We . . . declare sincerely and in good conscience, before the Lord, with this our subscription that we not only wholeheartedly feel and believe that all articles and heads of doctrine in the Confession and the Heidelberg Catechism of the Reformed Netherlands Churches, but also the explanation of certain points in said doctrine given in the National Synod at Dordrecht in 1619, agree in everything with God's Word. Promising therefore that we will diligently teach the said doctrine. . . ."
3. See the careful probing of conflicting statements in Volger, *Leer*, 12-19. Friesland's civil authorities had accepted the acts of Dordrecht, but did not accept the so-called *Post-Acta*. The latter contained the formula for ministerial candidates.
4. Volger, *Leer*, 39.
5. Supra, 12-13; a full review is to be found in Reitsma, *Hervorming*, 320-21.
6. Knappert, *Geschiedenis NHK*, I:263, names some of the classes and synods requiring ministerial candidates to sign such statements. In the Province of Groningen, candidates were required to sign statements condemning the teachings of Bekker and Roell, but not those of Vlak. Vos, *Groen*, I:201-202.
7. Difficulties over the *quia-quatenus* understanding of similar formulas had come up as early as 1769, when Johann Gottlieb Töllner, in his *Unterricht von symbolischen Büchern überhaupt*, attacked the *quatenus* interpretation because it implied the

supposition that the form or symbol does not agree with the Word of God. Walter Karowski, *Das Bekenntnis und seine Wertung* (Berlin: SW 68, 1939), 32-40.

8. The synod was the more able to do so because as Vos, Groen, I:199-224, has pointed out, the *quiatisten* were far from united. On the left, for example, was Isaac Da Costa, the converted Jew, who opposed what he called "Roman Orthodoxy" because it sought its strength not in the Word of God but in the manmade forms; and since the Synod of Dordrecht had started its forms *de novo*, Da Costa felt that a new synod could do so too.

9. Haitjema, *NGN*, 106-07. *Handelingen van de Algemeene Christelijke Synode der Hervormde Kerk in het Koninkrijk der Nederlanden* ('s-Gravenhage: Landsdrukkerij, 1854), 271. Henceforth: Handelingen, (*followed by the appropriate year*).

10. Oostendorp's statement that "Under the influence of men like Janssen and Van der Palm, the King reorganized the whole church," Scholte, 34, is misleading. He failed to consult the best authority on the subject, J. C. A. van Loon, who concludes on p. 211 of his *Het Algemeen Reglement*: "I have found no trace of King William's direct influence over and above what I said earlier concerning his appointing of the Commission of 1815 and editing the Constitution. His influence was far less than has been supposed." See also Haitjema, *NGN*, 94, who refers to a lecture by the late Professor G. C. Gerretson, proving for the early period of union with Belgium great care on the part of King William to be non-arbitrary and exactingly constitutional. I have been unable to trace this lecture.

11. Knappert, *Geschiedenis NHK*, II:271-74; Reitsma, *Hervorming*, 436-37; *Christelijke Encyclopaedie voor het Nederlandsche Volk* (zes delen; Kampen: Kok, n.d.; introduction 1925), IV:126-27, *sub voce* Mazereeuw, an article by J. C. Rullmann. Henceforth: *Chr. Encyclopaedie*.

12. Jane Leade's book, *Revelation of Revelation* (London, 1683), had been translated into Dutch and was published (at Amsterdam) by Wetstein in 1696.

13. Knappert, *Geschiedenis NHK*, II:24-27, states that as late as 1911 a few followers were still adhering to Mazereeuw's teachings.

14. Ibid., 275-80; Reitsma, *Hervorming*, 437-39; D. N. Anagraphaeus, *De Zwijndrechtsche Nieuwlichters (1816-1832) volgens de gedenkschriften van Maria Leer, met sen inleidend woord van J.H. Maronier* (Amsterdam: Uitgeversmaatschappij Elsevier, 1892). Henceforth: Anagraphaeus, *Nieuwlichters*.

15. Mulder, as did so many skippers of that day, frequented the conventicles. Maria Leer's account of her many contacts with these bodies provided a perceptive insight into the atmosphere prevailing there. Anagraphaeus, *Nieuwlichters*, 22-25, 33-37, 40-42.

16. Supra, 32-33.

17. Anagraphaeus, *Nieuwlichters*, 91-92.

18. By 1817, poverty was so widespread that pauperism constituted the nation's foremost problem. I. J. Brugmans, *De arbeidende klasse in Nederland in de 19e eeuw. 1813-1870* (5e druk; Utrecht-Antwerpen: Het Spectrum, 1961), denies the possibility of a comprehensive view of the situation because the available sources do not yield all the information necessary for a complete picture, pp. 151-52. Henceforth: Brugmans, *Arbeidende Klasse*. Verberne, *G.N.*, I:192-208, presents a cautious description of the laborer's misery. In 1817 the Province of South Holland, including The Hague and Rotterdam, listed twenty-three percent of the population as being on relief. The central government estimated that of the entire population, oneninth or even one-seventh could not support itself. Johannes van den Bosch formed his *Maatschappij van Weldadigheid*, translated, Benevolent Society, in 1818 to remove paupers from urban centers and resettle them on virgin land in the rural

districts. Within six months the society drew more than 17,000 voluntary supporters and was therefore able to start immediately on its first project: the colony Frederiksoord. Ibid., 198-203.

19. Mulder and Maria Leer married under the rules of the group and were called the Adam and Eve of the new "Garden of Eden." Anagraphaeus, *Nieuwlichters*, 46-47.

20. Historians differ considerably in their evaluations of this experiment. The socialist H. P. Quack sees them as a Dutch manifestation of Saint-Simonism: "De eerste dagen der Zwijndrechtsche Broederschap," published in *Mededelingen van de Koninklijke Academie van Weknschappen*, 3e reeks, IX (1892), 270-316. Brugmans, *Arbeidende Klasse*, 191-92, disagrees on the basis of G. P. Marang's dissertation *De Zwijndrechtsche Nieuwlichters* (Dordrecht: H. de Graaff, 1909), and holds that communism or socialism had little to do with the group's origin, because their way of life originated in their effort to emulate the first congregation of Christians. However, direct connections with Saint-Simonism did exist by 1829; Knappert, *Geschiedenis NHK*, II:275-77. Cf. G. P. Marang, "NieuwLicht over de Zwijndrechtsche Nieuwlichters," *Nederlandsch Archief voor Kerkgeschiedenis* ('s-Gravenhage: Martinus Nijhoff, 1936), XXVIII:129-53. Henceforth: *N.A.K.*

21. The surname is spelled either Vijgeboom or Vijgenboom; his Christian names are spelled Johannes Willem or Jan Willem. The best treatment of him is P. J. Meertens, "J. W. Vijgeboom," *N.A.K.*, XXVII (1935), 30-56. Henceforth: Meertens, *Vijgeboom*. Documents pertinent to his cause are found in *Archiefstukken*, I:1-59. Cf. Reitsma, *Hervorming*, 440; Knappert, *Geschiedenis NHK*, II:274-75. J. C. Rullmann in his article in the *Chr. Encyclopaedie*, 598-99, calls him Johan Willem Vijgenboom, V:598-99, but in his book, *Een Nagel*, pp. 65-67, he uses the name Johannes Willem Vijgeboom.

22. *Archiefstukken*, I:55-59, for the documents relating to his arrest and fine at Leeuwarden, capital of the Province of Friesland.

23. F. Staal Pzn, in his biography of the Reverend Mr. C. van der Meulen who arrived in Michigan shortly after Van Raalte in 1847 and founded Zeeland, states that Van der Meulen enlarged upon Vijgeboom's work in Axel where the latter "was . . . since 1822." See *De Apostel van Zeeland; uit de dagen der Afscheiding* (Bruinisse: J. van der Wal, n.d.), 25. Henceforth: *Apostel Zeeland*. It is true that Vijgeboom settled at Axel after a period of itinerancy that lasted from 1820 to 1823. But while at Axel during 1823 to 1833, Vijgeboom did engage in several preaching trips outside his congregation, and he was seldom long in one place during the last period of his life, 1833-45. He tried to receive ordination at the hands of the Seceded Church, but was unsuccessful because Albertus C. Van Raalte raised a question about his moral character. Nevertheless, he served the Seceded Church as an *oefenaar* or laypreacher at Bunschoten and other places. Henceforth: *Staal*.

24. *Archiefstukken*, I:31; cf. Meertens, *Vijgeboom*, 33.

25. *Archiefstukken*, I:19-20.

26. J. de Bosch Kemper, *Geschiedenis van Nederland na 1830, Met aanteekeningen en onuitgegeyen stukken* (eerste deel; Amsterdam: E. S. Witkamp, 1873), 30-31, states: "The Code Napoleon remained in effect until 1839 and was taught in Latin at Leiden by the dignified and strictly learned Smallenburg who also externally, with his white powdered wig, belonged completely to the old era. . . ." De Bosch Kemper's work was published in five volumes, the final one by Johannes Muller, in Amsterdam, in 1882. Henceforth: De Bosch Kemper, *GN 1830*.

27. Albert Hyma, *Albertus C. Van Raalte and His Dutch Settlements in the United States* (Grand Rapids: Wm. B. Eerdmans Publishing Co., 1947), 18-20. Henceforth: Hyma, *Van Raalte*. Cf. Elton M. Eeningenburg, *A Brief History of the Reformed*

154 *Sources of Secession*

Church in America (Grand Rapids: Douma Publications, n.d.), 78-79. Henceforth: Eeningenburg, *History RCA*. Cf. John Kromminga, *The Christian Reformed Church, A Study in Orthodoxy* (Grand Rapids: Baker Bookhouse, 1949), 18-19. Henceforth: Kromminga, *CRC*. Even the careful historian Henry S. Lucas did not call attention to the Code Penal being used against Vijgeboom and his group. Lucas, *Netherlanders*, 46, 119. In fairness to Lucas, it should be added that he mentions Vijgeboom in a context other than is presented here. An exception must be made for A. J. Pieters, *A Dutch Settlement in Michigan* (Grand Rapids: The Reformed Press— Eerdmans-Sevensma Co., 1923), in which these articles appear on p. 13. Pieters asserts erroneously that the articles ". . . several decades after his [Napoleon's] fall were revived by the government . . . against their own people" (p. 12). Henceforth: Pieters, *Settlement*.

28. *Archiefstukken*, I:xiii.
29. They referred to Article 190, supra, 32.
30. *Archiefstukken*, I:21-25, 24.
31. Ibid., 24-25. The closing part of this letter contains defaming remarks about the lowly estate of the seceders.
32. Ibid., 28. The phrase "confusion and irregularities" describes the fear typical of the conservative and rather autocratic government of that time.
33. This paragraph and the section dealing with the Restored Church of Christ are based on the appeal reproduced in *Archiefstukken*, I:29-36.
34. For the controversy over the hymns, see Reitsma, *Hervorming*, 409-11; Knappert, *Geschiedenis NHK*, II:224-27; Ter Haar-Moll, *Geschiedenis CKN*, II:583-609; Haitjema, *NGN*, 112-18. A review of each of these hymns together with a short introduction can be found in A. W. Bronsveld, *De Evangelische Gezangen verzameld in de jaren 1803-1804 en in Gebruik bij de Nederlandsche Hervormde Kerk* (Utrecht, Kemink en Zoon, 1917). Henceforth: Bronsveld, *Gezangen*.
35. Knappert, *Geschiedenis NHK*, II:224.
36. The Batavian Republic was rapidly nearing its end. In 1806, Louis Napoleon assumed royal power in the new kingdom of Holland.
37. The 162nd session of the *Post-Acta* allowed the church to sing (in addition to the 150 Psalms), the Ten Commandments, the Lord's Prayer, the Articles of Faith, and the doxologies of Mary, Zechariah, and Simeon. The hymn "O God, Who Our Father Art" was left at the church's discretion. Vijgeboom quotes the Dordtian article in full. *Archiefstukken*, I:30.
38. Ter Haar-Moll, *Geschiedenis CKN*, II:567-68. I have it on the authority of Dr. Otto J. DeJong, Professor of Church History at the University of Utrecht, The Netherlands, that a few traditional congregations still are using *Datheen* today.
39. Three versions were specified in the order of the States General. The committee selected ten psalms from the Psalter by Hendrik Ghijsen of 1686, itself the analect of seventeen different versions; eighty-two psalms from the Psalter by Johannes Eusebius Voet of 1758; and fifty-eight psalms from the Psalter composed by the society *Laus Deo Salus Populo* in 1761. In addition to making the selection, the committee improved the language of each verse.
40. E.g., riots occurred in the fishermen's towns of Maassluis and Vlaardingen, near Rotterdam. Ter Haar-Moll, *Geschiedenis CKN*, II:578-82.
41. Supra, 17-18.
42. Ter Haar-Moll, *Geschiedenis CKN*, II:568. The seceders of 1834 were at times seriously divided over the question of which Psalter should be used. The Reverend H. J. Budding quoted Luke 5:39 in defense of *Datheen*. J. H. Gunning J. Hzn.,

H. J. Budding, Leven en Arbeid (Rhenen: W. J. van Nas, 1909), 141-42. Henceforth: Gunning: *Budding*.

43. Haitjema, *NGN*, 116.

44. Another example is found in Hymn 177:

> If only ancestral virtue in the Dutch youth
> Would revive together with Religion!
> If thrift and industry
> Would live here again as in times gone by!
> That would indeed create hope of prosperity!

Haitjema, *NGN*, 116. According to Bronsveld, *Gezangen*, 242, Gezang 53 had at first been rejected by a subcommittee but was approved at a committee meeting in which the representatives of both North Holland and Groningen declined to vote. Bronsveld does not supply such additional details for Gezang 177, ibid., 445-46. It is of course obvious that many of the hymns became favorites.

45. The hymns continued to haunt the seceders who came to America. One of the reasons for the Secession of 1857 in Michigan was the opposition to the hymnbook at that time in use by the Reformed Church in America.

46. *Archiefstukken*, I:31.

47. In addition they quoted similar decisions of the provincial synods of Zeeland, held in 1591 and 1638, which had been in force in the Province of Zeeland. Ibid.

48. Volger, *Leer*, 58.

49. Within the confines of this study it is not possible to pursue this point further. There is, however, another aspect that should not be overlooked. The Lord's Supper was avoided in the late medieval church since the spectacle of the miraculous mass supplanted sacramental participation. The Dutch Reformation combated that tendency by placing a great stress on frequent communion. To the Dutch refugee church, leaders at the Synod of Wesel (1568) prescribed that "nobody shall be admitted to the Lord's supper unless he make prior confession of faith, and unless he submit himself to ecclesiastical discipline" (VI:7).

Since that time, the Reformed Church continued to maintain a close relation between confession and Supper. Starting in the seventeenth century, however, pietistic influences began to place great stress upon the believer and his confession. Thus, the believer was urged to abstain from bread and wine unless he manifested the presence of the Holy Spirit within him. This tendency, of which Jean de Labadie is an extreme example, may have been an instigating factor in Vijgeboom's protest. It is interesting to note that the seceders of 1857 in Michigan also objected to the practice of the Reformed Church in America, agreed to by Van Raalte, which allowed members of other denominations to share the Lord's Table. In the church of these seceders, later to be known as the Christian Reformed Church, it was for decades customary that only members of the denomination were allowed to partake of the bread and wine.

50. Handelingen, *1817*, 109.

51. The Reformed Church continued this practice until May 1, 1961. Her new church order then placed this matter in a more biblical, ecumenical perspective.

52. Handelingen, *1819*, 119. The entry is dated May 10, 1819. The absence of a reaction from the Remonstrant church may have been due to their earlier desire to take the greater step of uniting all Protestants into one body. Supra, 22.

53. Cf. the abortive attempt of *Christo Sacrum* to bring about union through sacrament and liturgy; supra, 23.

54. *Archiefstukken*, I:31.

55. Ter Haar-Moll, *Geschiedenis CKN*, II:622: W. F. Dankbaar, "De prediking bij de

bediening van het Heilig Avondmaal," *Handbook voor de Prediking, Bijzondere dagen en gelegenheden* (Amsterdam: Uitgeversmij. Holland, 1948), 102. A. F. N. Lekkerkerker, *Kanttekenkingen bij het Hervormd Dienstboek* (4 delen; 's-Gravenhage: Boekencentrum, 1956), III:154, points out that the custom originated under Lutheran influence in the Paltz, whence it was imported into Emden and hence into Groningen and Friesland.

56. Handelingen, *1817*, 87-88. For comparison, the four questions from Groningen and Friesland are quoted from Volger, *Leer*, 55-56:

The Christian congregation will please present itself before the countenance of the Lord and answer the following questions:

1. I ask you whether you do not wholeheartedly believe and confess with me that the books of the Old and New Testament are God's only true word and that in these according to the articles of the Christian faith is included the sole, perfect, and sufficient doctrine of salvation, as is being taught in our church. Those who confess and believe this join me in saying *yes*.

2. Whether you do not wholeheartedly believe and acknowledge with me that we, in ourselves totally depraved and unable to do any good, cannot at all obtain salvation in and because of ourselves, or because of our abilities and worthiness. Those who believe and confess this, join me in saying *yes*.

3. Whether you do not wholeheartedly believe and confess with me that we receive salvation and are saved and kept therein unto the end solely out of God's sheer love and grace, because of the completeness of the merits of Jesus Christ our only Lord and perfect Savior, by the illumination and powerful operation of the Holy Spirit. Those who believe and confess the same join me in saying *yes*.

4. Whether you resolve with me to persevere by God's grace until your life's end in this pure doctrine and confession of faith, and in addition thereto to use all diligence to hate and flee evil, and in true love for God and neighbor to experience [to give expression to] this doctrine by all good works of godliness, justice, and sobriety, to the honor of God and to the edification of the congregation. Those who are thus resolved join in saying *yes*.

57. Ibid., 56-57.
58. *Archiefstukken*, I:31.
59. Handelingen, *1917*, 89-109. It should be noted that when King William I attended the Lord's Supper he was not given special consideration in seating.
60. Smijtegeld became most famous of all for a collection of sermons written down and published by admirers under the title *Het gekrookte riet of 145 predicatieën over Mattheus XII:20-21*. They were very popular in conventicles and often reprinted. It is impossible here to treat this emphasis fully.
61. His book, *De godvruchtige avondmaalsganger*, was first published in 1715, and went through many editions. I used the edition by J. Teves Tzn (Groningen: R. Boerma, 1893).
62. Wilhelmus Brakel, *Logike Latreia, dat is Redelijke Godsdienst in welke de Goddelijke Waarheden van het Genade-Verbond worden verklaard, tegen partijen beschermd en tot beoefening aangedrongen, alsede de Bedeeling des Verbonds in het O. en N.T. en de Ontmoeting der Kerk in het N.T. vertoond in eene verklaring van de Openbaring van Johannes*. The first edition appeared in 1700. I used the second edition published by J. H. Donner (2 delen; Leiden: D. Donner, 1893), I:606. It should not be overlooked that Brakel does not refrain from advocating abstention under certain circumstances; ibid., 1039-40. But in combating the influence of Jean de Labadie (supra, 13-15), Brakel makes basic: "One does not need prior to partaking a perfect, steadfast, active assurance without solicitude that one is in the

state of grace . . . but it is sufficient that one is convinced of the outward acts of faith and of conversion even if one does not dare to conclude therefrom: I believe, I am converted." Ibid., 1040.

63. See the report of N. Borsboom (Sept. 1824), who became a Reformed pastor at Axel in 1824, in *Archiefstukken*, I:50-51.

64. Ibid., 47, 49, 50. The suggestion to use the monetary incentive had first been made by the governor of the Province of Zeeland. His information that part of the dissent was motivated by objections to financial responsibility for a portion of the ministerial salary proved to be correct.

65. The vacancy was created when the orthodox but quick-tempered pastor, H. Wesseling, accepted a call and left Axel in January 1824, ibid., 33, 47.

66. Ibid., 50-51. The report is dated December 18, 1824, and is addressed to the governor of Zeeland.

67. Ibid., 38-40.

68. A. W. Philipse, the prosecutor of the High Court, had reported to the minister of justice on October 16, 1823, that Articles 291-294 of the *Code Napoleon* had been unsuccessfully applied in the case of Herschel Lehren, the leader of a Jewish secession; *Archiefstukken*, I:42-43. J. Th. de Visser notes in *Kerk en Staat* (3 delen; Leiden: A. W. Sijthoff, 1927), III:264, three additional court cases extending from 1822-23 in which seceders were placed under similar judgments. The issue in these cases is complicated by the claim on the part of the accused that they alone represent the original body constituting the true church.

69. *Archiefstukken*, I:40.

70. Ibid., 39-40. It is apparent that the unity of the new kingdom was given high priority. Thus, it must have been a strong motivating factor for the conservatism of the administration.

71. Ibid., 37.

72. Ibid., 38.

CHAPTER IV

1. Supra, xi-xii.

2. Isaac Da Costa to Willem van Hogendorp in a letter preserved in the Government Archives at The Hague, as quoted by Z. W. Sneller, *Christendom en Historie Lustrumbundel uitgegeven van wege het Gezelschap van Christelijke Historici in Nederland* (Amsterdam: Uitgeversmaatschappij Holland, 1925), 262. Henceforth: Sneller, *Willem van Hogendorp*.

3. M. Elisabeth Kluit, *Het Réveil in Nederland*, 1817-54 (Amsterdam: H. J. Paris, 1936), x. Henceforth: Kluit, *Réveil*. The Roman Catholic author Dr. M. Staverman, O.F.M., arrived at the same conclusion in his study of non-churchmembership in the Dutch Province of Friesland: "The Réveil in Friesland was never a unified undertaking. It was not a system but a movement, not so much a party as a persuasion. Certainly in its infancy, religious sentiment dominated theological reflection." *Buitenkerkelijkheid in Friesland* (Assen: Van Gorcum en Comp., 1954), 104.

4. M. Elisabeth Kluit, *Maatschappij, School, en Kerk: Ottho Gerhard Heldring en het Réveil* (Hoenderloo: Strichting Hoenderloo, 1958), 20. Henceforth: Kluit, *Maatschappij*.

5. Supra, 39-41.

6. Isaac Johannes Dermout, 1777-1867, had been a minister in the Reformed Church at The Hague since 1805; in 1822 King William I appointed him as preacher for his court in The Hague. *Chr. Encyclopaedie*, I:581.

7. Vos, *Groen,* I:28-29. The text, 2 Timothy 1:7, in the Revised Standard Version reads "for God did not give us a spirit of timidity but a spirit of power and love and self-control."

8. Ibid., 31.

9. Knappert, *Geschiedenis NHK,* II:283.

10. Rullmann, *Een Nagel,* 51.

11. Popular Reformed historiographers early adopted the custom of describing The Netherlands and its struggle for independence in biblical and especially in Old Testament terms. Among the reasons for this development are (1) the rediscovery of the Bible and the ensuing reformation of faith and life, and (2) the intertwining of religious and politico-economic causes in the war against Spain. Cf. Joh. C. Breen: "Gereformeerde Populaire Historiographie in de Zeventiende en Achtiende Eeuw," *Christendom en Historie, Lustrumbundel uitgegevan vanwege het Gezelschap van Christalijke Historici in Nederland* (Amsterdam: Uitgeversmaatschappij Holland, 1925), 213-421. Henceforth: Breen, *Historigraphie.*

12. Acts 20:30-31 (RSV): "and from among your own selves will arise men speaking perverse things, to draw away the disciples after them. Therefore be alert." Revelation 16:15 (RSV): "Lo, I am coming like a thief! Blessed is he who is awake, keeping his garments that he may not go naked and be seen exposed!"

13. The Dutch title is: *Eerezuil ter gedachtenis van de voor twechonderd jaar te Dordrecht gehouden Nationale Synode, opgericht door Nicolaas Schotsman.* The Provincial Synod approved it for publication. The (permanent) secretary at that time was the Reverend Mr. J. Sluiter who was still in office when Albertus C. Van Raalte appeared before this body to be examined for licensure and ordination (1835).

14. This pun on the Dutch word *zuil,* pillar, appeared in an article whose author is unknown. It was published in *Vaderlandsche Letteroefeningen of Tijdschrift voor Kunsten en Wetenschappen, waarin de Boeken en Schriften die dagelijke in ons Vaderland en elders uitkomen oordeelkundig en tevens vrijmoedig behandeld worden,* 1819, 510ff.

15. Rullmann, *Een Nagel,* 54.

16. This practice was not uncommon. It is interesting to note that one of Schotsman's pupils, T. F. de Haan, became in 1839 the eleventh minister to join the secession. De Haan was from 1840 to 1860 a theological professor in the Seceded Church. It is probably more than a coincidence that prior to the secession De Haan, like Schotsman, considered King William I to be the foster-father of the Reformed Church. While minister of the Reformed Church at Hurwenen, 1821-24, De Haan appealed to William to follow the example of Judah's kings Jehoshaphat, Hezekiah, and Josiah, urging the king to no longer admit ministers into the church who were not preaching the old truth. Should the king fail to follow his advice, De Haan predicted that great calamities would befall the country, because the South would rebel against the North. Rullmann, *Een Nagel,* 49-66; cf. J. C. van der Does, *De Afscheiding in haar wording en beginperiode; tweede en vermeerderde druk* (Delft: W. E. Meinema, n.d. [1934?], 200-03. Henceforth: Van der Does, *Afscheiding.* See also W. de Graaf, *Een monument der Afscheiding, De Theologische Hogeschool der Gereformeerde Kerken in Nederland 1854-1954* (Kampen: Kok, 1955), 49-52. Henceforth: De Graaf, *Monument.*

17. M. Elisabeth Kluit points out that Schotsman was not the translator. "Wenselijkheden voor de Studie van het Réveil," *Nederlands Theologisch Tijdschrift,* XI, No. 5 (June 1957) 367. According to Kluit, Schotsman wrote the introduction. The authors mentioned in the previous note leave the impression that Schotsman was responsible for the entire Dutch edition. Cornelis Baron van Zuylen van Nijeveldt,

also called *Zwarte Kees, black Keith,* will be dealt with below, where his influence upon Hendrik de Cock, the father of the secession, will be noted.

18. Ami Bost was the son of a leader in the Brethren congregation established in Geneva by Zinzendorf in 1741. With his friend H. L. Empaytaz, later the secretary of Madame Von Krüdener, Bost studied theology and formed the Circle of Friends, which claimed to believe and defend the orthodox faith. Richard Wilcox, Robert Haldane, and Henri Drummond exerted influence upon this group and its adherents. Out of the turmoil came the secession of the *Bourg de Four,* Cesar Malan's *Eglise de Temeignage,* and ultimately L. Gaussen's *Societe Evangelique.* Good relationships developed between Geneva and The Netherlands, especially after 1835. See Kluit, *Réveil,* 7-16. A second edition of this work came out in 1970 under the title: *Het Protestantse Réveil in Nederland en Daarbuiten, 1815-1865* (Amsterdam: Paris). Since my thesis was completed prior to Kluit's second edition, the references pertain to the earlier edition. Where necessary corrections have been incorporated on the basis of the second edition and are so noted.

19. Volger, *Leer,* 73. Asher's book was translated from the French in 1822, the year that Schotsman died. Schotsman provided the foreword to this book, which had been written in answer to Joseph Priestley's *An History of the Corruptions of Christianity* (Birmingham, 1782).

20. *Nederlandsche Stemmen over Godsdienst, Staat-Geschied-en Letterkunde, onder 't motto: Gelijk er geschreven is: Ik hebbe geloofd, daarom heb ik gesproken: zoo geloven will ook, daarom spreken wij,* vol. II:37. This magazine was published by Van Peursem in Amsterdam, 1834-40. Da Costa, H. J. Koenen, and A. M. C. van Hall were the editors and were later joined by Willem de Clercq. The magazine became a monthly in 1838, changing its name to *Stemmen en Beschouwingen.* Henceforth: *Stemmen.*

21. Letter dated December 12, 1819; preserved in *Algemeen Rijksarchief,* 's-Gravenhage.

22. W. G. Byvanck, *De jeugd van Isaac Da Costa* (twee delen; Leiden: S. C. van Doesburg, 1894), I:33-37. The second volume was published by the same firm in 1896. Henceforth: Byvanck, *Da Costa.*

23. Jaap Meijer, *Isaac Da Costa's weg naar het Christendom, Bijdrage tet de geschiedenis der Joodse problematick in Nederland* (Amsterdam: Joachimthal's Boekhandel, 1946), 55-57. Dr. Meijer defended his thesis at the Municipal University of Amsterdam in 1941. After his miraculous return from Bergen-Belsen, he was able to publish the present edition. The work is the more valuable because it presents fairly the evidence that Byvanck (see previous note) studied Da Costa's youth too much from a Christian viewpoint and was not above twisting the evidence. Henceforth: Meijer, *Da Costa.*

24. Meijer, *Da Costa,* 64. Cf. Byvanck, *Da Costa,* I:44-47.

25. There is an enormous amount of literature on Bilderdijk. Within the limits of this study it is impossible to make reference to all of the publications. A sampling will appear below. The best factual account of Bilderdijk's life is R. A. Kollewijn, *Bilderdijk, Zijn leven en zijn werken* (twee delen; Amsterdam: Van Holkema en Warendorf, 1891). The following paragraphs are based on this work. Henceforth: Kollewijn, *Bilderdijk.*

26. Similar punitive steps were taken against ministers unwilling to swear allegiance. Supra, 19.

27. Geyl, *Bilderdijk-Huizinga,* 66. Geyl carefully analyzes how nineteen Dutch historians have treated Bilderdijk, especially with respect to his embarrassing support of the French and the shabby manner of his second marriage.

28. This is the net result of Geyl's penetrating study; ibid., 7-81.

29. W. van Oosterwijk Bruyn, *Uit de dagen van het Réveil* (Rotterdam: D. A. Daamen, 1900), 193. Henceforth: Van Oosterwijk Bruyn, *Dagen Réveil*. Van Oosterwijk Bruyn observes: "It is indeed a riddle how far a man's self-deception can go; and even the warmest admirer of Bilderdijk will have to acknowledge that his Christianity lacked much. In this field also he inexplicably confused fantasy and reality . . ." (ibid.). Geyl has indicated that Bilderdijk's reinterpretation of history is one of the reasons for this "confusion."

30. Jan Wagenaar, 1709-73, anonymously wrote *Vaderlandsche Historie* (Amsterdam: 1749-59) in twenty-two volumes. He published the second edition under his own name, again at Amsterdam, in 1770.

31. G. Groen van Prinsterer, *Archives ou correspondence énidite de la Maison d'Orange-Nassau, Première Série*, I-VIII (Leiden: S. en J. Luchtmans, 1835-47). This work has a register written by J. T. Bodel Nijenhuis. The second series of this work, the so-called *Deuxième Série*, I-V, was published at Utrecht by Kemink and Zoon, 1857-61. Henceforth: Groen, *Archives*. The references are found in series one, III:352, and in series two, I:30-31. It is customary to refer to the author by the shortened name Groen.

32. Rullmann, *Een Nagel*, 56; also Oostendorp, *Scholte*, 29.

33. Geyl, *Bilderdijk-Huizinga*, 34. As an example of Bilderdijk's speculations, Geyl quotes his explanation of the number 666 in Revelation 13:17. According to Bilderdijk, this number referred to Louis XVIII of France (if one only named him in Greek), and the passage should be understood to indicate the doom of the French monarchy. The beast with the horns rising from the earth was seen as representing Napoleon, for horn is *cor*, and Napoleon came from *Cor*-sica. Ibid., 48. Pierson, in *Oudere Tijdegenooten*, 151, gives a similar estimate of Bilderdijk.

34. For information concerning Da Costa's parents: Meijer, *Da Costa*, 30-39.

35. Supra, 63-64.

36. Meijer concludes that Da Costa was then still a Jew faithfully observing the holy days of Israel. But Abraham Capadose, Da Costa's Jewish friend and fellow-student who was also converted under the influence of Bilderdijk, reminisced in 1861 that "Neither he nor I ever visited the Synagogue in Leiden." His statement occurs in Capadose's letter to H. J. Koenen, May 25, 1861, and is quoted by D. Kalmijn, *Abraham Capadose* ('s-Gravenhage: Boekencentrum, 1955), 25. Henceforth: Kalmijn, *Capadose*. Meijer's evidence appears to be conclusive: Meijer, *Da Costa*, 66-74.

37. Kollewijn, *Bilderdijk*, II:70, 147.

38. Letter of January 27, 1817, Meijer, *Da Costa*, 71.

39. Kluit, *Réveil*, 44. For a brief characteristic of each student, ibid., 50-53.

40. Bilderdijk attracted the greater part of these students in the beginning. His course in 1822 opened with three students; in 1824 with three, and in 1826 with two. Kollewijn, *Bilderdijk*, II:236.

41. Pierson, *O.T.*, 151. A similar observation is made by W. van Oosterwijk Bruyn, *Dagen Réveil*, 259: "Bilderdijk was unable to create a school. He could inspire young men who worked out, who brought to life what his imagination held out to them, but what through him did not become marrow and bone. . . ."

42. When Abraham Capadose became ill with smallpox in 1817, Bilderdijk was the first to come to his room. Capadose recalled later: "his fatherly, tender words did me good; but before he left he offered a prayer in which sparkled such a glow of love, in addition to the prudence, over against a Jewish young man, that went already at that time through my soul." See Kalmijn, *Capadose*, 69. Another witness is Willem van Hogendorp in a letter to Isaac Da Costa, undated but probably written

in September 1824: "That we, and the few of his [i.e., Bilderdijk's] young friends agreed so completely with his insight and manner of thinking was solely the result of our personal intercourse." Letter in the Da Costa archives, Amsterdam.

43. W. Bilderdijk, *Opstellen van Godgeleerden en Zedekundigen Inhoud* (twee delen; Amsterdam: Immerzeel, 1833), I:24. Henceforth: Bilderdijk, *Opstellen*.
44. Ibid., 7-8.
45. Ibid., II:79.
46. W. Bilderdijk, *Verhandelingen Ziel-, Zede-, en Rechtsleer betreffende* (Leiden: L. Herdingh en Zoon, 1821), xv. Henceforth: Bilderdijk, *Verhandelingen*.
47. Bilderdijk wrote this in a letter to his friend Wiselius, police chief in Amsterdam, on January 1, 1821. The letter is quoted by Allard Pierson, *Oudere Tijdgenooten*, 180. Bilderdijk was extremely liberal toward those in whom he detected the presence of this "heart-felt relation to God." Thus, he defended Arminius and wanted to learn Arabic in order to prove that Mohammed had been a Christian at heart.
48. Ibid., 181.
49. Bilderdijk, *Geschiedenis des Vaderlands*, I:15, quoted by Kluit, *Réveil*, 41.
50. Bilderdijk, *Verhandelingen*, 1-94.
51. Blok, *Geschiedenis*, II:174-76. Geyl, *Geschiedenis*, II:340, characterizes it as a "completely secular document." Both Blok and Geyl understand it as a logical development of the medieval Dutch governmental tradition of limiting authority by a contract.
52. Geyl, *Nederlandes Figuren*, I:50-56.
53. G. W. Kernkamp, "Van Wagenaar tot Fruin," *Van Mensen en Tijden. Studien over Geschiedschrijvers* (Haarlem: H. D. Tjeenk Willink en Zoon, 1931), 11. Henceforth: Kernkamp, *Mensen en Tijden*. Kernkamp made the following judgment upon Bilderdijk's work: "What he substituted for Wagenaar is of little importance, but it lured to contradiction and therefore to new research" (ibid.). This latter point is also made by Kluit, *Réveil*, 50. Geyl gives Bilderdijk this credit, too: Geyl, *Bilderdijk-Huizinga*, 53. Both Kluit and Geyl point out that Van Pestel and A. Kluit, professors in Bilderdijk's student days, had called attention to Wagenaar's weak accusation that the stadholders were usurping power.
54. Gijsbert Karel van Hogendorp, supra, 8-9; 53.
55. A good essay on Willem van Hogendorp was written by Z. W. Sneller, "Willem van Hogendorp in zijne hetrekking tot het Réveil," 243-64, in Sneller, *Willem van Hogendorp*.
56. Kluit, *Réveil*, 56; Byvanck, *Da Costa*, I:213.
57. Kluit, *Réveil*, 59.
58. Byvanck, *Da Costa*, I:220, says that Wiselius, a friend of Bilderdijk, presented his report in a conciliatory manner, and adds that the king spoke disapprovingly of this new conservative tendency at Leiden's university.
59. Supra, 61.
60. Byvanck, *Da Costa*, I:221-28. Dirk van Hogendorp wrote extensively to Da Costa reporting the two attacks on Bilderdijk. In his letter of September 22, 1821, Dirk characterized Siegenbeek's oration as "a sneer at the house of Orange; among the students it has no success, but created indignation . . ." (ibid.).
61. In a letter of August 12, 1821, Kluit, *Réveil*, 60. Despite Gijsbert Karel's interest in his sons, there was a certain coolness in their relationship. He inquired for instance from the older son Willem: "Is Dirk making progress with his secret work?" Byvanck, *Da Costa*, I:240.
62. Byvanck, *Da Costa*, I:240. Da Costa had refused to supply such a poem for he wanted to avoid the impression that a conspiracy was brewing at Leiden. Ibid., 239.

63. Ibid., 247-51; Kluit, *Réveil*, 61.
64. Willem van Hogendorp's letter to Da Costa, May 10, 1822, Amsterdam, the Da Costa Archief.
65. Letter of December 9, 1821, in the Da Costa Archief.
66. Everard Gewin, *In den Réveilkring* (Baarn: Hollandia, 1920), 23-24. Gewin points out that many similar messianic prophecies were made in the aftermath of the Napoleonic upheavals. Henceforth: Gewin, *In den Réveilkring*. Cf. Byvanck, *Da Costa*, II:199.
67. "I have yet many things to say to you, but you cannot bear them now" (RSV).
68. Quoted by Byvanck, *Da Costa*, I:103-04, from a letter dated July 6, 1819. Hugo is the character in Müllner's play *Die Schuld* who stated in Act IV, Scene 4:

    Before this damned day is past,
    I desire to will nothing
    absolutely nothing, and to do nothing.
    Now my evil star is in command.

69. Byvanck, *Da Costa*, I:105; the letter is dated July 14, 1819. It is probable that Willem van Hogendorp was adversely affected in seeking a career because of his father's situation. The liberal Gijsbert Karel had been relieved of his civil duties by the king.
70. This letter is dated January 12, 1823, and is quoted by Sneller, *Willem van Hogendorp*, 251.
71. Byvanck, *Da Costa*, I:202-04, makes the point that Willem's nomination resulted from Gijsbert Karel's return to the king's favor. However, neither De Beaufort in *G. K. van Hogendorp*, nor Romein in *Erflaters*, mention this episode. Instead, they point out that Gijsbert Karel steadfastly refused to let the king appoint him to the First Chamber of Parliament, where he would have been without real influence. Was Willem's appointment an inducement? In 1825, Gijsbert Karel resigned his membership in the Second Chamber. Blok, *Geschiedenis*, IV:273.
72. Letter to Da Costa, November 3, 1821, *Da Costa*, I:204-05.
73. Letter to Da Costa, February 18, 1822, quoted by Sneller, *Willem van Hogendorp*, 251.
74. Bilderdijk expresses this sentiment in one of his poems quoted by Pierson, *O.T.*, 204:

    Affliction, Affliction alone has power of healing
    God gave it to him over whom his grace is watching.
    You who mourn, rejoice in this your lot,
    For no sweet its bitterness forsake.

    Is it night for us: once morning will dawn
    When no hindrance will longer obstruct our path
    And all your soul will thank God
    For every wound, for every tear,
    For every drop of blood.

75. Gewin, *In den Réveilkring*, 18.
76. Byvanck, *Da Costa*, I:205. Sneller characterizes Willem van Hogendorp as follows: "In nothing . . . so much the son of his father as in his gift for political economy." Sneller, *Willem van Hogendorp*, 256. Sneller also observes: "Say, Malthus, and Ricardo were [his] beloved literature out of which he created for himself a structure of political economy in its essence liberal, in which nevertheless the social element is also present," 257.
77. Oostendorp, *Scholte*, 331.
78. M. Elisabeth Kluit, "Mr. Isaac Da Costa, de mens en zijn tijd." *Isaac Da Costa,*

op 28 April 1960, honderd jaar na zijn overlijden herdacht; Uitgave in opdracht van de Maatschappij der Nederlandse Letterkunde te Amsterdam (Nijkerk: G. F. Callenbach, 1961), 9-38. Henceforth: Kluit, *Da Costa*.

79. Ibid., 17.
80. C. van Zuylen van Nijeveldt has been mentioned in connection with Schotsman. Supra, 62.
81. Oostendorp, *Scholte*, 30. Unfortunately, Oostendorp made no effort at all to clarify the sharp break that occurred between Bilderdijk and his pupils in later years.

CHAPTER V

1. Supra, 61-63.
2. Byvanck, *Da Costa*, I:108, from Da Costa's letter to Willem van Hogendorp. The letter is not dated.
3. Supra, 159, note 21. This letter of Da Costa contains the statement: "I am sorry that I cannot publicly speak more about this case. But the topic is so delicate for me that I cannot say much in my position. You understand and to you I can say it."
4. Byvanck, an undated letter, *Da Costa*, I:108.
5. Ibid., 146-47.
6. This point has been made by Meijer. He insists, however, that Da Costa was very much interested in making his law career a success: *Da Costa*, 74-75. Bilderdijk's influence affected Willem van Hogendorp in the same manner; supra, 71-72.
7. This is Meijer's conclusion, *Da Costa*, 77. Ibid., 11-12. Cf. for Da Costa's unhappy love affair.
8. Ibid., 15-25. Meijer devotes a chapter to this development. He points out that the Ashkenazim were little trusted by the *Patriotten* because of their love for Orange. A very small group was pro-French and sufficiently pro-Enlightenment to secede from the Ashkenazim congregation and form their own synagogue.
9. Ibid., 28-30.
10. Five Jews had established this society in 1807 as a protest against the progressive society *Tot Nut van het Algemeen*. The latter society excluded Jews from its activities. Meijer, *Da Costa*, 44.
11. Meijer calls attention to this boast: ibid., 152, note 24.
12. Cf. Bilderdijk, *Opstellen*, "Thoughts Concerning the Future and the Kingdom of Christ," II:116.
13. Meijer, *Da Costa*, 72-73. Corroborating evidence on Bilderdijk's influence is given by Kalmijn, the biographer of Da Costa's friend, Abraham Capadose. Kalmijn points out: "It has been Bilderdijk who, *without consciously wanting it*, led Capadose in the direction of Christianity." Cf. Kalmijn, *Capadose*, 24, italics mine.
14. Meijer, *Da Costa*, 64.
15. Meijer points out that the Sephardic Jew Isaac de Pinto underscored this fact in his polemics against Voltaire. The historical precedent for this at the zenith of their power was when the Iberian Jews wanted to prove ancient connections with their present homeland. See Meijer, *Da Costa*, 156-57, note 70.
16. Da Costa in a letter to Willem van Hogendorp, March 15, 1821; ibid., 81.
17. Da Costa in a letter of July 6, 1821; ibid., 97.
18. Byvanck, *Da Costa*, I:185. Unfortunately, Byvanck does not share the source supporting his statement.
19. Ibid., 221-81.
20. Isaac Da Costa was very proud of his Roman Catholic forefather Uriel Da Costa, who left Portugal in the early seventeenth century and settled in Amsterdam.

There he joined the Portuguese synagogue because of his disappointment with the Roman church. Finding the Jews to be not Christian enough, however, Uriel was so bitterly disappointed that he committed suicide in 1639. Ibid., 82-83.

21. The catalyzing agent in this process was Abraham Capadose, who considered it to be dishonest to be a Christian in the guise of a Jew. Cf. ibid., 107 and 154; Kluit, *Réveil*, 73-74; Byvanck, *Da Costa*, I:194-97.

22. Meijer limits himself to a factual account of Da Costa's life up to his baptism on October 18, 1822. Meijer's work makes it possible, however, to understand not only why Da Costa became a conservative like Bilderdijk, but also why he evolved later into an independent Christian.

23. This was published in 1823 by L. Herdingh en Zoon, Leiden. Henceforth: Da Costa, *Bezwaren*.

24. Supra, 73-76.

25. Meijer, *Da Costa*, 106, 100-01. Cf. Kluit, *Réveil*, 64-65. For Dirk van Hogendorp's estimate of Mrs. Da Costa, cf. Byvanck, *Da Costa*, II:224-25.

26. Byvanck, *Da Costa*, II:1-74; Cf. M. Elisabeth Kluit, *Briefwisseling tusschen Willem de Clercq en Isaac Da Costa, Bloemlezing uit onuitgegeven brieven berustende in het Réveil Archief te Amsterdam* (Baarn: Bosch en Keuning, n.d.). Henceforth: Kluit, *De Clercq-Da Costa*.

27. Van Oosterwijk Bruyn, *Dagen Réveil*, 314. Caroline was the former Caroline Boissevain, married to De Clercq in 1818; Kluit, *Réveil*, 68-69.

28. Kalmijn, *Capadose*, 28-43.

29. On September 4, 1822, Da Costa wrote to Bilderdijk: "As much as I have reason to thank God for the attitude of my beloved mother, as pitiable is the behavior of the Capadose family. They are enraged over us and they do not scruple to cast as much aspersion on us as they can." Kluit, *Réveil*, 79; cf. Meijer, *Da Costa*, 107.

30. D. Nauta, "Bilderdijk en de Kerk," *Opera Minora, Kerkhistorische verhandelingen over Calvijn en de Geschiedenis van de Kerk in Nederland* (Kampen: Kok, 1961), 139-71. Henceforth: Nauta, *Bilderdijk*.

31. Nauta observes: "As he [Bilderdijk] himself explained, his affairs occupied him to such an extent that Sunday observance was crowded out. Apparently, he was not at all upset by this development. He was perfectly at ease about it. . . . Bilderdijk's Sunday observance . . . was never in harmony with the rule formulated by the Dordtian fathers." Ibid., 149-50.

32. E.g., Rullmann, *Een Nagel*, 62-65.

33. E.g., supra, 46, note 15, where it is noted that conventicles formed the matrix of the *Zwijndrechtse Nieuwlichters*.

34. Nauta, *Bilderdijk*, 154.

35. Bilderdijk, *Opstellen*, II:43-53.

36. K. J. Pieters, D. J. van der Werp, and J. R. Kreulen, *Apologie. Is de Afscheiding in Nederland van het Hervormd Kerkgenootschap zooals het thans en sedert 1816 bestaat uit God of uit de menschen?* (Franeker: T. Telenga, 1856), 136.

37. Rullmann, *Een Nagel*, 67.

38. Oostendorp quotes this statement from H. Bultema; cf. *Scholte*, 32. Oostendorp quotes Nauta's essay, *Bilderdijk en de Kerk*, in defense of his conclusion: "Thus does the revival of Dutch Calvinism in church, school, and government owe a great debt to Bilderdijk." *Scholte*, 29. It is hard to understand, however, why he does not also comment on the following statement by Nauta: "It must be clear that what was strived after [by Bilderdijk] despite traits of resemblance which certainly are not lacking, is essentially something else than what later would be pleaded by

the Secession in 1834 and the *Doleantie* [i.e., Abraham Kuyper's movement] in 1886." Nauta, *Bilderdijk*, 162-63.

39. A letter dated November 11, 1823, as quoted by Kollewijn, *Bilderdijk*, II:242.
40. Cf. Nauta, *Bilderdijk*, 167-68.
41. Letter to Capadose, June 1823. Cf. ibid., 169.
42. Supra, 71-73.
43. An interesting light on the eschatological hope entertained by Bilderdijk and his pupils is given by Byvanck, *Da Costa*, II:238-39 in the quoting of Da Costa's letter to Willem van Hogendorp: "My insights differ from Bilderdijk's in that while he immediately expects the oppressive times of the Anti-Christ, I on the other hand believe that they will be preceded by a short-lived victory of the good cause on earth under the government of the Prince of Orange [i.e., the prince who in 1840 became King William II] that then the great kingdom of the Anti-Christ will form itself and that the glory of King Messiah will next close off these six thousand years with a millenium on earth." This letter is not dated, but was probably written in 1823.
44. Bilderdijk wrote to Capadose in June 1823: "I believe with you that Holland now and in its decay must become the center of true Christianity."
45. Nauta, *Bilderdijk*, 169-70.
46. Bilderdijk, *Opstellen*, II:90.
47. Nauta concludes: "What Bilderdijk missed was the living tie with the fullness of the Reformed understanding of the church. The view that dominated his practice had necessarily to lead either to the sect that segregates itself, or to the indifferent or passive attitude with respect to the external church. It is therefore incorrect to present him as a forerunner, in the strict meaning of the word, of the Secession and the *Doleantie*. In these two movements of the nineteenth century we see, other than with Bilderdijk, a struggle to grasp the Reformed understanding of the church." *Bilderdijk*, 171.
48. Kluit, *Reveil*, 81, states that Egeling was Bilderdijk's choice. Kalmijn, *Capadose*, 43, points out that Capadose had earlier met Egeling on several occasions and had been favorably impressed with him. It is probable that Bilderdijk and Capadose had collaborated on the choice of Egeling.
49. Oostendorp, *Scholte*, 32.
50. The letter was written in French on October 3, 1823, and may be found in Kalmijn, *Capadose*, 48. The passage reads: "Nous nouns entendons perfaitement pour ce qui regarde les dogmes de notre Eglise et les choses en elles-memes, mais il [i.e., Egeling] est excessivement tenace pour ne se servir que des propres mots de la Bible."
51. Kluit, *Reveil*, 80-81, from a letter dated September 21, 1822.
52. The complete Dutch title reads: *De Weg der zaligheid naar het beloop des Bijbels. Een leesboek voor mijn tegenwoordige en voormalige leerlingen. Ook voor anderen, die de kennis der waarheid liefhebben.* The first edition appeared in 1820, while the tenth was published in 1844 by Mortier Covens en Zoon, at Amsterdam. Egeling died in 1835. Henceforth: Egeling, *Weg*.
53. Ibid., II:vi.
54. Ibid., 531.
55. Ibid., 532.
56. Ibid., 531.
57. Ibid.
58. Ibid., 533.
59. Ibid., 624.

60. Ibid., 593.
61. L. Egeling, *Nadenkende Christen, die gaarne zichzelven en anderen behouden wilde* (Amsterdam: Mortier Covens en Zoon, 1832), 327. These rules appear in this work's tenth and final essay, "Aanprijzing van den Bijbel en deszelfs regt gebruik." (Translated: Recommendation of the Bible and of its Proper Use), 319-64. The italics are Egeling's. Henceforth: Egeling, *Christen.*
62. Ibid., 351-64.
63. Byvanck, *Da Costa*, II:219-20; the letter is dated early October 1822.
64. Kluit, *Réveil*, 81, from an undated letter.
65. It is, of course, not suggested that Bilderdijk was opposed to the instruction given by Egeling. The overpowering influence of Bilderdijk did not eclipse Egeling's contribution, however. The opposite would more closely approach the truth.
66. Kluit, *De Clercq-Da Costa*, 10-11, from a letter to De Clercq dated September 26, 1822.
67. Kalmijn, *Capadose*, 48; Kluit, *Réveil*, 81.
68. Meijer, *Da Costa*, 108, states that Da Costa was baptized on October 22. This is an oversight on his part.
69. Egeling conducted the service, preaching on Romans 11:5. The sermon was later published. De Clercq reports that Bilderdijk "sat there in subjection, in receptivity, and in an attention which I wish to be able to remember for a long time." Vos, *Groen*, I:35.
70. On March 23, 1823, Da Costa wrote to Willem van Hogendorp: "Since my baptism, I feel an irresistible desire to orally preach the Truth, so that I if I should yet have to choose a career would want nothing more ardently than to become a Preacher." Byvanck, *Da Costa*, II:241. Capadose wrote to Willem de Clercq on March 11, 1833, that he had desired nothing more than "to travel through the country preaching the Gospel." Cf. Kalmijn, *Capadose*, 64. Byvanck points out that Capadose wanted to leave behind his medical calling and warn the present generation against the prevailing understanding of nature. Byvanck, *Da Costa*, II:337-38.
71. Kluit, *Réveil*, 95-96.
72. Kalmijn presents a good summary of the tensions between the two converts. Cf. Kluit, *Réveil*, 119-21, and Kalmijn, *Capadose*, 54-59.
73. It should be noted that Bilderdijk tried to temper Da Costa's eagerness by cautioning: "Only, my dear friend, take care that you do not wish to do too much at once, but that you allow the Spirit of Truth time for his work." A letter dated November 28, 1833. Kluit, *Réveil*, 84. The warning must probably be understood in the light of Bilderdijk's suspicions concerning man's organizations as anticipating prematurely the work of the Lord. Supra, 80-82.
74. From an undated letter quoted by Byvanck, *Da Costa*, II:238-39. Da Costa explains in the letter that in this respect he differs with Bilderdijk.
75. Ibid., 235.
76. Ibid.
77. Quoted from an undated letter to Willem van Hogendorp. Ibid., 237.
78. Prince Maurice, siding with the strict Contra-Remonstrants, had broken Johan van Oldenbarnevelt's great power in the Province of Holland and in the United Republic. Oldenbarnevelt had given protection to the Remonstrants. Maurice's intervention made it possible for the Synod of Dordrecht to be held, which condemned the Remonstrants (also known as Arminians) in 1618-19. A biased court found Oldenbarnevelt guilty of treason and imposed the death penalty on him. Maurice declined to save Oldenbarnevelt from execution. Cf. Geyl, *Geschiedenis*, II:461-65;

Blok, *Geschiedenis*, II:471-93. This conflict in the Dutch republic inspired John Lottrop Motley to write *The Life and Death of John Barnevelt, Advocate of Holland, with a View of the Primary Causes of the Thirty Years War*, 1874. Groen van Prinsterer, editor of the Orange Archives, replied with his *Maurice et Barnevelt, Etude historique* (Utrecht: Kemink en Zoon, 1875). The prince of Orange was considered a hero because of his outstanding display of leadership when he fought against Napoleon in the battle of Waterloo, 1813.

79. Byvanck, *Da Costa*, II:238.
80. For the tendency to understand Dutch history as a kind of *Heilsgeschichte*, supra, 61.
81. Byvanck, *Da Costa*, II:238.
82. Ibid.
83. These were Da Costa's words in a letter to Willem van Hogendorp, dated March 1823. Ibid., 241.
84. From a letter to Willem van Hogendorp, dated April 4, 1823. Ibid., 242.
85. Kluit, *Réveil*, 85; cf. Byvanck, *Da Costa*, II:265-71.
86. De Groot says that Van der Palm reached his zenith in that address. De Groot, *Van der Palm*, 153.
87. The quotation is taken from the invitation addressed to Van der Palm. Ibid.
88. Byvanck, *Da Costa*, II:277.
89. According to Kollewijn, Bilderdijk had consulted Van der Palm on his "Ode to Napoleon," for which Van der Palm wrote a preface. Kollewijn, *Bilderdijk*, II:378. It is an irony of history that on July 5, 1830, the Society for Literature unanimously awarded its highest honor, a gold medal, to both Bilderdijk and Van der Palm for their achievements in Dutch literature; cf. ibid., 369. However, Kollewijn states that the relationship between the two began to change in 1816 when Bilderdijk turned toward a stricter Calvinism. Ibid., 83. The waning friendship was further cooled by Van der Palm's new translation of the Bible. In 1821, Van der Palm explained the Song of Songs in terms of a chaste love-poem, which caused Bilderdijk to write: "I abhor him for this Bible translation." Ibid., 259.
90. De Groot, *Van der Palm*, 100-02.
91. Kollewijn, *Bilderdijk*, II:260-69.
92. De Groot, *Van der Palm*, 153.
93. From an undated letter to Bilderdijk. Kluit, *Réveil*, 85. Da Costa correctly sensed the religious ferment in the celebration. The Reverend A. de Vries, a member of Haarlem's Centennial Committee, wrote to Van der Palm on March 18, 1823, "In the serious crisis of the struggle between the protagonists of the kingdom of light and that of darkness in which Europe now finds itself, this Celebration of Enlightenment fits gloriously." De Groot, *Van der Palm*, 153-54.
94. Dirk van Hogendorp noted in an undated letter to Da Costa: "Your objections begin piano and end fortissimo." Byvanck, *Da Costa*, II:271.
95. Sending a copy of the brochure to Willem van Hogendorp at Brussels, Da Costa wrote the following in an accompanying letter dated August 8, 1823: "I am following the dictates of my conscience in this publication. I have prayed to God that publishing should be prevented if in my intentions I were sinful." Ibid., 277.
96. Da Costa, *Bezwaren*, 1.
97. Byvanck, *Da Costa*, II:259-60. Byvanck has reconstructed this exchange in great detail. Ibid., 258-65.
98. Quoted from an undated letter. Ibid., 277.
99. Cf. Kollewijn, *Bilderdijk*, II:250.
100. Da Costa had written in his chapter on the constitution that the king was not bound to his oath of office "if he judges—and in this judgment he is amenable

only to his own conscience—that nullification of that oath . . . is demanded to
maintain his authority as Father, his dignity as Sovereign, his obligation as Vicar
of God in the temporal government of his people and his office of Christian King
who is called to adhere to and to protect the Reformed Confession of faith as were
his forebears." *Bezwaren*, 61.

101. Kluit, *Réveil*, 91.
102. N. G. van Kampen, *Verdediging van het goede der negentiende eeuw, tegen de
Bezwaren van den Heer Mr. I. Da Costa* (Haarlem: Kruseman, 1823). The title
reads in translation: "Defense of what is good in the 19th Century against Da Costa's
Bezwaren."
103. Da Costa, *Bezwaren*, 68-69. Da Costa was of the opinion that the abolition of the
slavery of the Negroes "belongs to the chimerical human wisdom wishing to an-
ticipate Almighty God." Ibid.
104. J. Roemer, *Voordelen van den Geest der Eeuw* (Leiden, 1823), 26. The title reads
in translation "Advantages of the Spirit of the Age." The italics are Roemer's. Cf.
J. A. Lotze's *Vijf Brieven behelzende eenige aanmerkingen over het zoo veel ger-
uchtmakende boek getiteld: Bezwaren tegen den Geest der Eeuw door Mr. J. [sic]
Da Costa* (Amsterdam, 1823), 16-36. Lotze counsels moderation in the process of
abolition, urging the development of a program to civilize the Negro slave prior
to freeing him. In The Netherlands slave trade was forbidden in 1814, but abolition
in the colonies came much later: in 1860 for the East Indies, now Indonesia, and
in 1863 for the West Indies.
105. The Dutch title reads, *De Bezwaren tegen den Geest der Eeuw van Mr. I. da Costa
toegelicht door Willem Bilderdijk* (Leiden: L. Herdingh en Zoon, 1823). Henceforth: Bilderdijk, *Toegelicht.*
106. Kluit, *Réveil*, 94-95.
107. Bilderdijk, *Toegelicht*, 2.
108. Ibid., 66. The biblical reference is found in Isaiah 30:9-11. Bilderdijk added in
parentheses the word *bastard*. The English translation follows the Revised Standard Version. The italics are Bilderdijk's.
109. Bilderdijk, *Toegelicht*, 52. The expression "supporters of Oldenbarneveld" refers
to the opponents of Prince Maurice of Orange; cf. supra, 166-67, note 78. Bilderdijk devoted the first chapter of his brochure to proving the thesis that Dutch
history had always been a battle between the genuine, God-inspired native strength,
as exemplified by Maurice, and the evils of foreign intrigue, exemplified by Oldenbarnevelt; cf. Bilderdijk, *Toegelicht*, 1-24. The issue of Maurice versus Oldenbarnevelt was a very hot one at the time. Willem de Clercq, despite his admiration
for Da Costa, objected to his friend's tendency to declare a Christian saved if he
agreed with Maurice but lost if he agreed with Oldenbarnevelt. Cf. Gewin, *In
den Réveilkring*, 150.
110. Bilderdijk, *Toegelicht*, 55.
111. Ibid., the italics are Bilderdijk's.
112. A. Capadose, *Bestrijding der Vaccine of de Vaccine aan de Beginselen der Godsdienst, der Rede, en der ware Geneeskunde getoetst* (Amsterdam: Sulpke, 1823).
The title reads in translation: *Fight against Vaccination, or Vaccination Weighed
Against the Principles of Religion, Reason, and True Medical Science.*" Henceforth:
Capadose, *Vaccine.*
113. Kalmijn, *Capadose*, 135. Capadose was even more infuriated over H. Collot
d'Escury's poem, translated by Van der Breggen from the Latin:

> To Jenner one is thankful, for Jenner altars stand
> And are decorated as if he were a benign God.

The offspring now being born and the coming generations
Will eternally claim Jenner's name as their father's name.

114. Cf. Capadose, *Vaccine*, 126. According to Meijer, the Jewish doctors were primarily responsible for and defending Jenner's discovery in The Netherlands. The first vaccination was used at Rotterdam in 1799 by Dr. R. Davids, who in 1801 translated into Dutch Jenner's treatise on smallpox. Meijer, *Da Costa*, 127.

115. Ibid., x.

116. Revised Standard Version.

117. Capadose, *Vaccine*, 68-72.

118. Ibid., 131-32. Capadose was also horrified that man was seeking refuge in the animal world: "Thus we see that we must seek our origin in the Ape, our first food from the Cow, and our health, or at least deliverance from one of the most devastating plagues, in the sickly condition of that animal." Ibid., 165.

119. Ibid., 216-20; italics are Capadose's.

120. Kalmijn, *Capadose*, 138. In 1822 the deacons of the Reformed Church in Amsterdam appointed Capadose as the medical doctor to whom indigents would be referred. Thus, Capadose became acquainted with the religious objections to vaccination through his contact with the poor. In 1818 the government had made vaccination obligatory for all pupils of public schools; only the well-to-do could afford avoiding the vaccination of their children, for private schools were not covered by the government's requirement. Capadose's moving style had caused much support for his position among the lower classes.

121. The Dutch title reads, *De Waarde der Koepokinenting gehandhaafd, en opnieuw aanbevolen aan de ouders en kunstgenoten, tegen de bestrijding derzelve van den Med. Doct. Abraham Capadose, of de Vaccinatie aan de Beginselen van Godsdienst, Rede, en ware Geneeskunde getcetst* ('s-Gravenhage: 1824).

122. Kalmijn, *Capadose*, 141.

123. Ibid., 139.

124. Ibid., 142.

125. Even his publisher suffered under the opposition, for he lost his contract to supply Dutch and German books to the University of Utrecht.

126. Capadose wrote his two last brochures against vaccination in 1872 and 1873. He died in 1874 at the age of 79.

127. Bilderdijk had coined this phrase in a poem in honor of Capadose, Kalmijn, *Capadose*, 151:

Thank you, my Friend, in the name of Religion and Conscience,
For the shield, taken up in the implacable battle,
To ward off the brute force that, forgetting God and obligation,
Throws innocent offspring in the infernal Moloch's arms.

Bilderdijk had opposed vaccination as early as 1806 in the poem, "De ziekte der geleerden," "The Illness of the Learned"; cf. *De dichtwerken van W. Bilderdijk, uitgegeven door I. Da Costa* (vijf delen; Haarlem: Kruseman, 1856), II:405.

128. Gewin, *In den Réveilkring*, 99-107; cf. Kluit, *De Clercq-Capadose*, 41-42.

129. Kalmijn, *Capadose*, 153.

130. Kluit, *De Clercq-Da Costa*, 42.

131. From an undated letter dealing with vaccination to the Rev. Hendrik De Cock, leader of the Secession of 1834. Gewin, *In den Réveilkring*, 100.

132. From Capadose's letter to H. J. Koenen, dated August 30, 1863. Kalmijn, *Capadose*, 157.

133. Through his determined action, Capadose made a lasting impact upon The Netherlands. To continue his battle, a "League against Enforced Vaccination" was es-

tablished in 1880. Its goal was that "the Jenner-Dagon idol of this age will not remain standing beside the ark of our salvation and the Word of God." Cf. Kalmijn, *Capadose,* 166. Formation of the league was also prompted by the enaction in 1872 of a law that forced private schools to admit no unvaccinated children. The battle continued into the twentieth century and was resolved by a law enacted in 1939 that guaranteed to conscientious objectors and their children freedom from compulsory vaccination.

134. Kluit, *Réveil,* 117-18; Kalmijn, *Capadose,* 223-34.
135. *Omstandig verhaal van de wederroeping der benoeming van den heer Hermanus Brasz als ouderling der Nederlandsche Hervormde Gemeente te Amsterdam, Met bijgevoegde aanmerkingen betreffende den toestand der Vaderlandsche Kerke,* Amsterdam in 1825.
136. Kalmijn, *Capadose,* 232.
137. J. L. van Essen, "De Betrekkingen tussen Willem Bilderdijk en Abraham Capadose," *Lucerna, Gereformeerd Interfacultair Tijdschrift,* V. No. 6 (March 1965), 270-88.
138. Byvanck relates how Da Costa and Capadose visited Bilderdijk at Leiden on November 20, 1823, in commemoration of their baptism. Da Costa was for the first time not sorry to leave Bilderdijk and observed: "The old man is weakening and is visibly failing." Byvanck, *Da Costa,* II:308-10.
139. Kalmijn, *Capadose,* 55.
140. Ibid.
141. Byvanck, *Da Costa,* II:338-42. Kluit tells of an incident that demonstrates the strained relation between Capadose and Mrs. Da Costa. When Capadose was asked to offer a prayer on a Sunday night, Mrs. Da Costa and her sister left the room. Kluit, *Réveil,* 120.
142. Supra, 85.
143. Unfortunately, this phase of the relationship cannot be fully reconstructed because Da Costa's letters to Capadose have been destroyed. The available evidence definitely points towards a break between the two friends, however. Kalmijn, *Capadose,* 55, note 2. Kluit observes that Capadose first had to grow in Christian love before he could become constructive: Kluit, *Réveil,* 119-21; "And even then he was to remain one of those difficult characters whose task it sometimes seems to be to create dissension in the circle of spiritual friends."
144. Kluit, *Réveil,* 120.
145. Kalmijn, *Capadose,* 276-84.
146. Kluit, *Da Costa,* 33. Da Costa changed so much that in 1848 he actually supported the adoption of the new constitution then proposed for the kingdom of The Netherlands. He even deplored the lack of a paragraph abolishing slavery. Ibid., 34. Despite his much more conservative attitude, Capadose favored abolition too. Thus, he became very active in the Dutch Abolition Society. Van Oosterwijk Bruyn, *Dagen Réveil,* 41.
147. Kluit, *Da Costa,* 22.
148. The mutual acquaintance was the Reverend Mr. L. G. James, minister of the Walloon Reformed Church at Breda.
149. Kluit explains that the custom of Bible study evenings was revived widely in 1824 and 1825, when extensive floods caused devastating damage in The Netherlands. Kluit, *Réveil,* 111-12.
150. Kluit, *Da Costa,* 22.
151. Ibid., 17.

152. *Oefeningen* had been characteristic of Dutch Protestant piety since the Reformation. Supra, 00.
153. Gewin, *In den Réveilkring*, 84.
154. Kalmijn states that *oefeningen* were common at Scherpenzeel prior to Capadose's arrival. Gewin states that Capadose waited prayerfully for three months before he began his *oefeningen*, finally beginning it not for the benefit of unbelievers but to strengthen the faith of God's children. Gewin, *In den Réveilkring*, 86. Capadose was so well liked for this leadership that trouble arose with the local Reformed church and its pastor. The latter tried to stop Capadose's activity by inciting the civil authorities to apply the articles of the *Code Napoleon* forbidding unauthorized meetings. Capadose left the area in 1833 before he got into serious difficulties. Scherpenzeel's consistory, however, refused to issue for him an unqualified letter of transfer to his new domicile in The Hague. Capadose was unsuccessful in his efforts to remove the notation on it that he was a restive person. Kalmijn, *Capadose*, 66-74.
155. Cf. M. Elisabeth Kluit, "Internationale Invloeden op de Voorgeschiedenis van het Réveil in Nederland," in *N.A.K.*, LIV, No. 1 (1961), 33-52.
156. Kluit, *Réveil*, 200-321.
157. Kluit, *Da Costa*, 31.
158. Supra, 15, 79.
159. M. Elisabeth Kluit, "Internationale Invloeden op de Voorgeschiedenis van het Réveil in Nederland," in *N.A.K.*, LIV, No. 1 (1961), 33-52.

CHAPTER VI

1. Isaac Da Costa, *De Sadduceen* (Leiden: L. Herdingh en Zoon, 1824), 29-30. Da Costa wrote this brochure as a complement to his *Bezwaren* and in it he again attacked the spirit of the age.
2. Pierson characterizes the attitude that prevailed in the *Réveil* and those connected with it: "They lacked absolutely the patience, the exactitude, the diligence necessary to find demonstrable truth. But how happy and blessed one was. One lived as in a dream. One did possess 'the Truth,' while others were slaving away along their erroneous ways." *O.T.*, 64.
3. Even Guillaume Groen van Prinsterer, who became the outstanding politician connected with the *Réveil*, described himself: "Not a statesman, but a confessor of the Gospel." He coined this phrase as the title of a pamphlet, the third in a series of twenty. The series was published in The Hague in 1866 under the title *Aan de Kiezers* (To the Voters).
4. Quoted from Lord's Day 2, Question 8, *Reformed Standards*, 25. A similar conviction is expressed in Answer 5: "I am by nature prone to hate God and my neighbor." Ibid. 24. This aspect of the *Réveil* has been treated with great insight by Pierson, *O.T.*, 50-57.
5. Kluit, *Réveil*, 200-321. M. C. T. van Lennep, *De ontwikkeling der inwendige zending in Nederland* (Den Haag: Boekcentrum, 1946), 7-35. The activities of the *Réveil's* most practical man, the Reverend Mr. O. G. Heldring, have been treated by Kluit, *Maatschappij*.
6. Supra, 92-93.
7. Supra, 89-90.
8. Th. Fliedner, "Collektenreise nach Holland und England," quoted by De Groot, *Van der Palm*, 167.
9. Chr. Sepp, *Proeve eener pragmatische geschiedenis der Theologie in Nederland*

van 1787 tot 1858 (Leiden: De Breuk en Smits, 1869), 127. Henceforth: Sepp, *Proeve*.

10. De Groot, *Van der Palm*, 243.

11. W. Faber, *Wijsgeren in Nederland* (Nijkerk: Callenbach, 1954), 72-81. Henceforth: Faber, *Wijsgeren*. F. Sassen, *Geschiedenis van de wijsbegeerte in Nederland tot het einde der negentiende eeuw* (Amsterdam: Elsevier, 1959), 298-303. Henceforth: Sassen, *GWN*.

12. Vos, *Groen*, I:70.

13. Sassen, *GWN*, 301.

14. Vos, *Groen*, I:71.

15. Cf. Hemsterhuis: Romein, *Erflaters*, 493-514.

16. Van Heusde taught the propaedeutic courses in Greek and history which were requirements for students of law, literature, and theology. Cf. Huizinga, *Verzamelde Werken*, VIII:140.

17. Huizinga quotes a student's report: "In Van Heusde's eye and face, in tone and voice, an enthusiasm revealed itself that made itself part of us through everything." Ibid.

18. Knappert, *Geschiedenis NHK*, II:280.

19. J. M. Kemper, *Proeve over den invloed der staatkundige gebeurtenissen en der godsdienstige en wijsgerige begrippen sedert ruim 25 jaren op de ware verlichting in het godsdienstige en zedelijke van de volkeren van Europa* (Haarlem: Teyler's Godgeleerd Genootschap, 1818), 25.

20. Both the liberal and orthodox theologians of The Netherlands agree on this fact of Dutch history. Cf. for the liberal position, K. H. Roessingh, *De Moderne theologie in Nederland, Hare voorbereiding en eerste periode* (Groningen: Erven B. van der Kamp, 1914), 7. Henceforth: Roessingh, *Moderne Theologie*. Cf. for an orthodox position, Th. L. Haitjema, *De richtingen in de Nederlandse Hervormde Kerk* (2e druk; Wageningen: H. Veenman en Zonen, n.d. [1953]), 35. Henceforth: Haitjema, *Richtingen*.

21. J. H. Scholten, 1811-85, studied theology at the University of Utrecht. In his student days he boarded with his uncle, Ph. W. van Heusde. There is abundant material on Scholten. I primarily used G. Brillenburg Wurth, *J. H. Scholten als systematisch theoloog* ('s-Gravenhage: Nijhoff, 1927). Henceforth: Wurth, *Scholten*. It is debatable whether Scholten or C. W. Opzoomer (who in 1846, at the age of twenty-five, became professor of philosophy at Utrecht) had the greater influence upon the rise of liberalism.

22. Ibid., 22.

23. Hyma, *Van Raalte*, 17-18.

24. Oostendorp, *Scholte*, 34.

25. Kromminga, *CRC*, 17.

26. Pieters, *Settlement*, 14.

27. *Classis Holland: Minutes 1848-58* (Grand Rapids: Eerdmans, 1950), 7-17.

28. How hymns were introduced in the Reformed Church has been noted.

29. *Classis Holland*, 12.

30. Supra, 16-19.

31. This is particularly the error of Oostendorp, *Scholte*, 34.

32. Pieters, *Settlement*, 14.

33. Reitsma, *Hervorming*, 431.

34. According to Knappert, the title of the oration, held in Latin, was *Oratio de eloquentiae sacrae natura*. *Geschiedenis NHK*, II:315.

35. See for Pareau, Hofstede de Groot, and Van Oordt: Roessingh, *Moderne Theologie*, 29-44.
36. P. Hofstede de Groot, *De Groninger Godgeleerden in hunne eigenaardigheid* (Groningen: A. L. Scholten, 1855), 26-33. Henceforth: Hofstede de Groot, *Groninger Godgeleerden.*
37. Cf. for a sound criticism of the decision to continue the use of Latin in the Dutch universities. Huizinga, *Verzamelde Werken*, II:319-20.
38. Reitsma, *Hervorming*, 453. In this circle of friends and colleagues was born the much-read periodical *Waarheid in Liefde*, Truth in Love.
39. Vos, *Groen*, I:79.
40. Hofstede de Groot, *Groninger Godgeleerden*, 26.
41. Haitjema, *Richtingen*, 27-29.
42. Roessingh states that Hofstede de Groot was more influenced by Herder, and especially the Dutchman, Frans Hemsterhuis, than by Schleiermacher. Roessingh, *Moderne Theologie*, 30.
43. Hofstede de Groot, *Groninger Godgeleerden*, 17.
44. Friedrich Schleiermacher, *Der Christliche Glaube* (delen; Gotha, 1889), I:201.
45. Hofstede de Groot, *Groninger Godgeleerden*, 136.
46. Roessingh, *Moderne Theologie*, 31-33.
47. Reitsma points out that since 1819 the number of students for the ministry increased significantly. While the General Synod of 1819 expressed concern about a shortage of ministers, by 1835 the number of theological students enrolled in the universities reached a peak of 653, more than sufficient to meet the need. Many of these students came under the influence of the *Groninger School*. *Hervorming*, 434.
48. Knappert states: "It is certain that Muntinghe, through numerous outstanding students, prepared the way for the upcoming evangelical persuasion, i.e., Groninger School." Knappert, *Geschiedenis NHK*, II:239.
49. Haitjema, *Richtingen*, 26. Cf. for an excellent characterization of Muntinghe: Huizinga, *Verzamelde Werken*, VIII:87-91.
50. The Dutch title reads: *Geschiedenis der menschheid naar den Bijbel.* The eleven volumes were published from 1801 to 1819.
51. Huizinga, *Verzamelde Werken*, VIII:88-89.
52. Ibid., 88.
53. Ibid., 89.
54. Hofstede de Groot makes the point that this was a unanimous feeling. *Groninger Godgeleerden*, 42.
55. Roessingh, *Moderne Theologie*, 37, from an article by J. F. van Oordt in *Waarheid in Liefde*, 1838, 305.
56. Hofstede de Groot, *Groninger Godgeleerden*, 43.
57. Ibid., 32.
58. Supra, 85-86.
59. According to Huizinga, Pareau was a specialist in the history of the ancient church. Huizinga, *Verzamelde Werken*, VIII:151.
60. Careful studies have proven that Hofstede de Groot, in spite of his insufficient research, had been right in his claim that there was a purely national reformation of the Dutch church. For an excellent treatment of this subject: J. Lindeboom, *De confessionele ontwikkeling der Reformatie in De Nederlanden* (Den Haag: Nijhoff, 1946).
61. Hofstede de Groot, in *N.A.K.*, II (1842), 188.
62. Hofstede de Groot, *Groninger Godgeleerden*, 24-25.

174   *Sources of Secession*

63. Ibid., 216.
64. Huizinga, *Verzamelde Werken,* VIII:149. Huizinga had access to private papers which were in the possession of descendants of Hofstede de Groot. Therefore, he was able to go into considerable detail concerning this aspect of the *Groninger School.*
65. Supra, 104.
66. Huizinga, *Verzamelde Werken,* VIII:149.
67. P. Hofstede de Groot, *Vijftig Jaren in de Theologie* (Groningen: C. M. van Bolhuis Hoitsema, 1851), 39.
68. Huizinga, *Verzamelde Werken,* VIII:157, 161.
69. For Guillaume Groen van Prinsterer see the biography by Vos, *Groen,* I-II. Cf. P. A. Diepenhorst, *Groen van Prinsterer* (Kampen: Kok, 1941), 17. Henceforth: Diepenhorst, *Groen.* Indispensable is Kluit, who quotes Groen's letter to A. G. A. van Rappard under date of November 20, 1831. Kluit, *Réveil,* 148-56.
70. Huizinga, *Verzamelde Werken,* VIII:154. The best treatment of the so-called *Adresbeweging,* Address-Movement, is in Volger, *Leer,* 171-220.
71. Kluit, *Réveil,* 247-49. Da Costa did not believe that a return to strict enforcement of the Three Forms of Unity as now demanded by the *Zeven Haagse Heren,* was the only orthodox way to overcome rationalism and *Groningen.*
72. For the immediate consequences of this difference: Kalmijn, *Capadose,* 256-61. Kluit describes the consequences in greater depth. Kluit, *Réveil,* 300-07.
73. Sepp, *Proeve,* 287-93. Sepp states as their main charge: "Neither the Biblical notion of revelation nor the New Testament concept of the logos have been studied anywhere by the *Groninger School.*" See p. 293.
74. Supra, 101-102.
75. Huizinga, *Verzamelde Werken,* VIII:157. A rapid decline occurred after 1860. In 1873 the periodical *Waarheid in Liefde* was discontinued.
76. Helenius de Cock, *Hendrik De Cock, Eerste Afgescheiden Predikant in Nederland* (tweede herziene druk; Delfzijl: Jan Haan, 1886). Henceforth: De Cock, *De Cock.* The author was a son of Hendrik De Cock. There are numerous publications dealing with De Cock, but Helenius's biography of his father has stood the test of historical criticism and is a reliable work. The character of Hendrik de Cock has been carefully described by M. Noordtzij, the husband of one of De Cock's granddaughters, who owned De Cock's papers. M. Noordtzij, *Herinnering en Waardering, Hendrik De Cock, de Vader der Reformatie van 1834* (Kampen: P. Zalsman, 1911).
77. Hofstede de Groot states in *Groninger Godgeleerden,* 223, that De Cock "was one of my friends at the University, although we were not on intimate terms." The friendship is acknowledged by De Cock, *De Cock,* 13.
78. The Province of Groningen is situated in the northeastern part of The Netherlands. The provincial capital is a city by the same name: Groningen. The university is still located in this city.
79. De Cock, *De Cock,* 18. Ulrum was De Cock's third parish. He had begun his ministerial career as minister of the Reformed Church at Eppenhuizen, 1824-27, and served the Reformed Church at Noordlaren from 1827 until 1829. Ibid., 14-15.
80. Supra, 107.
81. For the characteristics of this type of piety, cf. supra, 11, 13-14, 15. It is not suggested that this piety continued through the centuries without being influenced by others. It is, however, beyond the scope of this study to treat the deep influence of the Nijkerk Revival, 1750, and the preparatory work of pastor Wilhelmus Schortinghuis, 1700-50. Cf. Kromsigt, *Schortinghuis.*

82. G. Keizer, *De Afscheiding van 1834, Haar Aanleiding naar Authentieke Brieven en Bescheiden Beschreven* (Kampen: Kok, 1934), 172. Henceforth: Keizer, *Afscheiding*. From a professor ot church history at Göttingen, J. K. L. Gieseler, *De Bewegingen in de Nederlandsche Hervormde Kerk in de Jaren 1833 tot 1839* (Rotterdam, 1841). The book was actually ghost-written by P. Hofstede de Groot. Henceforth: Keizer, *Afscheiding*.

83. De Cock gives far less detail concerning De Cock's earlier, more "enlightened" period than does Keizer, *Afscheiding*, 140-69. Both accounts agree that De Cock was a sincere, hard-working pastor who loved his flock. De Cock, *De Cock*, 14-18.

84. In churches where the influence of Schortinghuis and like-minded theologians changed the piety characteristic of Voetius and Koelman, there would be found little appreciation of children's baptism, although this sacrament was faithfully administered. To make confession of faith was far more appreciated, because it was a sign of conversion. But the real test of faith was whether or not one dared to accept admission to the Lord's Supper and actually eat and drink the bread and wine. Congregations deeply influenced by Schortinghuis would pride themselves not only in well-attended church services but took far more pride in the very small number of members that considered themselves worthy partakers of the Lord's Table. Kromsigt, *Schortinghuis*.

85. Keizer quotes the names of such members from De Cock's letter to Hofstede de Groot, dated February 6, 1831: K. Barkema, K. Voet, Kornelia Harms, and the mother-in-law of Sievert Luninga. Keizer, *Afscheiding*, 205.

86. Ibid., 177.

87. De Cock, *De Cock*, 19.

88. Ibid., 20. The *Statenbijbel* was the translation financed by the government of the Dutch republic as a result of the Synod of Dordrecht. It was completed in 1635. The translation was so accurate and so unbiased that even the *Remonstranten*, condemned at the Synod of Dordrecht and excluded from the work of translation, adopted this Bible in their churches. Conrad Busken Huet gives a lucid account of the influence of this *Statenbijbel*: "One may say that a large majority of Dutchmen learned the Dutch language for the first time out of this book." Cf. Conrad Busken Huet, *Het Land van Rembrand. Studien over de Noordnederlandsche Beschaving in de Zeventiende Eeuw* (2de druk; Haarlem: H. D. Tjeenk Willink en Zoon, 1941), 326.

89. De Cock, *De Cock*, 20-21. Keizer adds that Mrs. De Cock had already attempted to guide her husband toward such an understanding of God's work. Keizer furiously rejects the charge, however, that Mrs. De Cock was a Xanthippe. Ibid., 263-64, 181.

90. C. Baron van Zuylen van Nijeveldt, *De Eenige Redding* (Amsterdam: J. H. den Ouden, January 28, 1831).

91. De Cock, *De Cock*, 22.

92. Kluit, *Réveil*, 133-34. Kluit states that the baron was such an arch-conservative that he was nicknamed Zwarte Kees, or Black Keith. The baron had been converted to a very conservative form of Christianity when he was searching the Scriptures in an effort to trace prophecies claiming that Napoleon had been foretold in the Bible. Ibid., 140.

93. Since several English-speaking authors have placed the blame for the more liberal attitude prevailing in The Netherlands on those who collaborated with the French, it may not be superfluous to point out that King William did not limit himself to persons from this liberal element in choosing civil servants. Cf. Oostendorp, *Scholte*, 34.

94. The address was published at Amsterdam by J. H. den Ouden, 1827. Molenaar withheld his name "so that nobody can think that I would place myself at the head of a secession." *Archiefstukken*, I:82.
95. Cf. for the *quia-quatenus* interpretations: supra, 44-45, 111.
96. Molenaar, *Adres*, 14.
97. Ibid., 10. Italics are Molenaar's.
98. Verberne, *G.N.*, II:33-45. Verberne gives a very balanced view of the king's language policies. He points out that a forceful program was necessary, and that increasing numbers of Flemish-Belgians began to support his efforts. At the same time, there were so many French-speaking Belgians that a slower pace should have been adopted. After all, Austria had ignored the Dutch language when it ruled the Southern Netherlands, while France had forbidden its use entirely.
99. Cf. for a very perceptive interpretation of King William's problems an essay by P. Geyl, "Hedendaagse Beschouwingen over het Verenigd Kominkrijk van Willem I." Geyl, *Noord-Zuid*, 173-94.
100. Cf. for the battle over the seminaries and the training of the priesthood: supra, 34.
101. Verberne, *G.N.*, II:40-44.
102. P. Geyl, "De Betekenis van 1830." Geyl, *Noord-Zuid*, 194-210.
103. Geyl, *Noord-Zuid*, 189. In a letter to his brother Dirk, Willem van Hogendorp spoke of the "damned principle that the church, the Reformed Church, is not represented on the committees for the schools." Sneller, *Willem van Hogendorp*, 253. It was Willem van Hogendorp's ideal in 1832 "to be able to serve as a Christian for God, for the Church, for the Fatherland, and for Orange." Ibid., 263.
104. William's effort to realize his dream of harmonious development in his realm is well described by Witlox, *Varia*, 50-55.
105. After the Belgian uprising of 1830, the North almost came to civil war when in 1853 the Dutch government sanctioned the official return to The Netherlands of the Roman Catholic hierarchy. Cf. efforts to de-escalate the tensions between Catholics and Protestants. Witlox, "Koning Willem II, 1840-1849, en de Katholieken," *Varia*, 57-60.
106. *Archiefstukken*, I:87. The committee's full report is reproduced: ibid., 83-89. A minority report is also reproduced: ibid., 93-94. The Minister of Justice, C. F. van Maanen, classified Molenaar with "Bilderdijk and his disciples Da Costa and Capadose."
107. Ibid., 77. The unsigned letter is reproduced in full. The wide distribution requested by Molenaar was indeed realized. The pamphlet was reprinted nine times in the course of one year.
108. Keizer describes J. H. den Ouden as "*the* bookseller at whose firm appeared before the Secession the one pamphlet after the other written in the circle of the Reveil to sound the alarm." The italics are Keizer's. Keizer, *Afscheiding*, 37-38.
109. *Archiefstukken*, I:108. The royal decision was mailed to the consistories of all Reformed churches. The documents dealing with Molenaar's *Adres* have been reprinted: ibid., 60-111.
110. C. Baron van Zuylen van Nijeveldt, *Het Liberalismus* (Amsterdam: J. H. den Ouden, 1828), 2.
111. Verberne points out that French agents were also creating proletarian revolutions in the German cities of Aachen and Cologne. Verberne, *G. N.*, II:72.
112. Ibid., 53-55.
113. The Liberals took heart when the French elections of 1827 brought the rule of Minister Villéle to an end. They, too, wanted a more democratic form of parlia-

mentary government and to obtain that goal they risked cooperation with the church that was, in their opinion, an enemy of democracy.

114. Colenbrander, *Afscheiding.*
115. Steinmetz, *England's Anteil.*
116. Belgium and The Netherlands signed the Agreement of London on April 19, 1839. Cf. Blok, *Geschiedenis*, IV:332-33.
117. Kemper says that support began to wane in 1833 when returning prisoners of war were so bombastically received the people became disillusioned with artificial hero-worship. In addition, the English blockaded Dutch harbors. The extended compulsory military service also caused the nation to review its unqualified support of the king. De Bosch Kemper, *G.N.*, 1830, II, 58-60.
118. Diepenhorst, *Groen*, 88, from Groen's weekly publication *Nederlandsche Gedachten*, Vol. II (August 1830). Groen cried out: "It is better to be dead than French." Ibid.
119. Van Oosterwijk Bruyn, *Dagen Réveil*, 353. Referring to the condition of The Netherlands, De Clercq wrote to Da Costa on February 12, 1831: "Rejoice in trembling.—For I may not doubt that God in these moments is resurrecting The Netherlands from the dead." Kluit, *De Clercq-Da Costa*, 24.
120. Kalmijn, *Capadose*, 332.
121. A. Capadose, *Het Plechtanker van Nederland's behoudenisse* (Amsterdam: J. H. den Ouden, 1832), 19.
122. M. Elisabeth Kluit, *Uit de Briefwisseling van C. M. van der Kemp (1799-1861) en J. H. Koenen (1809-1874) van 1833 van 1845*, 9. This work is a private printing and no publisher and date are specified. However, it had been previously printed in *Bijdragen en Meededelingen van het Historisch Genootschap* (Utrecht: Kemink en Zoon, 1941).
123. De Bosch Kemper observed that the Belgian revolt made the orthodox more orthodox and the liberals more liberal. De Bosch Kemper, *GN 1830*, I:45.
124. Amsterdam: J. H. den Ouden, 1831.
125. These pamphlets were also published by J. H. den Ouden at Amsterdam.
126. C. Baron van Zuylen van Nijeveldt died in 1833. A somewhat superficial description of this remarkable man may be found in Van der Does, *Afscheiding*, 34-39.
127. De Cock, *De Cock*, 22.
128. C. te Lintum, *Een Eeuw van Vooruitgang, 1813-1913*, (Zutphen: W. J. Thieme en Cie., n.d.), 96. Te Lintum devotes a full chapter to the cholera. Although cholera disappeared during the winter of 1832, the illness reappeared in 1833. In 1832 Rotterdam counted more than 1,400 cases, of which over 700 were fatal.
129. Keizer, *Afscheiding*, 184. Keizer points out that the North developed an intense hate of the Jesuits, suspecting them of instigating the Belgian revolt. Cf. A. C. J. Commissaris, *Van toen wij vrij werden* (Groningen: J. B. Wolters, 1928), 90-98.
130. The original title reads: *De Heilige eeuw-bazuin, oproepende alle soorten menschen tot bekeering en de komst tot de ware kerk des Nieuwen Verbonds, om bij den ingang het duizendjarig vrederijk met haar verreenigd to worden.*
131. De Bosch Kemper, *GN 1830*, II:17.
132. W. J. Formsma, "Groningen in 1848," H. P. Coster en W. J. Formsma, *Groningse Volksalmanak voor het jaar 1948* (Groningen: Erven B. van der Kamp, 1949), 33-80.
133. The village of Leens, for instance, was known as Little Brussels because of its rebellious spirit. Ibid., 41.
134. Ibid., 46-47. Dr. Middendorp subsequently escaped from prison and fled to Germany.
135. De Cock, *De Cock*, 23-24. Keizer, *Afscheiding*, does not mention this.
136. The Dutch title is *Ernstige en hartelijke toespraak aan mijne landgenooten, in*

deze zorgvolle en droevige dagen, vooral met betrekking hunner eeuwige belangen
(Veendam: T. E. Mulder, 1834). According to De Cock, the brochure was written
in 1832, but was not published until 1834. De Cock, *De Cock,* 29.

137. De Cock, *De Cock,* 34.
138. Hofstede de Groot writes: "Now and then I visited him in order to dissuade him
if possible from his exaggerations and especially from his habit to condemn others."
Hofstede de Groot, *Groninger Godgeleerden,* 223. But De Cock states emphatically that Hofstede de Groot was deceiving himself because he visited his father
only once. De Cock, *De Cock,* 37.
139. These are Hofstede de Groot's words, according to De Cock; ibid.
140. Ibid. Helenius de Cock remarks that his father gave Hofstede de Groot the brochure because "it contained the expression of his conviction."
141. The letters span the period from October 14, 1832, to January 8, 1834. They are
reprinted in full by Keizer, *Afscheiding,* 199-231. Keizer points out that both
Hendrik de Cock and his son Helenius honored Hofstede de Groot's request not
to publish the letters, even though the latter did not accurately represent De Cock's
position on the matter. Keizer, writing in 1934, felt that the time had come to
make the letters public.
142. Keizer, *Afscheiding,* 199.
143. Ibid., 205.
144. Ibid., 223.
145. Ibid., 202.
146. Ibid., 220.
147. Ibid., 223.
148. There is no letter from Hofstede de Groot dealing with this issue. Keizer says that
De Cock visited Hofstede de Groot in the city of Groningen, and wrote his letters
on the basis of what they discussed at that time. Keizer, *Afscheiding,* 217-18.
149. Ezekiel 33:3. For De Cock, this chapter was the key to the renewal of his ministry.
150. Keizer, *Afscheiding,* 230.
151. *Besluiten van de Nationale Dordsche Synode, gehouden in den jare 1618 en 1619,
te Dordrecht, uitgegeven door en met een voorrede van Hendrik DeCock, gereformeerd leeraar te Ulrum* (Veendam: T. E. Mulder, 1833), 2.
152. Supra, 74, 111-14.
153. De Cock, *De Cock,* 46. The entire letter is reprinted ibid., 46-50.
154. Ibid., 48-49.
155. Ibid.
156. Ibid., 49.
157. Ibid.
158. For De Cock's undated reply, ibid., 50-53.
159. Ibid., 71.
160. Ibid., 71-81. Cf., Keizer, *Afscheiding,* 296-312.
161. Cf. De Cock's letter to Rutgers dated November 23, 1833. De Cock, *De Cock,*
48-49.
162. W. J. deWilde states that such an article in fact did exist, and required the parents
of the child to have in hand a letter from their home pastor indicating that he and
his board of elders did not object to the baptism. W. J. deWilde, *Geschiedenis
van Afscheiding en Doleantic van Hervormd standpunt bezien* (2de druk: Wageningen: Veenman en Zonen, n.d.), 51. Henceforth: DeWilde, *G.A.D.* Volger,
Leer, 86, says that such an article was not formulated until 1842. *G.A.D., Volger,
Leer.* DeWilde is partly correct, however. In 1824 the General Synod decided to
issue a directive on baptism similar to that described by DeWilde. Cf. *Handelin-*

gen, 1824, 53-57. The final form of this directive was not mailed out to the churches until 1842. Cf. Handelingen, *1842*, 126.

163. *Verdediging van de Ware Gereformeerde Leer en van de Ware Gereformeerden bestreden en ten toon gesteld door Twee Zogenaamde Gereformeerde Leeraars, of de Schaapskooi van Christus aangetast door Twee Wolven en verdedigd door H. DeCock, Gereformeerd Leeraar te Ulrum* (Groningen: J. H. Bolt, 1833). Henceforth: De Cock, *Verdediging.*

164. Meijer Brouwer, *Noodige Waarschuwing en Heilzame Raad aan Mijne Gemeente in Twee Leerredenen* (Groningen: J. Oomkes, 1833); G. Benthem Reddinghiu, *Brieven over de Tegenwoordige Verdeeldheden en Bewegingen in de Hervormde Kerk* (Groningen: W. Zuidema, 1832).

165. *Archiefstukken*, I:235-37. It is obvious that Damste's letter is a reply to the Ministry's inquiry, dated November 30, 1833, as to what the classis is doing about De Cock's pamphlet in which he calls his colleagues: "Wolves, thieves, murderers, pharisees, hypocrites, devils." Ibid., 234-35.

166. Janssen: supra, 33, 36.

167. *Archiefstukken*, I:240. It should be noted that the Dutch verb *weren*, here translated as to bar, does not convey a notion of removal but of opposition.

168. The official citation is indeed no more specific. De Cock, *De Cock*, 101.

169. Ibid., 101-02.

170. Cf. for a detailed analysis S. Sybenga, *De Afscheiding en het Algemeen Reglement voor het Bestuur der Nederlandsche Hervormde Kerk van 1816* (Groningen: Erven B. van der Kamp, 1932). Henceforth: Sybenga, *Reglement Bestuur.*

171. *Archiefstukken*, I:241.

172. The official verdict is reproduced in De Cock, *De Cock*, 103-05. Helenius de Cock reports, however, that some payments were delayed. This was probably a deliberate attempt to cause financial difficulties for De Cock. Ibid., 172-73.

173. Ibid., 165-68.

174. Cf. for the difficulties with hymns: supra, 50-53.

175. The pamphlet is entitled: *De Evangelische Gezangen getoetst en gewogen en te ligt bevonden door Jacobus Klik, verwer en koopman te Delfzijl, met eene korte voorrede en uitgegeven door H. DeCock, Gereformeerd leeraar te Ulrum* (Groningen: J. H. Bolt, 1834).

176. De Cock, *De Cock*, 135. Keizer points out that De Cock also sponsored pamphlets written by laymen attempting to demonstrate that God was present in the simple people. Keizer, *Afscheiding*, 341-46; 262-63.

177. DeWilde, *G.A.D.*, 54.

178. Cf. the communication dated May 28, 1834: De Cock, *De Cock*, 200-04.

179. Ibid., 248-50. This action was taken on July 11, 1834.

180. Ibid., 287.

181. Ibid., 289.

182. Oostendorp, *Scholte*, 59-64.

183. The letter is reproduced by De Cock, *De Cock*, 121-24.

184. Ibid., 123.

185. Ibid., 293-94.

186. Ibid.

187. Cf. Smith's report to the classis in *Archiefstukken*, I:318-21. De Cock, *De Cock*, 294-97. Keizer makes a strong case against the innocence of the two men. Keizer, *Afscheiding*, 533-50.

188. It should be remembered that the Province of Groningen was also experiencing great difficulties. Cf. supra, 117.

189. De Cock, *De Cock,* 294-96.
190. Ibid., 297. The last sentence is hardly translatable because of its awkward construction.
191. Ibid., 298.
192. Oostendorp, *Scholte,* 60. Oostendorp adds: "Scholte is always too much the lawyer."
193. Ibid., 58. Oostendorp quotes a report of the governor of Groningen, W. F. L. Baron van Rengers, to the effect that Scholte incited the supporters of De Cock to secede. *Archiefstukken,* II:13; cf., Keizer, *Afscheiding,* 304.
194. Wagenaar, *Afscheiding-Réveil,* 178, from H. de Cock, *Verder Berigt* (Veendam: T. E. Mulder, 1834), 29.
195. Volger, *Leer,* 116-17.
196. Cf. the reproduction in Keizer, *Afscheiding,* 576-77.

CHAPTER VII

1. Oostendorp, *Scholte,* 37, 43.
2. Ibid., 61-63.
3. A. Brummelkamp, Jr., *Levensbeschrijving van wijlen Professor A. Brummelkamp* (Kampen: J. H. Kok, 1910).
4. The documents are reproduced in full in *K.U.,* 325-29.
5. A. Tjoelker, *Dr. S. van Velzen en zijn Betekenis voor de Afscheiding in Friesland* (Leeuwarden: A. Jongbloed, 1935).
6. The documents are reproduced in *K.U.,* 395-442.
7. Hyma, *Van Raalte.* Cf. J. A. Wormser, *In Twee Werelden, Het Leven van Albertus Christiaan Van Raalte* (Nijverdal: E. J. Bosch Jbzn., 1915); Henry E. Dosker, *Levensschets van Dr. A. C. Van Raalte* (Nijkerk: Callenbach, 1893). Henceforth: Wormser, *Van Raalte*; Dosker, *Van Raalte.*
8. Keizer, *Afscheiding,* 45-49.
9. Ibid., 49.
10. *Archiefstukken,* I:207.
11. The title of Le Febure's brochure is: *De Toetser Getoetst, of de Verdediging van het Adres aan alle Mijne Hervormde Geloofsgenooten: tegen de zoogenaamde Toetsing van Bernardus Verweij, aan de Geest der Waarheid, der Liefde, en des Vredes* (Amsterdam: J. H. den Ouden, 1828).
12. *K.U.,* 534.
13. Ibid.
14. Wormser, *Van Raalte,* 13. Cf. for Clarisse: *Biographisch Woordenboek van Protestantsche Godgeleerden,* onder redactie van J. P. de Bie en J. Loosjes (vijf delen; Den Haag: Nijhoff, 1919-41), II:60-73.
15. Dosker, *Van Raalte,* 5.
16. Hartog, *Predikkunde,* 274-78.
17. Minutes of the Provincial Synod of Zuid-Holland for 1835, pp. 18-19, preserved in holograph in the archives of the Netherlands Reformed Church in The Hague. Photocopies are on deposit in The Netherlands Museum, Holland, Michigan. Henceforth: *Minutes Z-H.*
18. Ibid.
19. Ibid., 18-19.
20. The two candidates were A. ten Bosch Corn. Zn, and J. P. Hasebroek. Ibid., 19. The same page shows an entry concerning the candidate Y. Loots, Jr., who appeared for a second examination because in his earlier examination "he had been found wanting in all subjects except Greek and Hebrew."

21. *K.U.*, 523.
22. This is of course a slighting reference to the visit of Scholte to De Cock prior to the secession at Ulrum.
23. *K.U.*, 524.
24. It is obvious that Van Raalte was a *quiatist*, while the board must have been dominated by *quatenussen*.
25. *K.U.*, 526.
26. Ibid. At this time Brummelkamp and Van Velzen had begun to apply pressure.
27. Ibid.
28. Ibid., 534.
29. A. Capadose, *Ernstig en biddend Woord aan de getrouwe Leeraren in de Hervormde Kerk in Nederland betreffende den tegenwoordigen Toestand in de Kerk en derzelver Synodaal Bestuur* (Amsterdam: J. H. den Ouden, 1835).
30. *K.U.*, 527.
31. *Minutes Z-H*, 24.
32. *K.U.*, 528.
33. Ibid.
34. *Minutes Z-H*, 25. The secretary sent Van Raalte a copy of that section of the minutes that applied to him.
35. *K.U.*, 529.
36. Ibid., 531-45.
37. Ibid., 533.
38. Ibid.

EPILOGUE

1. Elton J. Bruins, *The Americanization of a Congregation* (Grand Rapids: Wm. B. Eerdmans Publishing Co., 1970), 8-18.

Index of Persons

184

Haitjema, Th. L., 105
Hegel, G. F. D., 34
Hemsterhuis, Frans, 101
Herdingh, L., 89
Heusde, Philip Willem van, 101-2, 107
Hofstede de Groot, Petrus, 104-10, 118-20
Hogendorp, Dirk van, 66, 67, 70, 71, 94, 96
Hogendorp, Gijsbert Karel van, 3, 8, 9, 67, 69, 70, 96
Hogendorp, Karel van, 66, 67
Hogendorp, Willem van, 63, 66, 67, 69, 71-73, 78, 84, 85, 89
Holland, King of (Napoleon), 7
Holtius, Nikolaas, 17, 18, 52
Honert, Johannes van der, 18
Honig, A. C., 17
Hoop, Elisabeth M. M. van der, 109
Huguenots, 13
Huizinga, Johan, 2, 30
Hyma, Albert, 102

Immens, Petrus, 55

Janssen, J. D., 22, 34-36, 123
Jenner, Dr. Edward, 91, 93
Jesuits, 13, 28, 117
Jews—Ashkenazim, 76, 77
Jews—assimilation, 77
Jews—emancipation, 77
Jews—Sephardim, 76, 77, 87
Judah, 78

Kalmijn, D., 94
Kampen, N. G. van, 89, 100
Kemp, J. Th. van der, 23
Kemper, J. M., 70, 71, 102
Kerckhoven, H., 11
Klok, J., 124
Kluit, Dr. M. Elisabeth, 59, 60, 74, 95
Knappert, J. J., 36, 61
Koelman, Jacobus, 13-15, 110
Koenen, H. J., 115
Koenen, Mrs. F.A.C., 95
Kollewijn, R. A., 65
Kooten, G. van, 132
Koster, Laurens Janszoon, 86, 87
Krieger, W., 40
Kromminga, J., 103
Kromsigt, J. C., 14
Kuipinga, K. P., 110-11

Labadie, Jean de, 13-15
Labadists, 15
Lamennais, H. F. R. de, 114
Lampe, F. A., 55
Le Febure, Johannes, 130-31, 133
Leade, Jane, 45
Leer, Maria, 46
Lehmans, Mozes, 63
Locke, John, 16
Lodenstein, Jodocus van, 55
Louis Philippe, King of France, 114
Louis XIV, King of France, 15

Maanen, C. F. van, 50, 89
Mazereeuw, Jan, 45
Mazereeuwians, 48
Meijer, Jaap, 77-79
Mennonites, 22
Merle d'Aubigne, J. H., 109
Messiah, 79
Meyer Brouwer, L., 122
Molenaar, the Reverend D., 96, 111-14, 120-21, 130-31
Mollerus, J. H., 22
Mommers, J. M., 16
Moravian Brethren, 97
Mulder, Stoffel, 46
Muntinghe, H., 106-7, 110

Napoleon, 1, 6, 8, 9, 21, 22, 28, 30, 33, 34, 40, 48, 63, 77, 117
Nauta, 82
Nijenhuis, J. T. Bodel, 66
Nouhuijs, H. G. van, 131
Nuse, H., 117

Ontijd, Dr. C. G., 92, 93, 100
Oordt, J. F. van, 107-8
Oostendorp, L., 32, 73, 74, 81, 82, 103, 126
Orange, Frederik, Prince of, 6, 72
Orange, King William I of, 9, 24, 26-35, 45, 46, 48, 52, 56, 59, 61, 67, 69-70, 102-3, 109, 111-17, 125, 134
Orange, King William II of, 85, 86
Orange, Maurice, Prince of, 86
Orange, William I, Pr. of "the silent", 70, 113
Orange, William III, Prince of, 16, 69
Orange, William IV, Prince of, 17 .
Orange, William V, Prince of, 1, 5, 6, 9, 18, 64, 65

Index of Subjects